# CELTIC

## A · CENTURY
## WITH · HONOUR

# CELTIC
## A·CENTURY
## WITH·HONOUR

*Brian Wilson*

Willow Books
Collins
8 Grafton Street, London W1
1988

Willow Books
William Collins Sons & Co. Ltd
London · Glasgow · Sydney · Auckland
Toronto · Johannesburg

First published 1988
Reprinted 1988
© Brian Wilson 1988

BRITISH LIBRARY CATALOGUING IN PUBLICATION DATA

Wilson, Brian
Celtic: a century with honour.
1. Scotland. Association football. Clubs.
Glasgow Celtic Football Club, to 1987
I. Title
796.334′63′0941443

ISBN 0 00 218230 0

Photoset in Linotron 202 Plantin by
Rowland Phototypesetting Ltd
Bury St Edmunds, Suffolk
Made and printed in Great Britain by
Butler and Tanner Ltd, Frome, Somerset

# CONTENTS

# FOREWORD
## *by John C. McGinn*
### *Chairman, Celtic Football Club*

 T is my great, if unexpected, privilege to be the chairman of Celtic Football Club in the centenary year and it therefore becomes my pleasant task to write an introductory few words for the history of our very famous club.

During my lifetime as a supporter of Celtic I have witnessed most of the peaks and troughs experienced by various teams over a period nudging close to fifty years.

Many of these came back to me with stark realism as I read the author's words in galley proof form. I think he has quite brilliantly encapsulated the Celtic Story into a most readable and interesting book; no mean feat when one considers that the history has been committed to paper by at least half a dozen authors in the past.

I am not ashamed to say that I felt quite moved as I read the chapter on the tragic death of John Thomson, quite remarkable considering the tragedy occurred almost exactly one year before I was born.

I am delighted that we decided to ask Brian Wilson to undertake this onerous task and I am even more pleased with the finished product. I commend the book to all with an affection for Celtic Football Club.

# INTRODUCTION

ITH fifteen minutes remaining of the Scottish Cup Final, on 14 May 1988, Celtic were a goal behind to Dundee United. The events which followed will, for the next one hundred years, be part of Celtic folklore for, by the time the final whistle blew, Frank McAvennie had scored twice to ensure victory. It was, by any standard, an extraordinary climax to the game and to a wonderful centenary season. Better still, the manner of accomplishment epitomized the traditional Celtic characteristics – commitment to attacking football and an absolute refusal to admit defeat. With the great Celtic support urging the team on from the Hampden terraces, there was a sense of inevitability about the outcome.

While the players took their laps of honour, the other people most closely involved in the club's affairs carried on their own celebrations in front of the Hampden stand. Almost all of them had been part of the Celtic family for most of their adult lives. It was over thirty years since Billy McNeill had arrived at Celtic Park as a young player . . . thirty-six since Neil Mochan, now in charge of kit, had first pulled on a Celtic strip . . . yes, and over forty, since the much-loved masseur Jimmy Steele had become involved in the scheme of things. It was more than a quarter of a century since chairman Jack McGinn went to the Celtic board with the idea of a club newspaper, while each of his fellow directors represented a lineage which stretched back to the origins of the club. It was a scene which reminded me that commitment to Celtic tends to be measured in lifetimes, rather than in years; the true mark of a close-knit family.

The whole spectacle at Hampden on that glorious day encapsulated the spirit of the club and of the people who have made it what it is: the victory won in such dramatic fashion; the terraces ablaze with green and white; the extended family united in joyous self-congratulation. No football club has ever had such a perfect climax to its centenary celebrations.

It has been my privilege to research and write the story which led from St Mary's Hall and the aspirations of some far-sighted Irishmen, all the way to Hampden Park on 14 May 1988. I am deeply indebted to Jack McGinn and his fellow-directors for having asked me to write the club's official centenary history, and for having given me every possible assistance over the past two years. It has indeed been a labour of love, for I was brought up to admire, respect and support the Celtic Football Club and I have never had any reason to deviate from that approach. I have found out a great deal more than I had ever expected about the fascinating origins of the club, and the inter-relationship with other great events which were taking place in Scotland at that time. There is more social history in this book than would normally be found in the story of a mere football club. But I think it is important that the youngsters who stand on the Celtic terraces, and those who come after them, should have access to the story which, from the start, ensured that Celtic would be a very special club. For many readers, the world that Celtic were born into was also the world that their own forebears were born into and, through the story of Celtic, it is possible to gain initial access to the wider history of the Irish community in Scotland.

There are many people to be thanked for their advice and co-operation during the preparation of this book. I am grateful to all those who sent me material in response to items in the *Celtic View*; to the staff of the Mitchell Library in Glasgow; to the Archdiocesan Library in Glasgow; to Bernard Meehan of Trinity College Library in Dublin; and to Chris White, whose office I used while ploughing through the club records. I have been assisted in research by my friends Des Tierney and Malcolm Burns in Glasgow, and by Hugh Jordan and John Rush in Ireland. Glenn Gibbons of the *Observer* has provided me with invaluable background material and insights, covering the modern period, which he has reported and commented upon from an excellent vantage point. David Docherty has compiled a fine statistical section and his own book, which gives details of every Celtic game played since the Second World War, would make an excellent companion to this one. Donald MacLeod of the *Scotsman* has been largely responsible for assembling the pictures, including some old plates which he discovered in the inner recesses of Celtic Park. The Picture Library of the *Glasgow Herald* have also supplied some fine illustrations. I was particularly grateful to Mrs Angela Quayle of Stornoway, for putting at my disposal much valuable material about her grandfather, Tom Maley, and the rest of that interesting family. Celtic have been extensively written about, and I have given due recognition to quotes taken from the books by William Maley (1940) and James Handley (1960).

For more than a decade, I have spent my post-match Saturday evenings in the Dowanhill Bar, Partick, discussing Celtic and politics, past and present. I have owed this extension of my education and entertainment to Billy Connolly and his father, who died just a few months ago; to John and Eddie Connolly and Alex Lochhead. If my Celtic enthusiasm was ever in danger of flagging, these sessions soon revived it!

Among those who subjected themselves to interview were Roy Aitken, Jimmy Delaney, Sean Fallon, James Farrell, Mike Jackson, Bobby Lennox, Joe McBride, Malcolm MacDonald, Jack McGinn, Tony McGuinness, Billy McNeill, William Murphy, Benny Rooney and Bob Rooney. They were all of great assistance in building up a picture of the club at various stages in its development. Dr Michael Kelly offered many helpful suggestions and filled in details of his own family's involvement, and I am indebted to Bob Crampsey for having read and constructively criticised the proofs. Sadly, several important figures in Celtic's history have died in recent years – including Jock Stein, Desmond White and Tom Devlin. I was saddened by the death of George McLaughlin, chairman of the Industrial Tribunals in Scotland, who was in the process of assisting me with information about his grandfather, John H. McLaughlin, when he and his wife were killed in a car crash in Ireland. I was also sorry to learn of the death of that fine sports journalist Cyril Horne, who had promised to be of considerable assistance to me.

Celtic have celebrated their centenary with great style and panache. Events on the field of play were, of course, the highlights. But there has also been the novel idea of a musical, commissioned by the club and presented by the Wildcat Theatre Company, at the Pavilion Theatre. Splendid new facilities have been added to Celtic Park itself. I hope that this book will serve as a lasting memento of this centenary year, as well as being a testament to the history of a great club.

Brian Wilson
*Glasgow, May 1988*

# 1

## ORIGINS
### *The Irish Connection*

HE Celtic Football and Athletic Club was instituted for reasons closely related to Irish identity and Catholic charity. It emerged out of the poverty that prevailed in Glasgow's East End of the 1880s. This was an age of dreadful housing conditions, high infant mortality and little formal education. It was an age when Irish emigrants retained a passionate concern for the fate of their native land. But it was also an age of innovation and enterprise, when the willingness to accept daunting challenges was more commonplace than in any subsequent period. The men who founded Celtic would probably not, in any other context, have wished to be regarded as classic Victorians. But the spirit in which they set about their task, and the level at which their ambitions were pitched, were characteristic of that thrillingly productive and creative period.

Numerous attempts to found a distinctively Irish football club in the East End, to play at the highest levels, had come and gone. Dozens of teams had been formed by the Catholic parishes, but none of these had a strong enough organizational basis on which to build a 'senior' club. The inspiration for thoughts about a first-rate Irish club in the west of Scotland came in part from Edinburgh, where the Hibernians club had been prospering since 1875. It had been initiated by Canon Edward Hannan, and was run along exclusivist Catholic Irish and temperance lines, based on the Young Men's Catholic Society in St Andrew's parish. By the mid 1880s it had become one of the leading teams in Britain, and when Hibs won the Scottish Cup in 1887 it was a triumph in which all of Scotland's Catholic Irish shared. Before they could return to Edinburgh with the cup, the Hibs had to join in the rejoicing of the west of Scotland Irish, as later recalled by Tom Maley in the *Glasgow Observer*: 'They were fêted by their Glasgow supporters, who drove them to St Mary's Hall, East Rose Street, and gave them a dinner and later presented them with mementoes of their great deed.'

The Hibs' secretary, John McFadden, addressed the assembly and, having recounted the club's history, urged his audience 'to go and do likewise'. The listeners included several of those who were soon to found Celtic. They observed the way in which the Hibs' victory inspired community identity, pride and confidence, and that the banners carried by the Hibs supporters were often emblazoned with the words 'God Save Ireland'. There were those in that St Mary's audience who recognized that an Irish team in the west, operating at the highest level, would increase the self-confidence and strengthen the sense of identity of the Irish Catholic community as a whole.

The East End was, at this time, the only area of Glasgow which did not support a senior football team. Meetings were held among representatives of three parishes – St Andrew's, St Mary's and St Alphonsus. Willie Maley, who was to play a key role in the club's history, recorded his own version of subsequent events:

There emanated a desire to put the matter to the test, and several meetings were held to decide what course of action should be taken to put the proposed club right on the way. As in all things Irish at that time, jealousies arose and various good men drew out rather than submit to being shoved aside by the more pushing sort always to be found. St Mary's representatives, with the greatest enthusiasm, eventually forced matters to an issue, and at a big meeting held in St Mary's Hall it was decided to proceed with the formation of the club and to look for the necessary ground. The St Andrew's representatives felt themselves side-tracked and withdrew from the project, although several of their best folks stuck to their guns and helped the project along.

Yet a remarkable point was that, while the idea of forming a football club was accepted, there were other aspects of the Edinburgh formula that were not – including the Hibernians' name, the temperance emphasis, and the direct association with the Young Men's Catholic Society.

The initial discussions about the formation of a club involved priests and leading laymen of the East End and beyond. In particular, the headmasters of the Sacred Heart and St Mary's schools, Brother Walfrid and Brother Dorotheus respectively, enthused over the prospect of a football team. They had been fighting the effects of poverty, ignorance and alcoholism among the East Enders for decades, and were acutely aware that many of the children in their care were hopelessly under-nourished and prone to disease. Brother Walfrid especially had become adept at inspiring others to voluntary effort on behalf of the many charities upon which the East End parishes relied. Local politicians took a leading role in the discussions. John Glass, John O'Hara and Thomas Flood led the local Catholic Union committees (the Catholic Union was the body set up to contest school board elections). Dr Conway, a much-loved local GP, J. M. Nelis and Joseph Shaughnessy – all of them founder members of the St Aloysius Association in 1887 – represented Glasgow's small Catholic professional class, while James Quillan and William McKillop were leading figures in the Irish National League in Glasgow. Such a breadth of involvement indicates that, from the start, this was not simply a local East End initiative but a co-ordinated drive involving all sections of the Catholic community in the Glasgow area.

The landmark meeting at which the decision was taken to form the Celtic Football and Athletic Club was held in St Mary's Hall on 6 November 1887, with John Glass presiding. Glass was in business as a joiner, a member of St Mary's and a leading figure in Glasgow Irish political circles. His commitment and imaginative approach to the Celtic concept were to prove vital in bringing it to fruition and in sustaining it through the early years. He was later to be described by Willie Maley as the man 'to whom the club owes its existence' and by J. H. McLaughlin as 'the originator and motivator' of Celtic.

From the very earliest days, there were differing shades of opinion about what the precise nature and purpose of the new club should be. These centred largely on the extent to which the example of Edinburgh Hibernians should be emulated. But enough was resolved by the time of that November meeting for a committee to be formed and a constitution adopted. The name of Celtic was also agreed upon (with the strong support of Brother Walfrid), as opposed to the widely-canvassed alternative of Glasgow Hibernians.

Within a week of the St Mary's Hall meeting, six acres of vacant ground had been leased adjacent to Janefield Cemetery, and voluntary work was soon under way on constructing the new stadium. Meanwhile, fund-raising efforts were in hand and the following circular was issued in January 1888. It did not, it must be said, make any concession to ecumenism, and it cannot be accepted – as has tended to happen – as the definitive statement of Celtic's aims.

CELTIC FOOTBALL AND ATHLETIC CLUB
Celtic Park, Parkhead
(Corner of Dalmarnock and Janefield Streets)

Patrons

His Grace the Archbishop of Glasgow and the Clergy of St Mary's, Sacred Heart and St Michael's Missions, and the principal Catholic laymen of the East End.

The above Club was formed in November 1887, by a number of the Catholics of the East End of the City.

The main object is to supply the East End conferences of the St Vincent de Paul Society with funds for the maintenance of the 'Dinner Tables' of our needy children in the Missions of St Mary's, Sacred Heart and St Michael's. Many cases of sheer poverty are left unaided through lack of means. It is therefore with this principal object that we have set afloat the 'Celtic' and we invite you as one of our ever-ready friends to assist in putting our new Park in proper working order for the coming football season.

We have already several of the leading Catholic football players of the West of Scotland on our membership list. They have most thoughtfully offered to assist in the good work.

We are fully aware that the 'elite' of football players belong to this City and suburbs, and we know that from there we can select a team which will be able to do credit to the Catholics of the West of Scotland as the Hibernians have been doing in the East. Again there is also the desire to have a large recreation ground where our Catholic young men will be able to enjoy the various sports which will build them up physically, and we feel sure we will have many supporters with us in this laudable object.

The good and great of Catholic Glasgow headed the subscription list, with Archbishop Eyre's name at the top. The Archbishop of Glasgow 'knew nothing of football but was always prepared to support any scheme that had for its object the welfare of the poor of his flock'. In less than six months from the date of the St Mary's Hall meeting, a level pitch had been formed, surrounded by a cycle track. A rudimentary open-air stand, to accommodate 1000 spectators, was erected with dressing rooms and committee rooms underneath. The committee met weekly and the opening date for the new Celtic Park was fixed for 8 May 1888, with Hibs and Cowlairs as the attraction. Earlier that day, Queen Victoria was to be in Glasgow for the opening of the great Glasgow International Exhibition of Industry, Science and Art at Kelvingrove, described by its promoters as a 'vast encyclopaedia of innovation and manufacture'. In the East End of the city, however, enthusiasm was centred on the opening of Celtic Park rather than on the royal occasion. The event was advertised in the *Glasgow Observer*, and the paper commented:

The courage of the committee in venturing such a grand undertaking at the commencement is the surprise of many. Some idea may be formed of it when we state that it is the opinion of competent judges that the Celtic Park is second to none in the country, and that is saying a great deal . . . It is with unqualified pleasure we offer our Celtic friends our congratulations on the great success that has crowned their labours so far and we wish them a long and prosperous career.

The following week, the *Observer* reported:

On Tuesday evening the weather was all that could be desired; a trifle chilly perhaps, but bright and pleasant notwithstanding. In and around the pavilion were clusters of clergy and people . . . Prompt to the advertised time, Dr Conway and Mr Shaughnessy emerged from the pavilion and entered the field, heading the procession of players. The Doctor placed the ball amid the cheers of the spectators, who numbered fully 5000.

After a goalless draw had been played out, the players and officials adjourned to the Royal Hotel, George Square. Dr John Conway, who was the club's first chairman and honorary president, presided and proposed a toast to 'The Hibernians'. In response, Mr McFadden of Hibs declared that 'it would be a sorry day indeed for the Irish in Scotland when residents of one city should act in an unfriendly way towards those of another'. Mr Thomas E. Maley then gave a reciprocal toast to 'The Celtic'.

On Monday 28 May Celtic played their own first game in front of 2000 spectators. Rangers provided the opposition and Celtic, who won 5–2, wore white shirts with green collars and a Celtic cross in red and green on the left breast. With no Scottish League in existence at that time, players were not tightly attached to clubs and it was possible to assemble what was, in effect, a select side of players who might be likely to throw in their lot with the new club. The first Celtic team was: M. Dolan (Drumpellier), E. Pearson (Carfin Shamrock) and J. McLaughlin (Govan Whitfield); W. Maley (Cathcart), J. Kelly (Renton) and P. Murray (Cambuslang Hibs); N. McCallum (Renton) and T. Maley (Cathcart); J. Madden (Dumbarton), M. Dunbar (Edinburgh Hibs) and H. Gorevin (Govan Whitfield).

After the game, St Mary's Hall was once again the venue for supper and, with much toasting and music, 'proceedings were of the happiest character'. Celtic were in business. They now applied to join the Glasgow and Scottish Football Associations, and further games were quickly arranged.

The early history of Celtic, and the personnel involved, are of unusual relevance to the present day because of the remarkable continuity which has persisted throughout the century of the club's existence. One hundred years later, the inaugural aims are still frequently debated, the sense of identity is similar, and prominent personnel owe their Celtic connection to a lineage which stretches all the way back to 1888.

The man who dominated the first half-century of Celtic's existence, Willie Maley, played at right-half in that inaugural side, although he had come to be involved, by his own account, more by accident than design. Within a few weeks of the St Mary's Hall meeting, three of Celtic's founding fathers – John Glass, Brother Walfrid and Pat 'Tailor' Welsh – visited the Maley home in Cathcart, with a view to securing the services of Tom Maley, a schoolmaster, who had played with Partick Thistle, Third Lanark and Edinburgh Hibernians. It was a shrewd move by the emissaries, who must have known that, apart from offering his own considerable ability, Tom Maley was also the man whom others would follow westwards from Hibernians. Willie Maley recalled:

Tom was not at home, and I arranged to get him to meet the party in Glasgow to hear the proposals. Brother Walfrid said, 'Why don't you come with him?' I replied that I was only a second-rater and had almost decided to give up the game for cross-country running. He persuaded me to come in with Tom, and when Tom decided to join up my name went down too, and so I was at once initiated into the wonderful scheme of things that this committee of men, with no football knowledge at all, had built up, and which their tremendous enthusiasm eventually brought to fruition.

Willie Maley joined Celtic as a player, but quickly became a committee man. He then took on the duties of match secretary, and this post was later converted into the managership, which he retained until 1940.

John Glass was the architect of such recruiting efforts, and he shrewdly concentrated his attentions on another of the finest players in Scotland at that time, James Kelly. This was the other signing, before Celtic had kicked a ball, which had enormous implications for the club's subsequent history. The son of Irish parents who had migrated to Scotland in 1842, Kelly was born in 1865 in the village of Renton, on the banks of the Leven. His story is representative of those who would soon establish Celtic as one of Britain's leading football clubs. During James' childhood, the new sport of football was developing rapidly in the Dumbarton area; the spacious flat land along the Leven, and a tradition of team games such as shinty in the area, helped to ensure that football developed more rapidly there than anywhere else in Scotland. James Kelly started playing for Renton when he was eighteen. Throughout his youth, he was involved in the local Young Ireland Association and the Irish National League. No doubt he was present when Michael Davitt – the founder of the Irish Land League – addressed a rally in Dumbarton in 1887. His father, David, was a hammer-man in the local forge, and the extreme poverty of the family pushed him towards professional football, which did exist in practice, if not in theory, at that time.

By the time he signed for Celtic in the summer of 1888, James Kelly had been in a Scottish cup-winning side, and had also starred in Renton's celebrated 'world club championship' victory over West Bromwich Albion, just ten days before Celtic's first game. It had seemed likely that he would be attracted to the Edinburgh Hibernians, for whom he had played on several occasions, but he was wooed to the fledgling Glasgow club by the persuasive Irish tongue of John Glass. The signing of Kelly represented a huge success, which ensured that other high-quality players would follow. He quickly became very much involved in the running of the club, was one of the first directors in 1897, and initiated a Kelly dynasty within Celtic which survives to the present day. If John Glass had set his sights a little lower than Tom Maley and James Kelly, the subsequent history of Celtic would have been very different.

The second fixture at Celtic Park was against Dundee Harp, who went down 1–0 to the infant club in front of 6000 spectators. By the end of June, Celtic had drawn 3–3 with Mossend Swifts and lost 4–3 to Clyde. The life-span of new clubs tended to be brief in those days – a point illustrated by the company in which Celtic found themselves when being admitted to membership of the Scottish Football Association on 21 August 1888. The other successful applicants that day were Champfleurie and Adventurers from Edinburgh, Leith Harp, Balaclava Rangers from Oban, Temperance Athletic of Glasgow, Whifflet Shamrock and Britannia of Auchinleck! None survived to tell the tale.

Although the Scottish League did not yet exist, it was possible to put together a very full programme of fixtures during Celtic's first full season, 1888–9. Of fifty-six matches played, forty-two were won and three drawn. Celtic lost the major tournament, the Scottish Cup, to Third Lanark only in a replayed final at Hampden, after accounting for Shettleston, Cowlairs, Albion Rovers, St Bernard, Clyde, East Stirling and Dumbarton. The major power in the land were still Queen's Park, who deprived Celtic of the Glasgow Cup, while Renton gave them a quick knock-out from the Charity Cup. Cowlairs eliminated Celtic from the Exhibition Cup, but they won their first trophy by defeating the same club in the less prestigious North Eastern Cup at Barrowfield.

Celtic travelled remarkably far from home in that first season. There were games in Newcastle, Burnley, Bolton, London and Belfast. Their guests at Celtic Park included the mighty Corinthians, whom they beat 6–2 in front of a crowd of over 16,000 on 3 January 1889, although losing 3–1 when they went to London for a return challenge. Within their first year of existence, Celtic even acquired their first 'brake club' (a brake was a type of vehicle hired by a club's supporters to transport them to wherever their team was playing). Appropriately, it hailed from the parish of St Mary's, and the club's banner gave pride of place to the features of Tom Maley. Others quickly followed, usually under the auspices of a parish's League of the

Cross, a temperance organization. Each brake held twenty-five people; soon, they would start to assemble at Carlton Place and proceed to whichever ground Celtic were playing at.

By the time the club held its annual meeting in June 1889 there was already much to celebrate, and when Tom Maley responded to the vote of thanks, 'the meeting rose en masse and sang out lustily, "He's a Jolly Good Fellow"'. Prior to the election of officers, Mr Shaughnessy moved that Michael Davitt should be made honorary patron of the club, and 'this was received with acclamation'. Davitt had confirmed his popularity among the Glasgow Irish with a memorable St Patrick's Day address in the city hall when he condemned Irish landlordism as a system which 'breeds Irish poverty, nourishes Irish crime, feeds Irish discontent, disturbs Irish peace, paralyses Irish industry and enterprise, checks material and social progress and arrests in the works of development and expansion the genius of a nation. [Loud cheers] Home Rule or no Home Rule, Irish landlordism has got to go.' These were sentiments close to the hearts of those people who had founded, as well as of those who supported, Celtic. Most, perhaps all, of the inaugural committee were deeply committed to the politics of Ireland, and they included several who were to become at least as well known through their activities in that arena as through the Celtic connection. Once again, this strain in the club's tradition has remained relevant to an understanding of its nature and character.

Reports of the annual meeting in 1889 indicate that there were already 'malcontents' among the membership, none of whom was elected to the committee – 'for which the Celtic Football Club have every reason to be thankful', snorted *Scottish Sport*. The cause of unrest concerned the development of the club's nature and priorities. It had been clear from the start that Celtic would generate substantial sums of money and great community influence for those who controlled the club. The malcontents remained adamant that it should be Catholic, amateur and charitable. In particular, they disliked the connection which had developed with the licensed trade. For many in the Irish immigrant community, drink was undoubtedly a curse. For some, however, it was the only business opportunity apart from pawnbroking available to the immigrant community. Inevitably, therefore, the input of Glasgow's Catholic businessmen into Celtic came largely from publicans and restaurant owners, including the McKillops, J. H. McLaughlin and James Quillan. Equally inevitably, some of the players ended up with jobs, either nominal or real, in the licensed premises.

In spite of the great start the Celtic club had enjoyed, some of the malcontents sought to encourage Hibernians to move west as a rival club. The goodwill towards the new Glasgow organization exuded by Mr McFadden of Hibs in the early days had dissipated rapidly as several leading players had been lured to Celtic Park, particularly in the wake of James Kelly's decision to go there rather than to Hibs. When Celtic played them in Edinburgh in October 1888, there had been a hostile reception from the crowd – scarcely eased by the fact that Celtic won 3–0. However, negotiations with Hibs fell through and the malcontents made their own short-lived effort to establish a club called Glasgow Hibernians. The choice of name was significant, for here, indeed, was an attempt to establish an alternative club along the lines that Celtic had deliberately chosen not to follow. The rival school of thought about Celtic's proper nature and purpose would linger on. But it is important to note that the debate was there from the start and that it was consistently won by those who saw Celtic's charitable function as the by-product of creating a successful, well-organized club.

Within the space of the nineteen months which separated these two St Mary's Hall meetings, Celtic had not only been brought into existence but had also established themselves as a major power in Scottish football. They had won respect from further afield, both for their playing prowess and for the efficiency of their management. They had equipped themselves with a fine stadium and proven their crowd-pulling power. Never had a club enjoyed such an auspicious start and, for good measure, they were able to donate £421 19s 6d to charity, in addition to raising several hundred pounds by playing invitation games and distributing match tickets for sale by the local conferences of the St Vincent de Paul Society. That section of Scottish society which did not much fancy the idea of a football club that was largely Irish in identity and successful on the playing field would, for a century to come, have to learn to live with that reality.

# 2

## SOCIAL BACKGROUND
### *Religion and Politics*

LASGOW in 1888 was dominated by the hallmarks, both good and ill, of the Industrial Revolution. The credit side of the picture was amply illustrated in the Great Exhibition – the largest ever held outside London – opened by Queen Victoria on the same day as the inauguration of the first Celtic Park. The Exhibition was a testimony to the second city of the empire's primary place as a hotbed of industrial innovation, manufacture and trade. Glasgow was at the height of its powers as a workshop of the world, with the greatest concentrations of engineering works and factories in the city's East End. To the west, along the Clyde, shipbuilding was in its heyday and 234 ships were launched on the river in 1888. The volume of the Corporation-published *Statistics of Glasgow* for that year reported: 'In every department of the city's well-being – municipal, commercial, educational, artistic and philanthropic – evidences of conspicuous advance present themselves.'

And so they did, so long as one did not look much beneath the surface. For instance, the city chambers in George Square were completed in 1888 (the foundation stone having been laid five years earlier by Sir John Ure, Lord Provost, 'with full Masonic rites'). The citizenry watched the building's progress 'with ever-growing interest as it rose from the ground course by course and storey by storey, the interest intensifying as it effloresced into domes and towers'. When the Shah of Persia visited a few months later, the new chambers were described as 'an edifice which combines the solid purposes of a Western business city with Oriental ideas of splendour'. But for reasons that were political and cultural as well as social and economic, the grandeur of George Square was far more remote from the great majority of people in Glasgow's impoverished East End than mere geography suggested. It would, for example, be another decade before the first Catholic councillor was elected in the city.

In 1888, there were 11,675 registered deaths in Glasgow of which 4750 were of infants under five years. Another 1192 failed to reach the age of twenty, and fewer than 2000 had made it to sixty. Among the children, the principal plagues were measles, whooping cough and scarlet fever – diseases associated with poverty and overcrowding. In the jerry-built slums of the East End, the world into which Celtic arrived, conditions were at their most miserable. The Irish immigrant population was heavily represented in this area of the city, particularly since the great influx of refugees after the potato famine in Ireland in the 1840s. Catholic marriages in Glasgow between 1885 and 1888 accounted for almost one in six of the total – an indication of how the Irish had become a substantial minority within the city. Nineteenth-century Glasgow had, among British cities, been second only to Liverpool as a magnet for Irish immigrants.

The Irish had been driven to Scotland and other lands by the inability of their rack-rented, colonized country to sustain them. The political complexities of the situation, and the reinforced sense of grievance felt by the Irish people, were of little interest to most people in Presbyterian Scotland, who viewed the Irish influx with varying degrees of apprehension and hostility. Yet governments did nothing to stop it, because of the flow of cheap labour which it provided. The keeper of Glasgow's statistical records probably spoke for much of Presbyterian Scotland at this time, when he felt bold enough to offer the unscientific opinion: 'The sufferings of Ireland have not been the offspring of Saxon tyranny but of racial fertility beyond the capabilities of the soil.' He recommended emigration to North America rather than to the slums of Glasgow where, he noted, 'the practice amongst the poor of two families living together is on the increase'. The reality was a scene very different from the revelry that accompanied the Great Exhibition.

Scotland in the latter half of the nineteenth century was fired by fierce religious controversy, to which the Roman Catholic minority was peripheral. The ranks of Presbyterians had been split into deeply opposed churches by various schisms, notably the disruption of 1843 which created the Free Church of Scotland. Indigenous Scottish Catholicism had been marginalized by the Reformation, and had survived principally in remote areas of the Highlands and Islands. This meant, therefore, that Catholicism and Irishness became largely interchangeable terms in lowland Scotland as

the immigrant influx increased during the century. The feuding Presby-
terians found unity in their hostility towards the Catholic Irish incursion.
In 1867 Bishop Gray, who led the Catholic mission in Scotland, advised an
English visitor: 'The Scotch are animated by a strong hereditary hatred of
Catholicity, nor is the feeling of the country favourable to Irish settlers . . .
The religion, the history, the character and habits of the two peoples show
many elements not of difference but of antagonism.'

By and large, the Irish immigrants in Glasgow filled the more menial jobs,
being untrained for those aspects of industrialization which required skills.
Along with the displaced Highlanders they acquired the reputation of being
prepared to undercut their fellows in terms of wages and conditions in order
to obtain jobs at any price. This secular source of resentment went
hand-in-hand with the anti-Catholic propaganda which was maintained by
the Presbyterian churches. Signs of Catholic progress, such as the restora-
tion of the Scottish hierarchy in 1878, were meat and drink for those whose
vested interest was in warning against the Catholic-Irish 'threat'.

While never resting easily alongside mainstream Scottish Presbyterian-
ism, the Orange Order was another ingredient in the mix which ensured
that Glasgow's Irish population would create its own social structures and
defence mechanisms. The Order had its origins in supporting Protestant
landholding in Armagh in the late eighteenth century. Glasgow did not have
its first Orange Lodge until 1860, by which time the organization was
established as an all-purpose vehicle for anti-Irish Catholic sentiment as well
as for political Conservatism. The substantial number of Ulster Protestant
immigrants to Scotland formed the basis of Orange strength.

The religious distinctiveness of the Irish community was matched by its
political preoccupations. It was the politics of Ireland which held the
attention of the expatriates, and it was along Irish lines that they had
organized themselves politically. Irish Home Rule was the prime demand,
with land reform not far behind. Their interest in British politics had been
measured largely in terms of the relevance to Ireland; thus the Liberalism to
which most of Glasgow still subscribed in the 1880s was shared by the Irish
only in so far as Gladstone was seen to be delivering on Home Rule.
Lowland Scottish suspicion of that cause (and the Catholicism which went
with it) was regularly fuelled by Fenian outrages – the attempted bombings
in 1883 of Tradeston Gas Works, Buchanan Street Goods Station and
Ruchill Canal Bridge certainly helped to condition Glasgow attitudes in the
latter part of the same decade. From 1881, Michael Davitt, a former Fenian
prisoner and the most radical of the Irish political leaders, was an extremely
popular visitor to the Irish in Glasgow. The city's Catholic Irish press
reflected the political interests of the readership. The same issue of the
*Glasgow Observer* which announced the opening of Celtic Park carried much
more prominent headlines concerning such matters as: 'Double Execution

in Tralee'; 'Shocking Eviction' in Co. Carlow; and Pope Leo XIII's condemnation of the tactic known as boycotting in Ireland. The contrast with the news carried in the mainstream Scottish press was total.

The decision to form Celtic Football Club is rightly identified with the needs of Catholic charity in the East End of Glasgow. But the early nature of the club, and the direction it pursued, owe at least as much to the influence exercised by the political organization which spoke for the vast majority of the Irish in Scotland in the 1880s, the Irish National League, and specifically one of its branches in Glasgow, known as the Home Government Branch. Among those involved in setting up Celtic, John Glass, James Quillan, the McKillops and the Murphys were heavily involved in the Home Government Branch. Glass was its treasurer; Quillan, Celtic's first vice-president, was also vice-president of the branch. Hugh Murphy was president of the Home Government Branch and also a member of Celtic, while his brother Arthur would serve on Celtic's committee for its first decade. Later, Thomas White would also preside over the Home Government Branch.

The Home Government Branch of the Irish National League in Glasgow was founded in 1871 by John Ferguson, a Belfast Protestant described by Michael Davitt as the 'father of the Irish movement in Scotland'. It was the start of an organization which would grow to 600 branches throughout Britain by the mid 1880s. The Home Government Branch dominated Irish politics in Scotland and had the closest of links with the Irish parliamentary party, in its struggle for Home Rule. It raised large amounts of money for the parliamentary party and its own weekly meetings were known as 'the parliament of the Irish people in Glasgow'. Each year, it was the Home Government Branch which organized the St Patrick's Day celebrations in Glasgow and made sure that all the leading figures of the Irish movement visited the city, including Isaac Butt, Parnell and Davitt. The influence which the leading figures in the Home Government Branch exercised in the founding of Celtic ensured that the primary aim would be to create a club that was outward-looking, proudly Irish and excellent, rather than a 'Glasgow Hibernians' founded on the Catholic parishes.

The Irish National League was a non-sectarian organization, and the Home Government Branch was in the forefront of practising this doctrine, reinforced by the role of Ferguson, whose leadership had already been challenged unsuccessfully on the grounds that he was not Catholic. That matter had come to a head in 1875 over a commemoration rally for the Irish national hero Daniel O'Connell. The rally had physically split into two groups – those, under Church influence, who wanted to recall only O'Connell's role in achieving Catholic emancipation, and those – under Ferguson's leadership – who saw it as a more political occasion. Ferguson had emerged all the stronger from this dispute, and he remained the dominant figure in Home Rule politics in Glasgow until after the turn of the century. It is unthinkable that people who were his closest allies in the Home Government Branch in the following decade would have had any interest in forming a football club which retreated into Catholic exclusivism.

The choice of Celtic as the club's name can also be traced to the strategy of the Irish National League in Scotland at that time. By placing emphasis upon the struggle against Irish landlordism, of which the campaign for Home Rule was only a part, they were building bridges with the Scottish Highland community, both at home and in Glasgow. The impoverished state of the Highlands and Islands was the dominant political issue in Scotland at that time and it was a reasonable belief that identifying a common cause with the predominantly Presbyterian Highlanders would help to break down the suspicions within Ulster that the Home Rule movement would lead them into 'Rome Rule'. The Home Government Branch of the INL was most enthusiastic about applying this strategy – hence the repeated visits of Davitt to Glasgow and, indeed, the Highlands and Islands which he toured under the branch's auspices in 1887. The proceeds of the St Patrick's Day rally that year were given to the crofters' movement. Wherever he went, Davitt emphasized the common Celtic background of Scots and Irish. The main Catholic paper, the *Glasgow Observer*, accorded huge headlines to his visit: 'Davitt in Highlands – the Tribune of the Celtic Race'. When he met with John Murdoch, a leading figure in the crofters' movement, 'so loud and hearty was the cheering that the mountains as well as the buildings echoed in celebration of a meeting of Celt with Celt'.

A few months later, the name 'Celtic' was adopted for the new football club, with Brother Walfrid prominent in advocating it. This was consistent with the fact that he had previously organized teams under the name 'Columba', which evoked the common religious inheritance of Scotland and Ireland. The Catholic Irish had been naming teams for the previous fifteen or twenty years, and Celtic never appears to have arisen as a suggestion – Hibernians, Harp, Erin, Shamrock and Emerald were the popular choices. Even as late as August 1887, an Irish select team played Partick Thistle at Whiteinch under the name of Western Hibernians. The side included James Kelly, Willie Groves and John Coleman, all soon to be Celtic regulars. But over the next few months, the argument in favour of 'Celtic' was won. For those who wished to build bridges between the Scots and the Irish, it was perfect. So unfamiliar were the Glasgow Irish with the name that they immediately mispronounced it with a soft 'C'. To his dying day, Brother Walfrid maintained the proper pronunciation.

The divisions over how Catholic and charitable Celtic should be, and the Home Government Branch's crucial role in determining the outcome, were paralleled at exactly the same time, and involving many of the same people, by the vital debate over the political direction of the Irish community. Also in May 1888 the Home Government Branch endorsed Keir Hardie, the first Labour candidate in Britain, in the Mid Lanark by-election. John Ferguson became a founding vice-president of the Scottish Labour Party at its inception. Had the Home Government Branch supported instead the formation of an Irish Party in Scotland – as was being mooted in some Catholic circles at that time – then the subsequent political development of the country might have been very different.

By 1880 there were still only eighteen Catholic churches in Glasgow. One of the largest was St Mary's in Abercromby Street, founded in 1842, which served a population of 10,000 in the surrounding East End districts. A school had attached to the church since 1850, and it was run by the Marist Brothers from 1863. The 1872 Education Act had made the provision of schooling the responsibility of the state, but the Catholic Church continued to run its own 'voluntary' schools, in order to ensure the maintenance of Catholic education. They were entitled to state support only through parliamentary grant and not from the rates, which the newly-created school boards could levy. In 1874 another school, attached to the Sacred Heart church, was opened and Brother Walfrid moved from St Mary's School to this new charge. He continued to work closely with Brother Dorotheus, head of St Mary's School, in the common cause of fund-raising to sustain the schools, allow for expansion and provide assistance to those pupils who required it. The 'penny dinner' scheme was initiated by Walfrid in Sacred Heart and taken up by Dorotheus in St Mary's. As the centenary history of the latter school recalled:

For some lads it was not indifference but lack of means that made them absentees. Even in the cruellest days of winter then a barefooted boy was no uncommon sight and raggedness and an ill-filled belly were the daily lot of many an urchin . . . The penny was charged only when no great hardship was involved, to preserve the self-respect of the beneficiaries. Many parents whose children needed the meal would have baulked at the idea of receiving charity but were reconciled by the face-saving device of a token payment.

The scheme was off the ground by December 1885, and a few months later a football match was organized between Edinburgh Hibernians and St Peter's, Partick, to raise money for its funding, proceeds going to Sacred Heart, St Mary's and St Michael's in the Gallowgate. Organized football had by this time been around for some twenty years. Its attractiveness as a team game, capable of arousing mass enthusiasm, had grown steadily as Saturday afternoons off work became the norm. Queen's Park, founded in

1867, were deeply involved in codifying the rules of the game – the prerequisite for its popularity as a spectator sport. The extent to which the game had caught on in a big way among Glasgow's youth can be gauged from these recollections in the history of St Mary's school.

The use of footballs to kick in the yard before school was one of the schemes in St Mary's to encourage good time-keeping; and football matches for the perfect attenders with prizes for the winning teams helped in the good work. As the government grant to the managers of the Catholic schools varied with roll and attendance, teachers tried all kinds of schemes to ensure the highest possible daily attendance.

The same account notes, incidentally:

The attractions that lured the fickle attender from his duty, thought not so many as in modern times, were just as potent as today. Among other seductions the St Mary's logbook lists at various intervals the Paisley Races, the Wild Beast Show at Vinegar Hill, Buffalo Bill's Wild West Show – though staging it in Duke Street was surely demanding superhuman restraint from any St Mary's boy – and the Glasgow Exhibition of 1888.

Such were the temptations in the 1880s against which football in the playground was weighed!

When placed in the context of history, and given the nature of Scottish society and attitudes in the 1880s, Celtic's emergence as a club with a strong Irish identity is wholly understandable. Brother Walfrid's discovery of football – a game of which the cleric from Ballymote, County Sligo had little prior knowledge – as a splendid fund-raiser made the origination of a substantial club from within the East End parishes a very natural extension of this principle. The wonder is that the Edinburgh example had not been followed, and such a club successfully established, long before 1888.

The rapid flourishing of the St Mary's Hall enterprise was due entirely to the fact that several quite outstanding individuals invested their enthusiasm in it. Disparaging references to the 'bunch of publicans' who founded Celtic or carried the club through its inevitable transition to the status of limited company, can be based only on ignorance, for the truth is that Celtic's pioneers included several men of real interest and character, whose public activities extended well beyond football. The careers of Glass, Shaughnessy, Kelly, the McKillops, White (who entered the scene a little later) and others who were to the fore in these early years would all be worthy of study in their own right, and in each case the Celtic involvement would represent just one strand of the story to be told.

Just as the reasons for Celtic's emergence can be readily understood, so too it can be seen as inevitable that the club would attract hostility, with its roots in issues which had little or nothing to do with footballing prowess. It took time for this antagonism to develop into a clearly defined counter-force. But from the day of Celtic's birth, there must have been a sizeable proportion of Scottish public opinion which resented the club's very existence, as a manifestation of the Irish presence in Scotland.

That was the nature of the world into which Celtic were born and, as in so many other respects, the world has not entirely mended its ways in the course of the past century. Celtic have not sought to appease the unappeasable by denying their origins and identity. But success on the field of play, dignity in their affairs and adherence to the founding principles have transcended all prejudices other than those which exist in the minds of their harshest detractors.

# 3

# THE EARLY DAYS
## *Pioneering and Professionalism*

ITHIN a few months of Celtic taking to the field, sports writers were claiming to discern a distinctive style in their play. In November 1888, *Scottish Sport* commented upon 'the clever dribbling and short accurate passing which is characteristic of their play'. When they met Dumbarton in the third round of the Scottish Cup, the *Scottish Referee* observed:

'The Celts' style is modelled on that of Preston North End, and whilst it demands speed, strength and all the essentials which go to make up the stock-in-trade of the football player, the one thing needful is head. The cool, calculating, easy-going manner in which the Celts wrought the ball must have been a revelation to the Dumbarton people . . .'

Celtic's progress to the Final of the Scottish Cup in their inaugural season stands out as their first great playing achievement, which immediately commanded respect – however grudging – in Scottish football circles. Their progress was, however, accompanied by the kind of controversies that marked these pioneering days of the organized game. In the fifth round, Willie Maley as match secretary lodged a protest after Clyde had won 1–0 at Celtic Park, on the grounds that the last ten minutes had been played in darkness due to Clyde's late readiness for the game. The protest was upheld by one vote, and Clyde were so incensed by this outcome that at the replay they refused to change in the Celtic pavilion, arriving at the ground ready for action. They lost 9–2.

The Final itself was scheduled for 2 February 1889, and though Third Lanark won this game 3–0, a replay was again required. The match became known as the 'Snow Final': as the large crowd assembled, a blizzard swept Hampden Park. Under the guidance of a solicitor who was present, the two clubs drew up a joint 'protest' against the game being played in such conditions. Dr James Handley, author of *The Celtic Story* (published in 1960), wrote:

'The agreement was a quiet one. Only a rope separated spectators and players in those days and the playing pitch would probably have been the rallying ground for a demonstration on the part of an incensed crowd, who had paid to see a final and were being fobbed off with a friendly, particularly as the admission price had been raised for the occasion from the usual sixpence to a shilling . . .'

The final proper took place on the following Saturday, and Third Lanark won 2–1.

Celtic's second season was less auspicious than the first, losing the Glasgow Cup Final to still-mighty Queen's Park and going out of the Scottish Cup in the first round to the same club. But in 1890–1 they won the Glasgow Cup – a feat which, at that time, required victories in four rounds prior to the Final. This was Celtic's first major trophy, but the event of far greater significance in the 1890–1 season was the inauguration of the Scottish League, with ten clubs involved at the outset in the First Division. They were Abercorn, Cambuslang, Celtic, Cowlairs, Dumbarton, Heart of Midlothian, Rangers, St Mirren, Third Lanark and Vale of Leven. Celtic's representative at the SFA, J. H. McLaughlin, had been very much involved in advocating the establishment of a league, which brought a much-needed edge of competition to the Scottish game at a crucial time. In the first League season, Celtic had four points deducted for fielding ineligible players and finished in third place behind the joint winners, Rangers and Dumbarton. In all, Celtic played forty-nine games in 1890–1, winning thirty-four of them and losing only eight. A reserve team had been formed, and it won the Scottish Second Eleven Cup.

The early disagreements about the club's nature and purpose continued to fester, and came to the fore again at the annual meeting of members in 1891. The press apparently went to some trouble to be present on such occasions, and the correspondent of the *Scottish Referee* reported breathlessly that this particular meeting attracted 'a respectable but excited audience, who were so taken up with discussion amongst themselves that they did not observe me sliding under the table at the entrance and seating myself at the side of the platform to watch and hear'.

There was plenty to observe, for this turned into a showdown meeting between the rival camps, with each faction issuing 'slates' of candidates to vote for. Dr Conway, the man who had kicked the first ball on Celtic Park, led the attack on the officials of the club and, in particular, opposed the decision to pay William Maley a fee. Seconded by J. H. McLaughlin, he moved against this and declared that while there were plenty of men willing to work for the club for nothing, nobody should be paid for it. Clearly, Dr Conway's argument applied to players as well as to officials. He was challenging Celtic's whole approach, but his motion was lost by 102 votes to 74.

In the elections which followed, the malcontents were trounced by similar margins. Dr Conway lost his position as honorary president to Joseph Shaughnessy. He then stood against Glass for the key position of president (effectively chairman), and lost again. A leading member of the Irish National League, Arthur Murphy, was added to the committee. Willie Maley was confirmed as match secretary. 'The anti-officialites, as the opposition in the Celtic committee has been called, have been cleared out', stated *Scottish Sport*. (The reported role of McLaughlin as seconder of Dr Conway's motion remains puzzling. Far from being 'cleared out', he was appointed club secretary at this meeting, and was already at that time a leading advocate of 'honest professionalism' in football. Perhaps the covert reporter got it wrong!)

The early months of the following season brought potentially crippling news for Celtic – as Wilie Maley described it, 'an old affliction to Irishmen – the Landlord.' John McLaughlin went into detail at the club's half-yearly meeting in December 1891.

Being an Irish club, it was but natural that they should have a greedy landlord, and they had one who was working to take a place high among rack-renters in Ireland. In the old country these gentlemen were satisfied with doubling or at the worst trebling it, but the bright genius who boasted the possession of Celtic Park wanted nine times the previous rent for a new lease. Instead of £50 per year, he wished to increase the annual rent to £450.

With the lease due to expire at Martinmas 1892, consideration was given to moving out of the East End to Possilpark or Springburn, but as the Cowlairs club had 'sort of official rights to the northern district', the idea was abandoned. In the end, Celtic did not have to look far for their alternative. An expanse of waste ground – or 'quarry hole' according to Maley – situated between the old ground and London Road was leased from the estate of

Lord Hozier, initially for ten years. It seemed an unpromising, waterlogged site and 10,000 cartloads of infill were required to level it. But the work, much of it accomplished with voluntary labour, was completed in astonishingly quick time, and on Saturday 20 March 1892 the link between Michael Davitt and Celtic was reinforced when he laid a centre sod, fresh from Donegal that morning with a clump of shamrocks growing in it. What better man, the committee must have reasoned, to celebrate this triumph over a landlord's excessive demands? John Ferguson was another who was to the fore at the ceremony which, it was noted, was a much more secular occasion than the first ground opening.

To commemorate the occasion, an understandably anonymous poem appeared in one of the Catholic papers of the day.

> On alien soil like yourself I am here;
> I'll take root and flourish of that never fear,
> And though I'll be crossed sore and oft by the foes
> You'll find me as hardy as Thistle and Rose.
> If model is needed on your own pitch you will have it,
> Let your play honour me and my friend Michael Davitt.

When the centre sod was promptly stolen by a nineteenth-century vandal, the poet returned to the fray:

> The curse of Cromwell blast the sand that stole the sod that Michael cut;
> May all his praties turn to sand – the crawling, thieving scut.
> That precious site of Irish soil with verdant shamrocks overgrown
> Was token of a glorious soil more fitting far than fretted stone.
> Again I say, may Heaven blight that envious soulless knave
> May all his sunshine be like night and the sod rest heavy on his grave.

Almost fifty years later, Willie Maley recalled with pride how 'a seemingly impossible site . . . was converted into a palatial enclosure, and it looked, as one smart chap said, "like leaving the graveyard to enter Paradise". That title, seized on by a pressman, clung to the present ground for many years.' The new stadium was recognized as the best in Britain at that time. There were tracks for running and cycling, a grandstand for 3500 spectators and a two-storeyed pavilion.

In 1891–2, Celtic won their first Scottish Cup, beating Queen's Park 5–1 in a replayed final at Ibrox. Once again, there had been an agreement in the first match – at half-time on this occasion – to make the game a friendly, this time because the very large crowd of around 40,000 was occasionally spilling over on to the park. The gates had been closed, but thousands climbed over the barricades and, with no real protection against the press of the throng, there was frequent encroachment upon the area of play. There was an attendance of just 15,000 at Ibrox for the second game, scarcely justifying the presence of two hundred police.

The Scottish football press was not inclined to be generous towards Celtic in their hour of triumph. The *Scottish Referee* reported grudgingly: 'There are circumstances which tone down the triumph considerably, and make it pretty much a Pyrrhic victory. The Queen's had but a skeleton team . . .' *Scottish Sport* concurred that Queen's Park team difficulties and ultimate line-up had been more significant in bringing about the 5–1 scoreline 'than any inherent ability displayed by the Celtic team'. The first Celtic side to win the Scottish Cup was: Cullen, Reynolds and Doyle; W. Maley, Kelly and Gallacher; McCallum and Brady; Dowds, McMahon and Campbell. Celtic also won the Glasgow Cup and Glasgow Charity Cup in this season to give them their first 'treble'.

A mere handful of years into their existence, the season 1892–3 proved to be of landmark importance to Celtic. This was the season of their first Scottish League title. But the wider significance of the season was summed up by Willie Maley: 'It was a happy augury for the future, as it marked the opening of the new ground, and with the legalisation of professionalism, football seemed in a fair way to becoming a more honest and better organised sport.' The principal advocate of professionalism in Scottish football was John H. McLaughlin, one of Celtic's founders, who became the club's leading figure on the legislative side of the game. Of Donegal stock, he had been the organist in St Mary's and had had, like most of the Celtic founders, minimal knowledge of football prior to the Celtic initiative. According to Maley, indeed, his previous sporting interest was in cricket. When the club was founded, he was barely twenty-five years of age, but on his death in 1909, Tom Maley wrote of him:

The late legislator entered into football at a time most dangerous. Dangerous, because an older school of leaders – conservative as a tramcar – were at the head of affairs, and progress was slow, so very slow. The establishment of the Scottish Football League as well as the legalisation of professionalism, epochs in football, are monumental to his labours.

From the outset, Celtic had been prepared to spend money in order to build a team of merit. In theory, Scottish football was an amateur game, but only Queen's Park adhered to this principle with any sense of commitment. Football was capable of creating substantial income through the gates, and there was no obvious reason why the players who drew the crowds should not share in this wealth – then, as to some extent now, football offered one of the few legitimate devices by which young working-class men could rapidly improve their economic lot. Apart from anything else, professionalism had been recognized in England since 1875, so players were bound to drain away from Scotland as long as amateurism remained the reality there.

Celtic had from the start paid their players thirty shillings a week, and this rose to £2 in 1890 as other players went on strike for equality with those brought from England. This at a time when all were supposed to be amateurs! It was the signature of Dan Doyle from Everton that sparked off the revolt, and also caused some very reasonable questions to be asked in the sporting press. The *Scottish Referee* wondered:

How can an amateur club like Celtic outbid a very wealthy professional team in Everton? It is far easier to comprehend the weaving of one of Mr Gladstone's speeches than the exact process by which the Celtic can induce a Scot, well paid in England, to return to his native land and yet keep within the rules of the Scottish Association. That Doyle now proposes to cross the border to play for an amateur club like the Celtic imposes too great a strain on the credulity.

The tale of the 1890 strike was told by Willie Maley almost fifty years later in *The Story of the Celtic*. It did not last long, 'as the committee had to face the increases brought about by the return of Doyle and Coy'. The 'paid amateur' state of affairs was, Maley agreed, 'farcical', and it was to Celtic's credit that they were more open about their practices than others and also in the vanguard of campaigning for change. It was largely through John McLaughlin's advocacy within the SFA that the legalization of professionalism was approved almost unanimously in 1893, after his motion to the same effect had failed narrowly the previous year. 'To the Celtic lies the credit of bringing about this honest avowal of what had existed long before their inception, aye and in clubs too that had the audacity to pose as purists on the amateur question', said the Celtic handbook.

By the time of the half-yearly meeting in December 1892, Celtic were Scottish Cup-holders and on their way to their first League title. It was time for satisfaction to be taken from these achievements, and Mr Thomas Flood, who proposed the adoption of the secretary's report on that occasion, undoubtedly summed up the prevailing mood when he declared that the club's success 'not only reflects credit on the members of the team and their Glasgow followers, but will be welcomed by their countrymen all over Great Britain, who take a deep interest in the working of the Celtic club'. Warming to his theme, Flood elaborated upon the significance of this footballing achievement.

Irishmen in Scotland, in past years, have been made little of, because they have few of their number in business or in positions of responsibility. But they have lately demonstrated that not only in commercial life can they be successful, but they have proved the possession on their part of an amount of pluck and perseverance by the manner in which they have risen to the top of the ladder in the football world. The Celtic team is the pride of the Irish race in England, Ireland and Scotland . . .

His seconder saw Celtic's achievement as 'proof of the ability of Irishmen to manage any concern in which they took an interest . . .'.

Celtic were indeed at the forefront of progressive innovation. In December 1892, the honorary president, Joseph Shaughnessy, 'gave an explanation of the negotiations of the committee with regard to the erection of electric light in the park with a view to evening matches, and explanations respecting the preservation of the field from frost'. Lighting was actually introduced at Celtic Park late in the following year, and the first game the club played under artificial light was a friendly against Clyde on Christmas night, 1893. James Handley's account of the Heath Robinson structure makes amusing reading.

The experiment was not a success and after a few weeks' trial was abandoned. The wires, fixed to a dozen huge wooden posts 50 feet high, were stretched across the field, with lamps attached, and along the covered enclosure additional illumination was provided by a hundred gas-jets. Apart from the unsightly mass of wires and lamps, which detracted from the appearance of the ground, the structure was apt to sag and impede the flight of the ball. St Bernard, beaten 8–1 by Celtic in the quarter-finals of the Scottish Cup in January 1894, were moved to lodge a protest with the SFA – later withdrawn – on that account. The ball had struck the wires only twice during the course of the game, but the club claimed that its objection was based on principle. After their great centre-forward, the rigging went by the name of 'Madden's Shipyard' among the Celtic supporters.

# 4

## TOWARDS
## THE TWENTIETH CENTURY
### *Business and Battles*

EFORE the turn of the century, Celtic won the Scottish League Championship again in seasons 1893/4, '95/6 and '97/8. The Scottish Cup proved more elusive, and they did not recapture it after 1892 until 1899, when they beat Rangers 2–0 at Hampden. By the end of the 1893/4 season, only James Kelly remained of the original team. Names such as Johnny Divers, Jimmy Blessington and Barney Battles began to appear on the team-sheet. By winning the League title three times in the competition's first six years of existence, the paramount position of Celtic in Scottish football was clearly established, and this status was recognized when J. H. McLaughlin stepped up from the vice-presidency to become the second president of the Scottish League in 1896.

Celtic had quickly developed the largest following in Britain, and was probably the wealthiest club, in Scotland at least, within a few years of its inception – a conclusion supported by the manner in which the ambitious undertaking of a new stadium was embarked upon. This, in turn, became the source of further revenue and was, for a few years, recognized as Scotland's international ground. Scotland's four home games with England between 1894 and 1900 were played there, with 57,000 crowding in for the 1896 encounter. There was also a flair for showmanship at Celtic Park, with Willie Maley – himself a Scottish champion sprinter – an enthusiastic advocate of athletics, boxing and cycling events as ancillary activities to the club's major business. From 1890, the Celtic Sports became an important two-day fixture on the athletics calendar each August.

The conflict of convictions which had been around since the club was first mooted had carried over to a new issue, following the defeat of the 'anti-officialites' in 1891. Most leading members of the club believed that, if it was to survive, it had to be organized on a more commercial, business-like footing, and as a limited company. A majority of the rank and file were determined that it should remain as a club in which all members were equal. Feelings ran high on both sides of the argument, and some of those who had rejected the purist approach of Dr Conway were, none the less, unhappy about the proposed transition to a limited liability company (which eventually occurred in 1897). The spirit of the debate, and the legends to which it gave rise, are reflected in the fact that the centenary history of St Mary's parish school, published in 1963, recalled the affair in starkly unequivocal terms.

The Penny Dinner tables lost the financial aid of the Celtic Football Club. Brother Walfrid, who had founded Celtic as a charitable trust, was changed by his superiors to London in August 1892 and the committee, freed from his restraining hand, ignored the end for which the club had been founded. The last contribution to the Poor Children's Dinner Table was made at the AGM of session 1891–92. The committee after a bitter struggle against the honest element among the team's supporters got their way at last and turned the club into a business with themselves as directors and shareholders.

James Handley, himself a Marist brother (Brother Clare), in *The Celtic Story*, scarcely took a more understanding view and referred to 'this betrayal of a charitable trust'. When this book appeared in 1960, the Celtic chairman, Robert Kelly, had his thoughts minuted at the annual general meeting of shareholders, demonstrating just how sensitive an issue it continued to be.

It has been brought out [by Handley] that the club was founded in the cause of charity, primarily to provide free dinners for the poor people of the East End of Glasgow. The club was eventually transformed into a limited company, and it has been expressed that the club has in consequence not done as much as it should for the charitable purposes for which it was formed. The original members had undoubtedly built a very fine stadium in those days for the club, and it is questionable whether the club could have survived had this not been done. Indeed, we must come to the conclusion that the club in its present form has over the years done more in the field of charity than it could have done had it remained in its original state.

In his foreword to Handley's book – and probably with the same controversy in mind – Kelly observed saltily:

'It was a great handicap to him that many vital records and books were lost in the fire which razed the old pavilion. Dr Handley had to rely on newspaper reports for much of his material, and as we well know writers then, as now, could be something less than neutral.'

That, in summary, was the case for the defence, and the general caution which Kelly offered should be respected. The arguments in favour of creating a limited liability company were not necessarily based on personal avarice, and the problems inherent in running a large organization on strictly club lines were bound to increase as time went on.

Willie Maley, writing in 1939, recalled the controversy in quite straightforward terms:

Various schemes were tried to put the club on a sound business footing, but each year saw the best efforts of the real managers of the club thwarted by the change of new men, who had neither the knowledge nor the time to keep the club up to standard, being elected to the committee . . . The matter came to a head when at a special meeting called in 1896 to consider the club's financial position, the 'Heads' stated distinctly that the club must be put on a sound footing or else close down . . . Thereafter the men who actually made our club proceeded to put it on a real business footing. They felt the club must expand and the only way to do so was by making it a limited company, and so Celtic became such with a capital of £10,000. The old members had all the liabilities wiped out and each received £1 Founders share, which has since been added to by another share with 10s paid on same out of profits.

Put that way, it all sounded business-like and reasonable – a far cry from talk of 'a bitter struggle against the honest element among the team's supporters'. The two interpretations of events are as far apart today as they were in the 1890s, but there can surely be no doubt that Celtic would not have continued indefinitely both as highly successful competitors on the football field and as an organization run by committee. There is certainly no other example of such a combination having flourished.

The change to full professionalism and the expenditure on the new ground had put Celtic into debt, and this required guarantors. The first motion to form a limited liability company was put forward in 1893. It was in the name of the committee which had voted 11–4 in favour of it, but the membership threw it out by 86 votes to 31. The motion was proposed by Joseph Shaughnessy and seconded by J. H. McLaughlin. The main speaker against was Arthur Murphy – 'the Keir Hardie of the Celtic' as one newspaper described him, and a leading figure in Home Rule politics – evidence that the 'club *v.* company' dispute cut across previous alliances.

In the months that followed, the bickering intensified. Some of the committee's critics deplored the absence of charitable donations and, at the 1894 annual meeting, put forward a motion 'that no member of the committee, either ordinary or ex officio, shall, on and after this meeting, do any work for the Celtic club, directly or indirectly, receive payment for such work'. This move was defeated, but it reflected both the suspicions that existed and the gulf that separated the rival interpretations of the club's purposes. The *Glasgow Observer* – strongly pro-temperance and still distinctly agnostic towards Celtic – complained in August 1894:

The thing is a mere business, in the hands of publicans and others. Catholic charities get nothing out of the thousands of pounds passing through the treasurer's hands. Can we not get a club that will carry out the original idea of Brother Walfrid? The income of the Celtic club is drawn largely from our own people.

The row flared again when changes in the club constitution were put forward by McLaughlin. One of these would have made members liable for sums determined by the committee, to meet the club's debts. This was widely interpreted as a move towards shedding the club's less well-off members, and was heavily defeated. McLaughlin wrote:

Not a single argument worthy of the name was brought to bear against the proposition . . . I had the misfortune to be sponsor for the rules as a whole, and this one in particular, and had to bear the brunt of the flapdoodle it provoked . . . and just to put a fitting climax on the absurdity, another commenced to talk of charity. Imagine a club with £1500 of debt on its head asked to consider what it is going to give to charity.

The limited company issue remained prominent, and the committee again recommended the change to the half-yearly meeting in December 1895. Tom Maley objected to such an issue being raised at a half-yearly meeting, and suggested an extraordinary meeting to debate it. This obstruction further irritated the leading lights on the committee, and was overruled. Shaughnessy said that the question of limited liability must be considered because of the club's financial responsibilities. McLaughlin threw in the information that there was a sum of £500 hanging on the settlement of the question – the Scottish Cyclists' Union had offered this amount for the use of Celtic Park for three days in 1897, subject to the cycle track being brought up to international standards. The committee had taken the view that this investment could not be carried through without the safeguard of limited liability. But scepticism among the membership again triumphed, and the suggestion that a committee should be set up to examine the pros and cons of limited liability was again thrown out by a large majority. Most members of the committee were determined, however, to press ahead with improvements to the ground – and that fact alone guaranteed that the question of limited liability would remain firmly on the agenda.

When it had been established that it would cost £900 to make the alterations necessary to the track and banking, to meet the requirements of the Scottish Cyclists' Union event, the committee summoned a special general meeting to discuss the club's future constitutional status. On 25 February 1897, about a hundred members of the club attended a meeting in St Mary's Hall, presided over by John Glass. They were told that the committee was not prepared to incur further personal liability to meet the balance of the outlay. Faced with the ultimatum that the track improvements would not go ahead on the basis of the club's existing status, this meeting finally agreed to the formation of a committee to draw up a plan for submission to a special general meeting. This was done with remarkable rapidity, and – at the same venue which had played such a significant part in the club's inception – approval was given on 4 March to the formation of a limited company. Each club member would have one fully paid-up share, carrying a vote, but otherwise only each block of ten shares would carry a vote. (Not every shareholder realized the potential value of what he was getting. William Murphy, the veteran Catholic journalist, recalls that his father sold his share in order to buy a bike to take part in the Celtic Park cycle races!) The seventh article of association – dismissed by Handley as 'a sop to the simple' – decreed that 'after paying a 5 per cent annual dividend, the directors shall have power to give for such charities as they may select such sum or sums as they may think proper'.

The first directors of the new company were Michael Dunbar, John Glass, James Grant, James Kelly, John McKillop, John H. McLaughlin and John O'Hara. To an extraordinary extent, their election – based almost wholly on their willingness and ability to subscribe to the first share allocation – has determined the future pattern of control over the club. The immediate effect of the changed commercial status was dynamic. Before the end of 1897, when the ten-year lease was half completed, the club bought the freehold of the ground from the landlord, Sir William Hozier. To support this enterprise, the issued share capital was increased by £5000, exclusively among existing shareholders, and the ground capacity was increased to around 70,000 in the hope of attracting further international matches.

One of the directors, James Grant, was permitted in 1898 to erect football's first double-decker stand as a private enterprise. Advertised as providing 'comfortable chair accommodation with entire freedom from all atmospheric inconveniences being covered and protected on all sides by windows', it proved unpopular due to the long climb and the fact that the windows tended to steam up during games – much like the present-day press box! Grant eventually sold it to the club for a small sum having lost all his initial investment.

Willie Maley later reflected:

From the changeover to limited liability position in 1898 [*sic*], the club gradually settled into a real business state, and much good work was done in making Celtic Park one of the best grounds in the country. It was a beautiful sight when on a big match or sports day, a huge crowd filled up what was then the last word in terracings. The coloured cement cycling track set off the whole field and the huge Grant stand added to the *tout ensemble*. Celtic at that time had a great opportunity of crowding out all opposition, if they had had the foresight to see what the game was coming to. They had then the chance of taking in all the ground right down to London Road, where the big school is now, and if that had been done the present ground could have run north to south, with room for terracings equal to Hampden of today.

With three League titles in 1893/4, '95/6 and '97/8, the team's playing record remained impressive throughout this troubled period, though the Scottish Cup, still the most prestigious honour, proved elusive. Celtic's worst result in their early history was probably the 4–2 defeat at the hands of lowly Arthurlie at Barrhead in the first round of the 1896/7 competition. The loss of the League title that season was attributed by Willie Maley to the second strike in the club's short history. This resulted from the sensitivity of some players in the face of adverse press comment.

Three of our players, Battles, Meechan and Divers, as a protest against the unfair, even brutal, criticism of a certain section of the press, refused to turn out against Hibernian at Parkhead unless the representatives of the offending paper were ejected from the press box. To this the management could not consent, although they had considerable sympathy with the malcontents, and promised to make representation in the proper quarters. The players, however, were adamant in their decision and after some delay, although I had given up the game, I turned out along with Barney Crossan, while a message was hurriedly dispatched to Hampden Park for Tommy Dunbar who was playing there for the second eleven, and he arrived long after the game had started.

Maley continued his account of this episode with that air of certainty which characterized his explanations for every adversity encountered by Celtic:

30

The result was a draw, and those of the remaining matches were not in keeping with our previous returns – the affair costing us the Championship, as the players were naturally suspended and the playing strength suffered in consequence.

After three seasons in which Celtic's Scottish Cup run had not extended to more than two rounds, the 1898/9 competition took the Cup back to Celtic Park after an unaccustomed lapse of seven years. The quarter-final tie with Queen's Park was abandoned due to fading light with Celtic leading 4–2, but the replay was won 2–1. They went on to win a 2–0 semi-final victory over Port Glasgow, which took them through to a Final with Rangers. The players, who won 2–0 at Hampden and thus qualified for a handsome £20 bonus, were: McArthur, Welford and Storrier; Battles, Marshall and King; Hodge and Campbell; Divers, McMahon and Bell. McMahon and Hodge scored the winning goals.

The *Glasgow Herald* published a highly complimentary report of the match.

The feature of the game was the grand play of the Celtic half-backs and the utter incapacity of the Rangers forwards. It was the best-behaved and most orderly concourse of spectators of recent times. There were 25,000 and even at that number there was not the slightest indication of overcrowding at any part of the enclosure. When the increased rate of admission is considered, the attendance is a high testimonial to the drawing powers of the clubs engaged.

As the bells chimed in the year 1900, Celtic could look back on an extraordinarily progressive first twelve years. They had won the Scottish Cup twice (and were on their way to a third success). The club had been instrumental in forming the Scottish League, which it had then won four times in nine seasons. In days when the Glasgow Cup and Glasgow Charity Cup competitions were of some standing, they had won these four and six times respectively. They had a stadium second to none, the largest support in Britain and a far-flung reputation to match. The attacking style of play, which has stayed with them throughout their history, was already a Celtic hallmark.

Another great Celtic tradition, that of rearing the club's own talent, was in the making. This, wrote Maley, was in preference to the first decade's tendency towards 'gathering in men from all over the country and from England, many of whom had been in the game for a considerable time'. As in future periods of team-building, 'it was not to be expected that success would immediately follow, as it took several years to blend the youngsters satisfactorily'.

Any other club would have bowed out of the century gracefully, satisfied with its accomplishments. Characteristically, however, Celtic were in the middle of a thoroughgoing Irish row in the last days of 1899. The villain of the piece, in the eyes of many Celtic followers, was the club's chairman, J. H. McLaughlin, a brusque man who was almost unique among its leading figures in having no apparent involvement in Irish politics. As one letter-writer to the *Glasgow Examiner* put it: 'He has been conspicuous by his absence, personally, spiritually and otherwise, from the contaminating effects of membership of any Irish national organisation having for its objects the attainment of the national aspirations of the people of Ireland.' His footballing interest had developed in the direction of how the game was administered, and the sensibilities of his own club's supporters were not among the foremost of his concerns.

When the subject of the Boer War came up at a meeting of the SFA, of which he was president, McLaughlin went out of his way to speak in support of a hundred-guinea donation to a 'patriotic fund' for the families of those fighting in South Africa. He denounced opposition to the war as being the prerogative of 'demented Irish politicians who do not represent 5 per cent of the population of Ireland'. All hell broke loose in the columns of Glasgow's Irish and Catholic press. In the midst of the uproar, the Scottish League presented McLaughlin with a 'magnificent diamond ring' for services rendered, and the president congratulated him on having 'spoken like a true British citizen'.

This sealed McLaughlin's fate in the court of public opinion. For most Irishmen, the Boer War was being fought against British imperialism – the curse that also afflicted Ireland. In the same week that the newspapers reported McLaughlin's outburst, John Glass was seconding the vote of thanks to an Irish MP who declared that 'the hearts of the people of Ireland go out to the people of the two South African republics who are fighting for their independence, and whom England has forced into war in order to destroy their liberties, just as they did in Ireland in 1798'.

There were widespread calls for McLaughlin's removal from the Celtic chairmanship. Scottish branches of Home Rule organizations passed resolutions of condemnation, as did the United Celtic Brake Clubs, who resolved that McLaughlin would never be given a place of honour in their association. The mood was summed up by a letter to the *Glasgow Observer* of 30 December 1899, asking if the 'silence on the part of the Celtic Ltd means approval of the denunciation of Messrs John Dillon and Michael Davitt, which would have come more fittingly from a member of any Orange Lodge than from a director of a club which lives on the money of its Irish supporters'. The writer continued: 'With such a politician at the head of its affairs, it is small wonder that there has been a mournful slump in the Celtic enthusiasm and a corresponding ebb in Celtic gates.' Not for the first or last time, there was excited talk of forming a rival Celtic club.

Personal feelings must have been intense within the club itself, since men such as Glass, John McKillop and, indeed, James Kelly had a very public identification with precisely those 'demented Irish politicians' referred to by McLaughlin. But the calls for his removal were to no effect, and he remained as chairman until the time of his death in 1909. Willie Maley, forty years later, wrote that McLaughlin 'never held power such as did John Glass, and never was the aid to the club the cheery East End joiner was all his days'. When McLaughlin – a publican in Lanarkshire – died, there was none of the normal glowing obituaries in the Catholic press, though the fastidious Tom Maley did pay tribute to his legislative contribution.

By the turn of the century, the legendary rivalry between Rangers and Celtic was well established. Rangers had been around a lot longer – since 1872, in fact – but it was with their move to a permanent home in Govan in 1887 that the way was clear for them to build mass support. With the advent of Celtic on the other side of the city, with very distinctive origins and a natural support base, the formula for rivalry clearly existed. The clubs could meet as often as ten or twelve times in a season during the 1890s, and there were invariably good gates. Rivalry was strong, but relationships cordial, as epitomized by the fact that when a benefit match was played for the early Celtic 'great', Sandy McMahon, in September 1899, Rangers provided the opposition. 'In the directors' room, Mr J. McIntyre, Rangers, eulogised the worthy Celt to such an extent that there was nothing for it but to reply . . .'

But the seeds of future problems were being sown at the same time in Belfast, which had also acquired a 'Celtic' football club in 1896. Also in September 1899, readers of the *Glasgow Examiner* learned of 'outrageous attacks' on Catholics following a Belfast Celtic–Cliftonville game. 'The rowdies sang snatches of Orange Party songs, interspersed with staves of Rule Britannia.' Sadly, football's potential as a vehicle for sectarian hooliganism had already begun to be realized, and was soon to be imported to Glasgow.

# 5

## A TASTE OF SUCCESS
### *The Six-in-a-Row Side*

MONG the crowds who gathered at Glasgow Cross to welcome the year 1900, 'the almost universal topic of discussion was the war in South Africa, although the disputed problem as to the beginning of the new century also formed the subject of conversation'. From Celtic's point of view, it is convenient to regard 1 January 1900 as the first day of the twentieth century, since on that basis a most auspicious start was made to it, with a 3–2 victory over Rangers. The team that day was: McArthur, Davidson and Turnbull; Russell, Marshall and Orr; Bell, Somers; Divers, McMahon and Campbell. It was the age of the steamship, and the advertising columns offered an exotic array of destinations, at relatively modest cost, from the great port of Glasgow. Of more immediate interest to Celtic supporters than the option of sailing to Shanghai or the River Plate, however, might have been the advent of 'the magnificent new steamer, the *Duke of Rothesay*' on the Glasgow–Dublin service.

The Glasgow Irish newspapers continued to chronicle the progress towards constitutional change in Ireland and, as the Labour movement gathered strength, to reflect the historic debate about the compatibility of Catholicism and socialism. More prosaically, their advertising columns reflected the fact that those members of the Irish community who went into business normally looked to the licensed trade. It was no off-chance that six of the seven founding Celtic directors had gravitated in that direction.

The early years of the century's first decade were trying ones for the Celtic supporters. In 1900, the Scottish Cup was won for the second successive season, with a 4–3 victory over Queen's Park in the Final. This was to be the amateur club's last appearance at that stage of the competition. Celtic then contested six finals – two in each of the Scottish, Glasgow and Glasgow Charity Cups – before returning to their winning ways with the Charity Cup in 1903. The most noteworthy of these unsuccessful ventures was the 1901/2 Glasgow Cup Final against Rangers, which was played at Ibrox and finished in a draw. Celtic held that the replay should be at Celtic Park, and when the Glasgow Association ruled against them, withdrew from the replay.

This was only one of a number of episodes around this time which laid the foundations for frosty relationships between the two clubs. Rangers, who had followed Celtic in becoming a limited company, had invested heavily in developing Ibrox and in 1902 the SFA preferred that ground to Celtic Park as venue for the international match against England. Tragically, this led to disaster when part of the terracing collapsed and twenty-six spectators were killed. That year's Charity Cup competition was subsequently opened up to Edinburgh teams, to boost the Ibrox disaster fund, and Hibs beat Celtic in the Final.

In another fund-raising event, which came to be regarded as the British Championship, Rangers offered for competition the Exhibition Cup which they had won in the previous year. Celtic defeated Sunderland, thus qualifying to meet Rangers, who had overcome Everton. In the Final at Cathkin on 17 June 1902, the teams drew 1–1. They met again two evenings later and, in the final minute of extra time, Celtic scored to make the trophy their own. It is, to this day, one of the finest exhibits in the trophy room.

In the normal competitions success did not come immediately, but Willie Maley was building one of the greatest Celtic teams of all time, as the imported players of the 1890s phased out. Jimmy Quinn – destined to become one of Celtic's 'immortals' – was signed from Smithston Albion in 1901. Rutherglen Glencairn supplied Jimmy McMenemy, whose connection with the club was to span forty years, and Alex Bennett. Davy Adams, a junior international goalkeeper, came to Celtic Park from Dunipace. The juniors had become Celtic's main breeding ground, while from senior ranks 'Sunny Jim' Young, who had experience with Bristol Rovers, was signed from Kilmarnock, and Peter Somers returned from Blackburn Rovers – both modest acquisitions. It was at this time that the Celtic tradition of not seeking to buy success was inaugurated. However, in the 1902/3 season, the club suffered its worst record since its inception – nineteen games won, twenty-two lost and fourteen drawn. This was the slump before the storm.

For the 1903/4 season, Celtic adopted a new strip of green-and-white hoops in place of the previous vertical stripes. The major honours drought was ended in 1904, when Celtic beat Rangers 3–2 in the Scottish Cup Final at the new Hampden Park before 65,000 spectators. The team that day was Adams, MacLeod, Orr, Young, Loney, Hay, Muir, McMenemy, Quinn, Somers and Hamilton. Two down at half-time, Celtic won through a hat-trick from Jimmy Quinn. By this time, Maley was able to conclude that 'the team is now a splendid blend of youth and experience'. In the final League match of the season, against Kilmarnock a week later, Quinn scored five of Celtic's six goals. Alex Bennett had not been available for the Scottish Cup Final but replaced Muir on the right wing for the Charity Cup Final on 6 May 1904, also against Rangers. Arguably the most famous Celtic team of the club's first half-century therefore lined up for the first time on that occasion: Adams, MacLeod and Orr; Young, Loney and Hay; Bennett, McMenemy, Quinn, Somers and Hamilton. Quinn was injured early on, and Celtic's ten men lost 3–2. But the way was now well paved for Celtic's 'six in a row'. Maley considered that Young, Loney and Hay 'will go down to history as one of the most perfect half-back lines of all time, both for vigour and science'. The attack 'was a treat to watch in their sinuous movements and deadly attacks'.

On the evening of 9 May 1904, the 3500-seater north stand at Celtic Park was destroyed by fire. The *Glasgow Observer* reported: 'After a brief but savagely furious conflagration, the splendid stand and the palatial pavilion were reduced to cinders.' The cost of the damage was put at £6000, and Celtic were under-insured. But such was the security of the club's financial position by this time that no great hardship was suffered. The incident caused the club to purchase the Grant stand, which had previously been owned privately by a director. Before the start of the new season, Willie Maley had secured the signature of Alex McNair from Stenhousemuir, who for the next twenty years was to give sterling service to Celtic, mainly as a full-back.

The intensity of rivalry between Celtic and Rangers was, by this time, reaching the point of unhealthiness. The cynics noted that this was good for business, and even the *Glasgow Observer*'s 'Man in the Know' gave the impression of slight weariness with the frequency of meetings. 'In Glasgow, the rivalry of the Celtic and Rangers is responsible for a vast amount of interest, and if these teams met every day in the week for months it is not quite certain that the public would totally ignore any one of the games.'

The semi-final of the Scottish Cup, when the sides met yet again, provided one of the incidents which were to enter folklore where they could serve only to reinforce prejudice and encourage paranoia. Celtic were already down to ten men when Jimmy Quinn, one of the Celtic players most revered by the supporters, was ordered off for allegedly kicking Craig of Rangers. A section of the Celtic support invaded the pitch, and the game was abandoned with J. H. McLaughlin of Celtic promptly renouncing any right to a replay. But the matter did not end there. Several newspapers made savage criticism of Quinn and Celtic. The *Glasgow Observer* hit back at 'the ruffianly shrieking of a bigoted section of the anti-Irish press' and complained that 'as Quinn retired' one of his opponents had observed: 'Serves you right, you Papish . . .' Quinn denied that any kick had been involved, and Craig confirmed this. The affair ended up in court, with Quinn suing a newspaper which had reported him as having 'savagely kicked' Craig in the face. Quinn won the somewhat Pyrrhic victory of a shilling in damages – the sheriff found that he had stamped on Craig but not kicked him deliberately! It was a minor sensation in its day, but it was the kind of episode which poisoned relations between supporters of the clubs, rather than the clubs themselves – Craig and his mother both gave evidence for Quinn! But more than sixty years later, Robert Kelly devoted a whole chapter of his book to the affair.

A more poignant example of how mass interest in football and footballers had developed was given in February 1905, when Barney Battles died at the age of thirty-two. By then a Kilmarnock player, Battles had been a heroic defender for Celtic and was one of the players involved in the strike over hostile press comment. It was reported that 40,000 people lined the route to Dalbeth Cemetery in Glasgow's East End, to pay tribute to him.

Celtic won the League in 1904/5 by the narrowest of margins. They finished level on points with Rangers after twenty-six games and, fortunately, neither goal average nor goal difference applied in those days. A play-off was held at Hampden, and Celtic won 2–1 – the first of six successive League titles. Their league record over these seasons was as shown in the table.

|         | P   | W   | D  | L  | F   | A   | Pts |
|---------|-----|-----|----|----|-----|-----|-----|
| 1904/5  | 26  | 18  | 5  | 3  | 68  | 31  | 41  |
| 1905/6  | 30  | 24  | 1  | 5  | 76  | 19  | 49  |
| 1906/7  | 37  | 23  | 9  | 2  | 80  | 30  | 55  |
| 1907/8  | 34  | 24  | 7  | 3  | 86  | 27  | 55  |
| 1908/9  | 34  | 23  | 5  | 6  | 71  | 24  | 51  |
| 1909/10 | 34  | 24  | 6  | 4  | 63  | 22  | 54  |
| Totals  | 192 | 136 | 33 | 23 | 444 | 153 | 305 |

In the course of this remarkable title-winning run, which the Scottish League marked by striking a special shield bearing the names of all the players who had participated in the Championship successes, Celtic also won the Scottish Cup in 1906/7 and 1907/8; the Glasgow Cup in five of the six seasons, and the Glasgow Charity Cup in two. The team which brought this great run of honours to Celtic Park had cost less than £200 to assemble,

Willie Maley proudly affirmed. He wrote of these six great League-winning seasons:

Only once during that period did we fail to gain an additional honour – in 1908/9 – when after a drawn battle with Rangers in the final, the Cup was withheld following the regrettable Hampden riot. I mention this in order to show that our players not only proved their consistency in the League competition but in others also, and it will ever stand as a memento to the judgment and foresight of the management that the number of players included in the teams of that wonderful six seasons was comparatively small.

The 1909 Cup Final riot resulted from the old, vexed question of whether finals and replays should be pursued to a conclusion rather than strain the pockets of the paying public. Celtic and Rangers drew 2–2 in the first game and then 1–1 in the replay. The SFA rules said that there should be no extra time, and that a decision should be left to a third game. However, there had been some press speculation about the clubs agreeing to go into extra time in the event of the second replay finishing level. The rules did not permit this, but expectations had been aroused. Even some of the players seemed to expect extra time. When it became clear that this was not to be, hundreds of people spilled on to the park, lit a bonfire, fought with police and generally created the worst scenes so far experienced by the Scottish game. The *Glasgow Herald* thundered:

'Never in the memory of even the oldest inhabitant of the football world have scenes like Saturday's been witnessed. There have been outbreaks from time to time, but for downright malevolent, cowardly and brutal conduct, Saturday's display, one is glad to think, has no parallel.'

The directors of Celtic and Rangers met promptly and issued a joint statement:

'Although it was mooted during the week that extra time might be played in the event of a draw, it was found that the Cup competition rules prevented this. On account of the regrettable occurrences of Saturday, both clubs agree to petition the Association that the final tie be abandoned.'

The SFA council accepted this course of action by a vote of 15 to 11. The motion passed was: 'That to mark the Association's disapproval of the riotous conduct of a section of the spectators at Hampden Park, and to avoid a repetition, the Cup competition for this season be finished and the cup and medals be withheld'. Maley described it as 'the most unsatisfactory competition in the history of the Scottish Cup'.

The break-up of the great Celtic side began in 1908 with the transfer of Alex Bennett to Rangers. Ironically, his place was taken initially by Willie Kivlichan, who had earlier been transferred by the Ibrox club to Celtic. (Kivlichan, a native of Galashiels, was one of the handful of Catholics ever to be signed by Rangers. He later became a police surgeon in Glasgow and, for a time, Celtic club doctor.) Several careers then began to tail off simultaneously, and by the 1910/11 season the whole transition process was under way. Peter Somers moved to Hamilton, after thirteen seasons at Celtic Park. Jimmy Hay was transferred to Newcastle. Orr retired, and the great Jimmy Quinn's best days were behind him. In his lyrical account of the six-in-a-row side's qualities, Willie Maley chose to concentrate on two of his charges from this great Celtic era. He described 'Sunny Jim' Young as:

. . . the greatest clubman of them all. Jamie would play night or day, in sunshine or rain, and never spared himself. He was a source of inspiration to the rest of the team and never ceased to urge them on to greater effort. He was a man and a half in any team, and his place has never been filled since that fatal day he twisted his knee at Paisley and had to give up the game, to die tragically through a motor-cycle accident a few years later at Hurlford.

Maley was equally lyrical on the subject of Jimmy Quinn, the quiet pipe-smoking miner from Croy.

The picture of Quinn set for goal with his sturdy well-knit frame in the perfect condition he always kept himself in, and striving all the way to keep the ball in control as he charged off attacking defenders, was a sight never to be forgotten, and when to crown all, the finishing effort of a cannon-ball shot came from him, he would be a very cold-blooded enthusiast who could refrain from cheering the sturdy collier laddie whom I signed for £2 a week in the row where he was reared.

Celtic did not at that time operate a reserve side, but the rebuilding process was carried out with a speed and efficiency which once again reflected favourably upon Maley's skills. He recalled:

Towards the end of our record run Joe Dodds, Peter Johnstone, Andy McAtee, John Brown, Tom McGregor and John Mulrooney had been discovered and were by this time able to take their place in the team. And, in November 1911, a slip of a lad, who was afterwards to carve a niche in the history of the game, was signed, and forced his way almost immediately into the League side. I refer to 'Patsy' Gallagher.

For many of the generation which watched him, Patsy Gallagher was the greatest player of them all. Signed from Clydebank Juniors, this frail lad soon revealed himself as an inspired inside-forward – fast and skilful on the ball, he could also pass superbly and score extraordinary goals. 'Gallagher is a marvel,' wrote one observer. 'He has no stamina to make a song about, but he takes risks that many a bigger and heavier man would not think of, and the marvel is that he comes out of it scatheless.' James Handley recalled him as 'a shrimp of a man, whose frolics on the field were the wonder of the football world'. Around him the team could be rebuilt, and in the period prior to the outbreak of the First World War this was accomplished with near-complete success. They won the Scottish Cup in three seasons out of four from 1910/11 until the outbreak of war. In 1913/14 they achieved the League and Cup double for the first time since 1907/8. But the tragedy of war and the slaughter of a young generation now intervened.

To mark Willie Maley's silver jubilee with the club – as player, secretary and manager – Celtic gifted him three hundred guineas at a celebration in June 1913. With Celtic on the crest of a wave, the tributes to Maley's twenty-five-year reign were ecstatic. One admirer wrote in the *Glasgow Observer*: 'What price Mr William Maley of the Celtic FC as our greatest living Scotsman?' The scribe explained:

Mr Maley seems somehow to possess the knack of 'roping in' players rich in those vital qualities of ardour, aggressiveness and resolution. He catches them young and breathes into them the old traditional Celtic fire, of which he himself appears to be the very living fountain and source . . . Yes, a great man is William Maley, Prince of Team Managers and Discoverer of Quinn, McMenemy, Hay, McNair, Gallagher and all the other 'gems of purest ray serene' – not forgetting the one and only 'Sunny Jim', the truest Celt of the lot.

The season 1913/14 was a marvellous one for Celtic and their supporters. Patsy Gallagher was the sensation of Scottish football and, in an age when poetry and football went hand-in-hand, amateur bards vied with one another to pay adequate tribute to Peerless Patsy. This was one of the better efforts:

> You're a funny little nipper, oft I've watched you wriggling through,
> Even Sunny Jim, our skipper, never caused a laugh like you.
> Though in size you're not imposing, it's miraculous what you do.
> So, dear Patrick, just in closing, here's my heart and hand to you.

The New Year's Day game against Rangers was won 4–0. The football writers praised Celtic's 'iron-clad defence' as they put together a run of twenty-three games without defeat, during which fifty-two goals were scored and only two conceded. After a goalless draw with Hibs, the Scottish Cup was won 4–1 at Ibrox in the replay. The team was: Shaw, McNair and Dodds; Young, Johnstone and McMaster; McAtee and Gallagher; McColl, McMenemy and Browning.

The League title was also won in that season, after a three-year break, and Celtic set off on a European tour in the finest of fettles, little knowing that the dark days of war would soon be upon the continent. For good measure, the major political aspiration of many Celtic supporters appeared to be on the verge of fulfilment, through Asquith's Home Rule Bill. With Belfast Celtic due to play a friendly match in Glasgow in March 1914, the *Glasgow Observer* was concerned that the football crowd should pay due attention to the performance of the Rory Oge Pipe Band.

Apart from the interest taken in the rival Celtic clubs, the pipers are well worth seeing and now that Home Rule is practically certain, sympathisers with the old country should take the opportunity of seeing the national dress and listening to the music of Ireland as a nation, for what our dear isle once was, it will become again.

Along with much else, this prediction was promptly overtaken by war.

The 1914 annual general meeting of shareholders was a happy occasion. One observer wrote: 'I never remember such an enthusiastic meeting of the club, and the harmony was in marked contrast to the brave days of old . . .' Fourteen Celtic players, accompanied by directors Kelly, Dunbar and McKillop, 'with Mr Maley as guide, philosopher and friend', set off on the adventurous journey into Central Europe. The *Glasgow Observer*'s 'Man in the Know' accompanied the party, and was able to report that, after the stately twenty-seven-hour journey across mainland Europe, the first sight-seeing call in Budapest was to 'the great church of St Stephen's dating from the 12th century . . . of the 48,000,000 people [in Austro-Hungary], fully 80 per cent are Catholic and proud of it'. Celtic won their first game against local opposition, allowing 25,000 spectators to see 'the real football, for once'.

By the following week, even 'Man in the Know' had forgotten twelfth-century cathedrals and reassuring statistics on the state of Austro-Hungarian Catholicism. 'Wild Scenes – Players at Loggerheads' was the headline on his report of a game against Burnley in Budapest, to raise money for the unemployed, which ended in an undignified draw. Celtic travelled home early in June, via Vienna, Berlin and Leipzig. 'Man in the Know' assured the faithful at home: 'Of course, the players enjoyed themselves to the full during their three weeks out, but always in a rational manner, and it was a case of early to bed when a game was due next day.'

# 6

## THE GREAT WAR
### *Hostilities at Home and Away*

EARS of war cannot be accepted as normal periods in the organization of football, or of anything else. The call to arms takes young men away from their homes and careers. Diversions and entertainments must carry on, but are inevitably relegated in significance and acquire a makeshift quality. An air of unreality develops, as reports of incidents on the football field jostle for newspaper space with accounts of battles which cost tens of thousands of lives. The First World War, it was fondly believed by British public opinion, would all be over by Christmas. The irrepressible 'Man in the Know' reflected a mood of detached interest in this minor skirmish when he wrote: 'None will follow the fortunes of the present war with greater keenness than the Celtic players and officials, for few saw more of the various combatants than those who made the last two trips to Austro-Hungary and Germany.' At Mass in Prague, 'the German soldiers struck us as well set-up, well behaved young fellows, many of them showing by their manners that they have come from good families'.

Most Celtic supporters were, in these early days of war, at least as interested in the news that was coming out of Ireland, where Sir Edward Carson was engaged in playing 'the Orange card' against the prospect of Home Rule.

Life went on quite normally at first, and Celtic held their two-day sports event as usual – though for the first time there were no cycling events, as the cycle track had been removed in order to increase spectator accommodation. Willie Maley nostalgically recalled the era which had brought the World Championships to Celtic Park:

The public went simply mad on the sport around the end of the last century and the beginning of the present . . . we old timers cannot help sighing as we recall the days when Celtic sports, with a galaxy of champions – track, field and cycling – were events anticipated and enjoyed as the greatest of the year.

Military recruitment at football grounds, including Celtic Park, became a regular feature, prompting the 'Man in the Know' to comment:

There will come very little out of this football ground recruiting. The only fellows likely to fall in there are those who are disgusted at their club's non-success. Instead of going home and beating their wives because their team lost, they will now set about beating the Germans for spite.

Half-time announcements urging potential recruits to 'join up before the fun's over' were broadcast at Celtic Park, and there were recruiting events at the ground. This was symptomatic of the fact that the Irish community, under guidance from the Scottish hierarchy, adopted a much more 'British' attitude towards the First World War than had ever previously been the case. British reaction to the Easter Rising of 1916, and the impact of the unanticipated slaughter in the war itself, would however, soon cause many loyalties to be reconsidered.

Celtic opened the 1914/15 season by beating Burnley 2–1 in the return match following the angry encounter in Budapest. But there was by then considerable public debate about whether or not football and other public entertainments should continue at all for the duration of what, it was beginning to be recognized, would be a long and bloody war. The argument against carrying on was that the incentive for young men to sign up for the trenches would be enhanced if there were no counter-attractions at home. Indeed, in the first year of the war, the Scottish and English FA agreed to abandon international matches, and the Scottish Cup was also scrapped after consultation with the Government.

But the more general argument against the continuation of professional football did not prevail. Players' wages were cut to ensure that they took their places in the factories; League matches were confined to Saturdays and holidays; when the team had to travel, no early release was available for players from workplaces. Willie Maley's account of the period states:

With all our regulars and a few new recruits to bring along, our prospects for 1914/15 were bright indeed, but as the season was on the point of beginning, the drums of war resounded throughout the land. A number of the lads answered the call immediately, although no one realised that it was going to last so long, and as time went on our ranks were depleted gradually. Still, the game went on – it was the expressed wish of the authorities – but those who remained at home did their bit in the factories and workshops that were so necessary for the service of the country. The other clubs were similarly affected, so that the competition was just as keen as before . . .

Celtic retained the League title in 1914/15, finishing six points ahead of Rangers and using only sixteen players in the course of the campaign. The normal team that season was: Shaw, McNair and Dodds; Young, Johnstone and McMaster; McAtee and Gallagher; McColl, McMenemy and Browning. Jimmy Quinn, now concluding his playing career after fourteen seasons of the highest distinction, turned out six times in the course of 1914/15 and young men came to gaze upon the near-legendary figure. The Glasgow writer Colm Brogan recalled the character of Quinn many years later:

Quinn was a quiet, rather shy man who played football because he loved it, and wanted to be left to live his private life alone. The partisan passions of his most devoted supporters did not please him at all, and he was strongly opposed to that excess of passion which interpreted a Celtic–Rangers match in terms of civil war. No man gave heavier punishment on the field and no man had heavier retaliation . . . The power of his spectacular attack sometimes blinded both friend and foe to the fact that nobody could challenge a whole team as he did without suffering. But he took his wounds, if not meekly, then without rancour. In the only true sense of an abused word, he was an amateur. He played the game because he loved it, he gave his whole heart to it and, if he had had another source of living, I fancy he would have played for nothing. But he was a miner (who had to return to the pits in his later days) and he never made more than a very modest living from a prowess that was unique, and a fame that was without parallel.

Off the field, James Kelly handed over the chairmanship during the first wartime season to Tom White, the lawyer who had joined the board in 1906 on the death of John Glass. There was speculation about backroom disputes, but Kelly insisted that he merely wanted to devote more time to his duties as parish councillor and school board member, as well as his business interests. White would now preside over the club's destinies for a record period of thirty-three years. On the death of director James Grant in Toome Bridge in 1914, it was recorded: 'He never pretended to know much about the playing abilities of the boys, and took no great interest in the selection of the team, knowing that Messrs Kelly, Dunbar and Maley were able to deal with that sort of thing.' He had, however, bequeathed the Grandstand to the club and had superintended steady improvements to the ground over his years of service.

The annual report submitted to shareholders by Willie Maley on 1 June 1915 provides an interesting glimpse both of Celtic nostalgia and of attitudes in these troubled times. First, Maley reflected on the deaths which had occurred over the past year. Brother Walfrid had been 'the last of the leading founders of the Celtic club . . . He must have spent a considerable period near the blarney stone in his young days, as his persuasive powers once experienced could never be forgotten.' His work for Celtic had been 'a labour of love' and, until the time of his death, 'he remained as keen as ever to hear how his "boys" as he termed the team, were doing'. James Grant and John McKillop, said Maley, had been 'of the old school' and had triumphed over 'the hardships of an Irishman's struggles for existence in this city forty years ago'.

Three hundred footballs had been sent out by Celtic to 'the men whom we all hope will bring us the victory in this awful war'. Director John Shaughnessy, with the rank of Lieutenant Colonel, 'has been honoured by the City of Glasgow with the command of the 18th Battalion Highland Light Infantry, and out of his command of 1600 men you will be glad to know there are 500 of our Faith under his command'. Maley continued: 'Most of our players are working in Government employment, and three of the young ones in Cassidy, Gilhooly and O'Kane have joined the colours . . . The cruel war is still with us and God alone knows where it will all end.'

Once again, Celtic won the wartime League Championship in 1915/16, but Maley's recollection of this season indicates just how *ad hoc* the competition was.

'Although we were often in sore straits to field a team, the players, sometimes almost complete strangers to our regulars but proud to wear our colours, with traditional enthusiasm upheld our reputation so well that another title was won, with the loss of only eight points in 38 games.'

The season ended with a rush of games, and a unique curiosity in the club's history arose on 15 April 1916 when they were forced to play two League games on the same day. With games limited to Saturdays and holidays, Celtic ran out of match days when snow forced a cancellation at Motherwell as late as 25 March. Three weeks later they undertook the Saturday double. The team which lined up against Raith Rovers at Celtic Park at 3.15 p.m. was: Shaw, McNair and McGregor; Young, Dodds and McMaster; McAtee, Gallagher, O'Kane, McMenemy and Browning. They polished off this task with ease, Patsy Gallagher scoring a hat-trick in the course of a 6–0 victory. The team then motored to Motherwell, where the game kicked off at 6 p.m. Trooper Joe Cassidy, home on leave, replaced the injured O'Kane and Celtic won this game 3–1. For good measure, in the course of the evening Celtic beat the record for the number of League goals in a season. Quite a day!

The only Celtic regular to miss that day's play was McColl, who was injured, but the *Glasgow Observer* reported that he was 'the happiest man in the Bank Restaurant where the boys met for a snack and a chat on Saturday night' – an indication that Willie Maley's establishment had, by that time, become a regular Celtic retreat. Celtic had by 1916 won the League title thirteen times – as often as all other clubs put together. Rangers had been successful on seven occasions, as well as tying with Dumbarton in the inaugural competition. Hearts had been champions twice, and Dumbarton, Third Lanark and Hibs once each.

Recruitment for war service continued to eat into Celtic's playing re-serves, and the club had some difficulty in assembling a team for the following season. But they recruited several players from other clubs who were working in the Glasgow area. A fourth successive title was duly won, but a clean sweep of wartime flags was averted the next season when Rangers pipped them by a single point, beating Clyde on the last day of the season while Celtic could manage only a home draw with Motherwell. The Ibrox club had assembled an all-star line-up on wartime 'temporary transfers' from all over Britain – a policy which incensed their detractors. 'League Flag for Ibrox – Title Without Honour' opined the *Glasgow Observer*, going on to expand upon this theme: 'When the Scottish League clubs have to be fine-combed, English and Irish clubs asked for drafts to furnish an eleven that will hold its own with Celtic, that is the right way of showing the dread some people have of our fellows.'

There was consolation for Celtic in the shape of the War Fund Shield, yet another acquisition for the trophy room, which was secured with a victory over Morton at Hampden after the Greenock club had ousted Rangers in the semi-final. The state of relationships between the two major Glasgow clubs had declined sharply by this time, and a substantial number of Rangers supporters went along to cheer on Morton. 'Man in the Know's' reflections on this behaviour provide an interesting insight into how Celtic supporters – a category into which the *Glasgow Observer*'s correspondent most certainly fell – viewed the development of Scottish football rivalries at that stage. He wrote:

The present war is said to mean much regarding the future. The press is never tired telling us that we shall have to look upon things in a different light, that such things as wages, politics, social and economic life in general will have to undergo many changes . . . But after what we saw and heard at Hampden on Saturday, we may count one feature as to remain unchanged. Blind and unreasoning hostility to the Celtic team will continue; the anti-Celts will carry on pretty much as they have done for the last 30 years. New generations will arise; the old spirit will remain.

I can remember when Rangers occupied a minor position in Scottish football; when the gates at Kinning Park and old Ibrox were very moderate. Queen's Park, Clyde, Thistle, Cowlairs, Northern, Partick, Pilgrims, Battlefield and Pollokshields Athletic all ranked higher in public esteem; the majority of them had better support than Rangers. Things are very different today. Rangers are the most popular team in the city, in the country – I might say in the world as far as Glasgow enthusiasts are concerned. The fact is undeniable, the explanation very simple.

When the Celtic club began business in 1888, it immediately proceeded to make history – and enemies. For a time, Queen's Park, Third Lanark and Cowlairs managed to hold their own with the new club, and the two city clubs scored heavily in national and local cup ties. But gradually the Celts drew ahead, and took a clear lead in league and club football. None of the others had a look in, and after a time people began to get disgusted at seeing the Irish club getting the better of every opponent.

Then Rangers got a good eleven together, won the league championship four times in succession and became first favourites. Those who had got tired of waiting to see Queen's Park, Cowlairs, Third Lanark and other clubs take it out on Celtic flocked down to Govan to cheer on the long-awaited and anxiously-expected conquerors of the Irishmen, and from that day to this Ibrox has become the Mecca of the anti-Celt.


In the view of the *Glasgow Observer*'s correspondent – who must be regarded as the best available source of the official Celtic view from this era – the 'anti-Celt' category extended into the ranks of officials responsible for army recruitment, in these latter stages of the war. The inconsistent nature of the call-up selection process was the source of controversy and anger in the wider community, and the uneven impact on Scottish football clubs was a minor manifestation of this debate.

The feelings of 'Man in the Know' on this emotive subject spilled over when, during the summer of 1918, Jimmy McMenemy – one of whose brothers had been killed in the war, with another maimed – was notified of impending call-up for the trenches. 'There are several good reasons why a well-conducted chap like the Parkhead favourite should be left at home, at least until the streets and public works are cleared of the fit, the undesirables and unwilling currently masquerading as munition experts.' Players of other clubs who were on military service were 'to be seen in the city at the week-end, never having smelt powder or poison gas – and we have Peter Johnstone dead, John McMaster wounded, Dodds sent over after 11 weeks training, an entire Celtic eleven on the unsafe side of the Channel. I fear that kissing is not the only thing that goes by favour.' (Johnstone, the centre-half, had been killed in France in 1917.) In fact, the armistice came on 11

November, without McMenemy having departed for the field of battle, though 'for a long time to come, Dodds and McAtee might do all their football on a barrack square somewhere in Germany, and both are badly wanted on the home front'.

Though many players were still in uniform, something approaching normality returned in the 1918/19 season and Celtic took their fifteenth Scottish League title. This time the single-point difference between them and Rangers was to Celtic's advantage, and the neck-and-neck position at this time exacerbated a rivalry that had already grown too bitter. Of the condition of the Celtic side at this time, Willie Maley wrote: 'It was only to be expected that following the conclusion of war a process of rebuilding would require to be faced, as those who had carried the flag during these four awful years could not fail to show the strain.' Once again, Celtic set about signing young players, and Tommy McInally, from St Anthony's, was one of future 'greats' who was recruited at this time.

In 1919 Jimmy McMenemy, a veteran of the six-in-a-row side from before the war, was finally transferred to Partick Thistle for the autumn of his career (where he promptly helped them to win the Scottish Cup). James Handley wrote of the man known to a generation of Celtic supporters as 'Napoleon':

McMenemy was a master of the deceptive movement. His facility for shaking off a cloud of opponents by one simple unexpected turn was unequalled. Nobody excelled him in the art of making an adversary look foolish. It was quite impossible to anticipate his moves . . .

The last of the pre-war personalities to leave the club was the full-back McNair. We stay with James Handley for an assessment of that Celtic giant:

He would have been the perfect subject for a 'time-and-motion' study if they had troubled about such things in those days. No footballer was his peer in the science of achieving the maximum result with the minimum of effort. The most dashing forward seemed to be mesmerised by his presence . . .

Celtic had come through the war era, and were once more embarked on a youth policy which would take several years to come to fruition. But they left the appalling First World War years behind with their reputation as Scotland's leading club intact, while Maley's managership, particularly in the crucial matter of developing young talent, was recognized as the best in the land. With all the waste of human life at home, the war years had also given Celtic further opportunity to maintain their charitable traditions. It was recorded in the *Glasgow Observer* of 26 May 1917:

As everyone knows, the Celtic club was founded for charity's sake, and that object has never been lost sight of. But everyone does not know that the Celts are always giving, that never a week passes without an appeal coming before the directors from some of our local orphanages or other deserving institutions. The club, founded 30 years ago to provide dinners for hungry little ones, still keeps up the good work; Smyllum, Nazareth House, St Joseph's Home have reason to know this. Broken men and jaded women know also that a Celtic 'line' has enabled them to get over a bad accident or long illness, and secure a new lease of life in one or other of our convalescent homes.

In the pre-welfare-state age, such generosity mattered much.

As the First World War drew to a close, the attention of the Scottish Catholic community was diverted to the passage of the 1918 Education Act, which enshrined the position of Catholic schools within the state system. Section 18 of the Act allowed for the transfer of Catholic schools to the local education authorities, to be financed from the public purse. It was a vital development in determining the future identity and status of Scotland's Catholic minority. Inevitably, it was attacked by Protestant extremists as 'Rome on the Rates' and provided them with a convenient peg on which to hang their anti-Catholicism. But the rights won by the Catholic community in 1918 have been jealously safeguarded ever since.

A by-product of the schooling settlement was to ensure a permanent reservoir of footballing talent upon which Celtic has had first call, while always also looking to other sources. It might be that the links between the Catholic Irish community and the club to which it gave birth would, in any case, have remained strong. But the existence of denominational schools has undoubtedly minimized the dilution in identity which might otherwise have occurred. The wider implications of the 1918 Act continue to be debated passionately. But it is worth remembering that the legislation was introduced as a response to Catholic fears, based on hard experience, of seeing their religious rights trampled underfoot by an unsympathetic majority. It was not responsible for creating the attitudes which had given rise to these fears.

# 7

# THE TWENTIES
## *Taking a Back Seat*

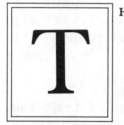 HE 1920s are generally regarded as having been a period of rather modest achievement by Celtic, during which supremacy in Scottish football passed decisively, for the time being at least, to Rangers. That acknowledged, there were still three Scottish Cup triumphs to celebrate in 1923, 1925 and 1927. The League title was won in 1921/2 and 1925/6, but a gap of ten years was then to occur before the flag was again hoisted over Celtic Park. Clearly, the inter-war years did not match the almost continuous success which had characterized the club's development pre-1914. Perhaps this was inevitable, as the financial stakes had become higher and the competition accordingly fiercer.

There had been a change in regime at Ibrox, where the death by drowning of the manager, William Wilton, had led to the emergence of William Struth as his successor in 1920. Here was the iron disciplinarian who turned Rangers into a much more consistently effective playing force than they had previously been. Sadly, he also came to personify that club's adherence to the policies of religious sectarianism which have done so much to divide Scottish football and Scottish society. Rangers came to be regarded as a hard-nosed business concern, willing to invest in order to achieve success. Celtic preferred financial caution. Under Struth, Rangers also acquired the reputation which has stayed with them for physical play. In October 1920, the *Glasgow Observer* complained:

As kickers the Rangers' rearguard could vie with the most competent of Army mules; as tacticians they could give the Black-and-Tans a long start and a whacking. If there were to be any extension of the liberty taken by the Blue defence on Saturday, the Rangers might as well arm their men with hatchets.

In the seasons 1919/20 and 1920/1, Rangers won the League title, while Celtic had to make do with the modest consolation of carrying off the two Glasgow trophies in each season. However, things looked up in the 1921/2 season when Celtic won their sixteenth League title with the recognized team of: Shaw, McNair and Dodds; Gilchrist, Cringan and McMaster; McAtee, Gallagher, McInally, Cassidy and McLean. They played twenty-three successive League games without losing a goal, and dropped only two points at home. The title was won on the last day of the season, in dramatic fashion. With 23,000 packed into Cappielow Park and thousands more outside, Celtic secured the draw which they needed to win the title with only eight minutes remaining, McAtee being the scorer. But that team did not stay together. Joe Dodds, recognized as one of the finest left-backs in the club's history, dropped out of League football. The quixotic Tommy McInally was sent packing to Third Lanark early in the 1922/3 season, after the Celtic board had held his wage demands to be unreasonable.

There were serious long-term implications in the winding-up of the reserve team, also in 1922. On the credit side, youngsters were being signed who would take their places in time among the greatest players to wear the Celtic colours. Alec Thomson was recruited from the Fife junior side Glencraig Celtic, and Jimmy McGrory, signed from St Roch's, made his Celtic first-team debut, as stand-in for Patsy Gallagher, against Third Lanark at Cathkin on 20 January 1923. McGrory, the great centre-forward from Garngad, who was to have over fifty years' involvement with Celtic, signed in the St Roch's chapel house after Bury had had him on trial – and rejected him.

That season Celtic finished third in the League, but won only nineteen of their thirty-eight games. They did, however, make amends by beating Hibs in the final of the Scottish Cup. According to contemporary accounts, the forty-year-old McNair stood head and shoulders above the rest of the players. James Handley wrote lyrically:

'Like the veteran actor who summons to his aid all the dramatic skill and experience of a lifetime to give the greatest performance of his career on the eve of his retirement, Alec, realising probably that this was his last appearance in a Scottish Cup Final, proceeded to illustrate, in the effortless way that was characteristic of his play, what perfect defensive work could look like.'

This was Celtic's tenth Scottish Cup success, equalling Queen's Park's record, but as far as the League title was concerned, Rangers were reigning supreme. They took the Championship three times in a row from 1922/3.

Peter Wilson, from Barrmill in Ayrshire, was among those signed by Maley in time for the following season, which yielded only the Glasgow Charity Cup as the young, new-look team took time to settle. Small wonder, when one considers the following extraordinary story, as attributed to Wilson, who signed for Celtic when he was just seventeen:

All I knew about Celtic was what I had read in the newspapers. I had never seen them play. Indeed, I had never been out of Ayrshire in my life. After a match for Beith Amateurs a man with a raincoat over his arm asked me if I would like to play for Celtic. I grinned and said 'Yes'. He then produced a form, which I signed, and handed me £20. The money I took home to my mother. She wouldn't believe that anybody would give me such a big amount of cash for playing football, and put it in a vase on the mantelpiece, saying she would keep it there until somebody or other came along and claimed it. I wondered if she thought I had stolen the money.

Anyway, several months went past until one day I received a postcard instructing me to report to the Bank Restaurant, Glasgow. That restaurant was run by Mr William Maley, manager of Celtic. I had never been in Glasgow before, and when I arrived at St Enoch Station I enquired of a policeman the way to the Bank Restaurant. He looked at the wee country laddie, and led me by the hand to the howff. I wasn't even wearing long trousers, but a suit of schoolboy knickerbockers.

At the restaurant, I asked for Mr Maley, and met him for the first time. He eyed me up and down, and led me into a private room. 'Better have some lunch', he said, and brusquely introduced me to the others at the table. I was meeting famous players whom I faintly recognised from their photos in the press. They made me welcome, and I tackled a bowl of soup.

Half an hour later, I was on a bus. I didn't know where I was going. I was too shy to ask. The bus stopped at a football ground. I got out with the others and passed through the official entrance. While the rest of the players went into the dressing-room, I hung about the corridors. There I met a middle-aged man. 'Where am I?' I queried. He looked at me in a strange sort of way, concluded that I wasn't cheekily attempting to pull his leg, and answered 'Fir Park'. I was in Motherwell. I knew Celtic were to play Motherwell that day. A few minutes later, Mr Maley came along. 'Come on, sonny,' he said. 'It's time you stripped', and led me to the dressing-room.

I had brought my own boots with me. Nothing else, and was thrown pants, socks and jersey by the hamper-man. The jersey was several sizes too big for me, and the sleeves had to be sewn to make them nearer my arms' length. I felt like a laddie wearing a fully-grown man's suit.

Mr Maley reappeared. 'You're playing at right half, sonny,' he intimated. 'Motherwell have an outside-left called Ferrier. He has a good left foot. Possibly you've heard of him.' Heard of Bob Ferrier! He was one of Scotland's star players, and I was opposed to him.

However, the following season brought the Scottish Cup back to Celtic Park, after a campaign of great character and incident, culminating in 'Patsy Gallagher's Final'. In the 5–1 defeat of Third Lanark at Cathkin in the first round of the cup, McGrory – by now revered by the fans as at last a man worthy to take on the mantle of Quinn – scored a hat-trick and 'Gallagher gave a brilliant performance in swerving, feinting, side-slipping and distribution'. Alloa Athletic and Solway Star were disposed of before Celtic faced St Mirren in the fourth round. After two drawn games, the sides met at Ibrox. James Handley takes up the story.

McGrory scored a goal and the game had almost run its course when Gillies of St Mirren, darting towards Shevlin, was tackled by McStay and fell on the penalty line. The referee, Mr Craigmyle, knelt down dramatically to examine the spot closely and awarded a free kick against Celtic. St Mirren would have none of it. A penalty was their demand, and they refused to touch the ball, which the referee had placed for the free kick. The teams faced each other, immobile and silent. The seconds ticked off without anyone stirring. Then the expiry of the game solved the dilemma and Mr Craigmyle whistled for the game to finish.

There were persistent suggestions throughout the early 1920s that disputes over the club's alleged parsimony towards the players were rife at Celtic Park, and had contributed to several unwelcome departures. In September 1923, the *Glasgow Observer*'s 'Man in the Know' complained of 'the seeming mercenary spirit of the players, who were expected to respect the proud traditional and exalted spirit of the green-and-white brigade and wear the famous colours more for love than money'. This was after the directors had turned down the idea of bonuses to the players, who were on £8 per week, for wins and draws. Chairman Tom White regarded it as 'an impossible request', since there was no guarantee that wins and draws would secure the League Championship, for which the club had traditionally paid substantial bonuses. Celtic's attitude throughout this period was apparently to accept a few seasons of little achievement while waiting for the promise of youth to bloom. It is a phlegmatic approach which has recurred from time to time in the course of the club's history.

There was a crowd of 100,000 at Hampden for the semi-final with Rangers, who had not won the Scottish Cup for twenty-two years. This turned out to be one of the great Celtic performances against the Ibrox club. The team which provided a memorable 5–0 victory was: Shevlin, W. McStay and Hilley; Wilson, J. McStay and McFarlane; Connolly and Gallagher; McGrory, Thomson and McLean. McGrory and McLean both scored twice, with Thomson getting the other. And so on to a Final with Dundee, which might have proved an anti-climax had it not been for the contribution of 'Peerless Patsy'. Over to Handley:

Dundee opened the scoring and with seven minutes to go they were leading by one goal to nil. Great excitement and pleasurable anticipation prevailed among the Dundee supporters in the park and at home, where the game was being relayed movement by movement. In the final few minutes Peter Wilson passed to Gallagher and Patsy, with that peculiar dragging motion of his, meandered past man after man until the Dundee left-back made a desperate effort to stop him. Gallagher fell to a roar of 'Penalty!' from the Celtic supporters, but in falling the crafty Gallagher had kept the ball gripped between his feet and somersaulted with it right over the goal-line and into the back of the net, from the cords of which his team-mates had to extricate him before they could shake his hand. It was a wonderful bit of individualism.

According to Willie Maley:

It was one of those incidents which has to be seen to be appreciated, and it was with difficulty, so I was told after the game, that the Dundee players refrained from joining in the tribute to that wonderful little player.

This was indeed the stuff of which legends are made, especially since a Jimmy McGrory header gave Celtic victory in the closing minutes. For McGrory it was his first Scottish Cup Final, and for Gallagher his last.

After three seasons in exile, Celtic brought Tommy McInally back from Third Lanark in time for the 1925/6 season. Providing grand service to Adam McLean on the left wing, he made a considerable contribution to the club's quite unexpected success in bringing the League title to Celtic Park after a gap of three campaigns. Rangers had emerged triumphant on each of these occasions, and this break in their run proved to be a very temporary success for Celtic supporters to savour. The League flag would not be hoisted over Celtic Park for another ten years, while Rangers would capture eight out of the nine intervening titles.

This was indeed the Ibrox club's golden age. It was a time of great poverty and unemployment, culminating in the General Strike of 1926 as the response to an attempt to cut miners' wages. Many could not afford the charges of admission to football grounds, in spite of Celtic's practice of operating a special cheap gate for the unemployed, and the *Glasgow Observer* commented in December 1925:

How often you and I have seen and pitied the forlorn groups hanging around outside Celtic Park gazing longingly and enviously at lucky fellows able to plank down their shillings at the turnstiles . . . the 'great excluded' shivering in the rain outside the barricade and trying to figure out what was happening within, reading a meaning into the crowd's cheers, yells and groans, and visualising Gallagher, McLean, McGrory or McFarlane shining like demi-gods in the unseen fray.

For Celtic supporters both inside and outside the ground, the news for that season at least was an uplift at a time of deprivation. With Rangers languishing in sixth place, Celtic took the title by eight clear points from Airdrie – but it was very definitely a case of one 'off-season' for the dominant Ibrox club.

In that season Celtic had high hopes of achieving the fourth League/Scottish Cup double in their history, but these were thwarted by St Mirren, who unexpectedly beat them 2–0 in front of a 98,620 crowd in the Final at Hampden. For a time it appeared as if Celtic could maintain their League supremacy in the 1926/7 season, with Jimmy McGrory scoring so freely. Three times that season he scored five goals in a game, and on three other occasions he made a personal contribution of four goals in the course of setting a new Scottish League record of forty-nine goals in a season. An injury which kept him out of the season's last few games prevented the tally from becoming even more unbeatable. On 12 February 1927, Willie Maley introduced an eighteen-year-old goalkeeper into the side for a League game at Dens Park, Dundee. This was the debut of John Thomson, signed from Wellesley Juniors in his native Fife, and Celtic won the match 2–1. However, they allowed the prospect of retaining the League title to slip away from them as Rangers came through strongly.

Securing the Scottish Cup for the third time since the competition had been revived after the war was a significant consolation, giving Thomson and John McMenemy – son of 'Napoleon' – winners' medals in their first season. In the Final, Second Division side East Fife provided the opposition, and after taking an early lead, the underdogs went down 3–1. With McGrory missing, McInally returned to his old position as centre-forward and clowned his way through the game. The Celtic team was: J. Thomson, W. McStay and Hilley; Wilson, J. McStay and McFarlane; Connolly, A. Thomson, McInally, McMenemy and McLean. The fine defender Hugh Hilley subsequently retired from the game, and Peter McGonagle took over as left-back for the new season.

It opened brightly, with Celtic retaining the Glasgow Cup when they beat Rangers 2–1 in front of 90,000 spectators. Progress was maintained into the New Year and, on 14 January 1928, the incredible Jimmy McGrory set a new world record (or so it was believed) when he scored eight goals in a game against Dunfermline. But Celtic again faded in the Championship race and finished behind Rangers. Twice in the course of the season McInally was suspended for indiscipline. Willie Maley was away from Celtic Park through illness for much of the season and, one way and another, the auguries were not good when the team returned to Hampden for the Scottish Cup Final against Rangers. The Celtic team which lined up in front of a record crowd of 118,115 was: J. Thomson. W. McStay and Donoghue; Wilson, J. McStay and McFarlane; Connolly, A. Thomson, McGrory,

McInally and McLean. A scoreline of 4–0 in the Ibrox club's favour brought them their first Scottish Cup in twenty-five years – an extraordinary contrast with their League record. The famous Rangers attack which broke Celtic hearts that day comprised Archibald, Cunningham, Fleming, McPhail and Morton. Maley wrote:

It was truly a meeting of giants in which tactics, strategy and craft were ever in evidence; and while Rangers eventually triumphed as they merited, they were indebted to many 'breaks' which, I willingly agree, had been denied them during their quarter of a century's failure to win the national trophy.

It was a characteristically grudging analysis of a result which emphasized the gap which existed between the sides at that time. Inevitably, the crushing defeat accelerated the pace of change at Celtic Park.

The wayward genius of Tommy McInally was transferred for a second time – to Sunderland at a fee of £2500. An inside-forward of legendary skills who had replaced Patsy Gallagher in the affections of the Celtic supporters, he had never found it easy to live with the disciplines of Celtic Park. It was ironic that, though he was a great personality and humorist, he took a very dim view of practical jokes which were played upon him. One of the flare-ups which led to his second estrangement from Celtic occurred at Seamill, when a fellow player, egged on by colleagues, phoned up McInally at his hotel, posing as a press man. McInally duly parted with some indiscreet information about team injuries, to the great amusement of the Celtic players crowded round the other end of the phone. When he found that he had been tricked, albeit with no malicious intent, McInally walked out of training in a sulk on the eve of a Cup tie against Motherwell, and caught the train from Ardrossan back to Glasgow. He was suspended indefinitely and, though he returned briefly to the team, he was transferred at the end of the season, soon to be followed to Roker Park by his left-wing partner, Adam McLean.

One unlikely side-effect of McInally's departure was that it upset the close-season holiday plans in which he had been involved. This story captures curious aspects of a Celtic age long gone. It had been planned that McInally, the boxer Tommy Milligan, Jimmy McGrory and Willie Maley would go off together for a pilgrimage to Lourdes. McInally and Milligan dropped out of these plans, leaving the manager and the goal-scorer to travel together. At this time Celtic were engaged in all-out efforts to sell McGrory to Arsenal – a remarkably shortsighted course of action, which was thwarted only because of the player's absolute reluctance to leave Celtic Park, unless for a very large sum of money (£2000 was the figure McGrory mentioned, against the legal maximum signing-on fee of £650). The free-spending

Arsenal manager, Herbert Chapman, came to Glasgow and the Celtic directors set up a meeting between him and McGrory. 'If a way had been found out of the impasse to grant my terms – my word, I'd have been a sorry man', wrote McGrory later. A record fee – around £10,000 – was being offered by Arsenal, and Celtic wanted to do business. But McGrory turned down the move, and two weeks later set off to Lourdes with his manager.

They first caught the train to London and, to McGrory's astonishment (though presumably not to any great surprise of his fellow pilgrim), Chapman and two Arsenal directors were waiting there to greet them. The party went off to a West End restaurant and then Chapman, Maley and McGrory headed for Drury Lane to see Paul Robeson in *Showboat*. They parted company without a transfer being mentioned. However, after five days in Lourdes, Maley and McGrory returned to Victoria Station to be met again by Chapman. After a private chat between the two managers, Chapman got to work on McGrory once more. But the player remained adamant that he would move only on terms which he knew to be impossible. Chapman gave up, and McGrory subsequently wrote: 'I came home next day with a light heart. I'd be carrying on for Celtic.' Whether the supporters would have been quite so light-hearted at the time if they had known of the club's efforts to sell the star player is another matter.

Maley's own position was called into question, after forty-one years at the helm, and the decade ended with Rangers winning the League and Kilmarnock – conquerors of Celtic in the semi-finals – the Scottish Cup in the 1928/9 season. In part, Celtic's willingness to sell players was connected to the need to raise money for ground improvements. The Grant Stand had become unsafe and was in the process of being demolished when, on 28 March 1929, fire also destroyed the old pavilion. Most of Celtic's early official records were lost in this fire – an immense loss to subsequent chroniclers of the club's history. The remainder of the season's home games had to be played at Shawfield.

At the end of this disappointing campaign, which yielded only the Glasgow Cup, the clear-out of players continued with the departure of veterans Willie McStay and 'Jean' MacFarlane. The following season started with the opening of a fine grandstand which was to serve the club well until 1971. But success on the field of play remained elusive, and Celtic finished 1929/30 with their first 'bare cupboard' since 1901 – usually, even in lean years, either the Glasgow Cup or Glasgow Charity Cup competition could be relied upon to provide a piece of silverware. This time, Rangers had won all four major competitions.

The 1920s, that decade of poverty and depression, had been an increasingly unsatisfactory period in the club's history, far from comparable, as James Handley put it, 'in brilliance with the decade that had immediately preceded the war'. As in so many other walks of life, adjustment to post-war conditions had been difficult for a football club which carried so many of a poor community's hopes. But by the turn of the decade, and notwithstanding that season without honours, it did look as though another outstanding Celtic team was on the verge of making its appearance. The fine young players who had been drawn to Celtic Park were maturing, and the scene seemed set for a return to dominance of Scottish football when Celtic triumphed in the Scottish Cup Final of 11 April 1931.

Motherwell provided the opposition for a long-remembered match. The names of the Celtic players that day would trip off the tongues of generations yet unborn: J. Thomson, Cook and McGonagle; Wilson, McStay and Geatons; R. Thomson, A. Thomson, McGrory, Scarff and Napier. At half-time the score was 2–0 to Motherwell, and it was still the same with eight minutes left for play. Then Jimmy McGrory scored, and this was followed, in the closing seconds, by an own goal from a luckless Motherwell defender, Alan Craig. It was 'one of the most exciting finishes one could hope to see', wrote Maley, and Celtic won the replay 4–2 with two goals each from Jimmy McGrory and Bert Thomson. The League title was lost only in a tight three-way finish with Rangers – who again prevailed – and Motherwell.

From the early years of the century, Celtic had been contemplating a tour of the United States of America – a land where they were bound to receive a huge reception from the population of Irish descent, which had been further boosted by emigrations from Scotland during the 1920s. Finally, on 13 May 1931, a party of about two dozen boarded the Anchor Line's *Caledonia* at Yorkhill Quay, with 'crowds occupying every point of vantage from Yorkhill to Greenock to cheer their heroes on their journey to the far west'. There were four directors – Tom Colgan, James Kelly, James McKillop and Tom White – in the party, while the seventeen players comprised the Cup-winning side plus Morrison, Whitelaw, Currie, Hughes, McGhee and Smith. Nine days later (for transatlantic travel was a civilized business by this time) they landed in New York to a rapturous reception, at the start of a tour which will always hold memories of special poignancy for the club, for nobody could have foreseen the tragedy that was soon to ensue.

Expatriates, even in the United States of the Depression, travelled hundreds of miles to see a game and catch a glimpse of the Scottish Cup, which Celtic had taken with them. The *Glasgow Observer* stated: 'The Celts have countless thousands of followers in the States but they are all Irish and will expect to see their favourites in an Irish atmosphere.' Sure enough, it transpired that some of the local organizers either did not understand, or did not want to understand, the fact that Celtic were at least one step removed from the old country. In Chicago, for instance, they were billed as 'Irish Holders of the World's Championship'.

The non-stop round of receptions, allied to the unaccustomed heat, made it a gruelling experience for the Celtic party. Thirteen games were played, all against American opposition, and Celtic won nine, with one drawn and three lost. They beat the New York Giants in front of a 40,000 crowd. When Fall River beat them 1–0, the hero was a young American goalkeeper by the name of Joe Kennaway. Against the New York Jewish team of Hakoah, Jimmy McGrory had his jaw fractured while Napier and Scarff were sent off with two of the opposition. Football in the United States was a rough, tough affair. Back home in Glasgow, 'Man in the Know' protested: 'The Yankee game as exploited by most of the clubs savours more of the menagerie or the bull-ring than of the sports field.' Exhausted by their American endeavours, the party sailed back from New York on the liner *Transylvania* – stopping at Moville, Co. Donegal, where Jimmy McGrory disembarked for his wedding!

Since the end of the season, one of the main talking points in the Scottish sporting press had been the possibility of John Thomson pressing his apparent desire for a transfer from Celtic. The tragedy that was soon to follow was to call into question the whole tradition of hostility between Glasgow's two rival clubs.

# 8

## JOHN THOMSON
### *The Legend Lives On*

HE tombstone in the cemetery at Cardenden bears the epitaph: 'They never die who live in the hearts they leave behind.' For over fifty years the name of John Thomson has been living in the hearts of thousands who recall the nature of the man and the circumstances of his death, as well as in the folk legend of succeeding generations. He was only twenty-two, and at the height of his powers, when he died from injuries sustained during a League game at Ibrox Park on 5 September 1931. Desmond White, the late Celtic chairman, spoke for the collective Celtic consciousness of that era when he said of John Thomson: 'He was certainly the best goalkeeper I have ever seen. He was not a tall man, but he had the ability of a ballet dancer to jump much higher than other people. There was a great deal of magic about what he was doing, and this came across to those who watched him.'

Magic for the masses who followed Celtic in an age of depression was rare enough, and they had taken this complete football hero to their hearts. Thomson was the quiet teetotal lad from the Fife pits who, when he took the field, became a tiger full of courage and grace. Sir Robert Kelly, who saw him play his first game for Celtic in 1927, as well as his last, wrote of him:

It was the natural athletic gracefulness of Thomson that appealed to everyone. He was not tall as goalkeepers go, but at 5 ft 9½ in. and 11 st. he was perfectly built. He had the sure clutching hands and fingers of a world class fielder in cricket and he had ability remarkable in one of his tender years to read opponents' moves before they tried to complete them. Many a time he gave the impression of being off his mark in a leap or dive to save before the opponent had made the effort. But if young John made up his mind to go in a particular way he was right 19 times out of 20.

That fateful Saturday the *Glasgow Herald* reported: 'Many people will learn with regret that Sam English, the Ibrox centre-forward, is unfit to play.' But the unfortunate English did play on a wet and miserable Saturday afternoon, and the die was cast for an episode of poignant tragedy. The teams lined up. Rangers: Dawson, Gray and McAulay; Meiklejohn, Simpson and Brown; Fleming, Marshall, English, McPhail and Morton. Celtic: J. Thomson, Cook and McGonagle; Wilson, McStay and Geatons; R. Thomson, A. Thomson, McGrory, Scarff and Napier. The same newspaper reported on the Monday morning:

Shortly after the interval, Rangers centre-forward English worked past the Celtic backs and, in a desperate and daring effort to save his goal from imminent downfall, John Thomson, the brilliant young Celtic goalkeeper, threw himself at the forward's feet as the latter delivered his shot, and received the impact of the kick as both players fell to the ground.

The *Daily Express* said:

The accident which cost Thomson his life occurred five minutes after the start of the second half. The ball was sent forward towards Celtic's goal and English, the Rangers' centre-forward, and Thomson ran to gain possession. English arrived first. A goal seemed certain. Thomson threw himself at the centre-forward's feet. His head crashed against English's knee. The centre-forward fell, and rose limping. Thomson lay unconscious, his head bleeding.

The players shouted for a doctor and the ambulance men. The trainers of both teams rushed to Thomson's assistance, and Mr Struth, the Rangers' manager, and Mr Maley, the Celtic manager, also ran to the prostrate player. Dr Kivlichan, a former Rangers and Celtic player, examined Thomson, bandaged him hurriedly, and ordered his removal to the Victoria Infirmary. Eighty thousand spectators remained silent and sympathetic as Thomson was carried to the pavilion on a stretcher. A discordant note was struck during the tragic occurrence by the cheering of hundreds of Rangers spectators when they saw Thomson fall to the ground. They did not realise the seriousness of the accident. Meiklejohn, the Rangers half-back, went to the touch-line and quietened the cheering section. A young woman rushed to the pavilion where Thomson lay unconscious. Tears rushed down her cheeks, and a cry came from her lips as she saw him on the stretcher. She was Miss Margaret Finlay, of Bedlormie, West Lothian, Thomson's fiancée, who accompanied him to many of the games in which he played.

Many years later, John Thomson's brother Jim recalled the sense of dreadful foreboding that engulfed him as he watched the incident from the Ibrox stand.

I knew at once it was serious from the way his hand fell slowly. I left my seat and went straight to the dressing room. I went into the ambulance with him and one ambulance man said to the other, 'That's the end of him.' I was angry. I knew it myself, but I didn't want it confirmed.

He telegraphed to the Post Office in Cardenden, and his parents were informed by a policeman as they sat down to their evening meal. They rushed to Kirkcaldy to catch a train and arrived just a few minutes before John died at 9 p.m. without regaining consciousness. He had a depressed fracture of the skull. 'Nobody in the family ever questioned that it was a complete accident,' said Jim Thomson. 'They were both going for the ball. I felt very, very sorry for Sam English.' A fatal accident enquiry subsequently confirmed this conclusion. 'John had been injured a few times before, because he always went straight for the ball,' Jim recalled. 'I had asked him the previous time he was injured if he wasn't going to stop going in like that. He said he should, but it was the ball he was after. He didn't see anyone else or anything else.'

Though there was certainly no specific blame to be apportioned for the fatal incident, the death of John Thomson in the charged Ibrox atmosphere, and particularly the immediate response from a section of the 80,000 crowd, led to an angry debate in the press about the whole Rangers–Celtic syndrome. One commentator wrote: 'They tell me it is a tradition. I was brought up to believe that too, but I am now satisfied that it is not traditional at all, but a menace to Scottish football.' Old Firm games, he suggested, were 'events to satisfy the emotions of the partisan and bigot'. For a few brief days, however, the fires of pseudo-religious hostility were doused by common humanity and a sense of national loss. In a shop window at Bridgeton Cross, a wreath from the local Rangers Supporters Club was filed past by thousands.

John Thomson, like many of Celtic's greatest players, was not a Catholic. His family had belonged to a sect without ministers called the Church of Christ and it was in Trinity Congregational Church, Glasgow, that a memorial service was held the following Tuesday. Five thousand people crammed into the church and surrounding streets. Even at this distance in time the words of the minister, the Reverend MacLelland, are worth recalling, for their relevance is undimmed:

There is one way in which his death might bring a great gain. Those thoughtless crowds who call themselves Celtic or Rangers followers, whom both teams disown, who gather behind the goals of their respective favourites and cheer themselves hoarse when a member of the opposing team lies writhing in pain, if they can be brought to realize by this tragic happening the brutal cruelty of their action, John Thomson will not have given his young life in vain. Do they realize that their shameless jeering was the last sound that ever reached John Thomson's dying brain?

The emotional scenes at the memorial service were surpassed the following day, when John Thomson was buried at Bowhill Cemetery in his native Cardenden. Unemployed men had walked the fifty-five miles from Glasgow. Grown men wept openly on a day of unbridled emotion, at the end of which Mr Tom White, the Celtic chairman, thanked the huge assembly 'for this spontaneous demonstration of your love'. This moving account, from the *Daily Express*, stands the test of time:

### 30,000 PEOPLE AT A FUNERAL –
### JOHN THOMSON, LAST GREAT TRIBUTE

John Thomson has had a funeral worthy of such a Prince of Sportsmen. Amid banks of wonderful wreaths and through dense lanes of 30,000 people, the Celtic players carried him from his home in Balgreggie Road to Bowhill Cemetery, almost half-a-mile away. The only sound which disturbed the slow tramping of thousands was the mournful tunes of the pipe band heading the procession. On his oak coffin there was a wreath shaped in the fashion of goalposts and crossbar, the gift of the Bowhill Football Club, and immediately behind another wreath of lilies and heather on the top of which proudly lay one of his international caps.

From the early morning, people have poured into this village from all over Scotland. Most of them were the humble folk of football. The miners of Fife, among whom Thomson worked as a boy of fourteen, were there in their hundreds squatting, as miners do, by the roadside talking in subdued tones and now and then proudly picking out famous footballers as they walked past to the Thomson home. Hundreds of them climbed the high crags which overlook the Thomson home, and there from the road they looked like sentinels of sorrow silhouetted against the sky line.

The funeral service was due to start at three o'clock, but an hour before that the narrow streets of Cardenden were a seething mass of sympathisers. Many of the younger men climbed the roofs of the houses or on to the high walls and hedge rows which lined the road. People converged on Cardenden from every point of the compass. When I came up from Dunfermline, seven miles away, the road was black with silent mourners walking to the scene. Then when three special trains came in from Glasgow and motor-cars by the score unloaded their passengers there was hardly room to move. The surrounding pits were idle for the day. Neighbouring villages were deserted. Every man, woman, and child for miles around came to Cardenden to pay their simple tribute.

The scene at the Thomson home was magnificent in its simple grandeur. They had brought the oak casket out to the little garden in front of the house. There it rested, with a background of rambling roses waving in the sunshine, as if bidding sad farewell to their young master. There were gorgeous wreaths everywhere. They lined the tops of the privet hedges, lay along the garden paths, peeped out of every little corner, while dozens of mourners continued to arrive carrying more floral tributes. They filled two huge motor-lorries with them and even then there were more. Celtic players preceded the coffin carrying masses of floral beauty, and half-a-mile behind the cortege were mourners bearing their tributes, patiently waiting to lay them on the grave.

Mr Duncan Adamson, an elder of the Church of Christ, conducted the service in the garden. The players and officials of the Celtic club lined up on one side, on the other were the leading legislators of the Scottish Football Association and the Scottish Football League, while at the head of the coffin stood Mr Thomson, the father of the dead international, and his brother and sisters. The service was as simple as the homage of the village folk. Mr Adamson conducted the ceremony after the fashion of his church. He read a chapter from the Bible, and then delivered a brief address. Women sobbed, and the eyes of many men glistened in tears as he finished by saying: 'Good night, dear brother, good night!' Then when they had driven a lane through the obedient crowd the Celtic players hoisted the coffin on their shoulders and the pathetic procession moved off. High up on the crags the sentinels stood like statues looking down on an unprecedented scene.

I joined the procession along with John McMenemy and George Stevenson, of Motherwell, and Mr William McCartney, the manager of the Hearts. All the famous players of Scotland were there. I noticed Alec McNair and Joe Dodds, the famous Celtic full backs of a decade ago, marching side by side. As the procession crawled along a man in front of me, overcome by the heat, fell to the ground in a faint. He was carried to a near-by shop for attention. Then, when the coffin passed into the main road, an old man overcome by emotion fell on his knees crying 'Oh, John Thomson, we will never see your like again.' I had fallen in some twenty yards behind the bier, but as the procession had reached the cemetery I was far behind. Meanwhile the police had thought it wise to close the cemetery gates. Thousands of mourners stood outside while the service at the graveside proceeded. The Rangers players and some of the officials were among those caught in the dense crowd which jammed the roadway. Finally, however, a way was made through the crowd and, led by Mr W. Roger Simpson, the secretary, the Ibrox players pushed and squeezed their way through to the cemetery gates. Here again the Rangers were held up. One of the officers on duty doubted the identity of Alan Morton, and it was not until Morton had been vouched for by a colleague inside the gate that he and his colleagues were allowed to pass.

Inside a service was conducted at the grave by Mr John Howie, another elder of the Church of Christ. The grave was just inside the boundary wall, which was lined by hundreds of villagers. Now and then a crackling of twigs at the roadside wall indicated that another impatient mourner had climbed the railings from the outside and burst through the shrubbery. On the far side of the cemetery, bank upon bank of wreaths stretched for yards and yards along the foot of the wall. John Thomson is buried in flowers. When the service had concluded people filed past the open grave and threw their floral tributes on top of the coffin.

After Mr Howie had paid a long tribute to the dead international, Mr Tom White, the Celtic chairman, associated himself and his club with all that had been said by Mr Howie. Not till the service was over were hundreds of mourners able to enter the cemetery and look into the grave. They are still filing past as I write – people of all stations in life paying their silent tributes to the greatest boy Scottish football has ever known.

Thirty years later, James Handley reflected:

It is hard for those who did not know him to appreciate the power of the spell he cast on all who watched him regularly in action. 'A man who has not read Homer,' wrote Bagehot, 'is like a man who has not seen the ocean. There is a great object of which he has no idea.' In like manner, a generation that did not see John Thomson has missed a touch of greatness in sport, for he was a brilliant virtuoso, as Gigli was and Menuhin is. One artiste employs the voice as his instrument, another the violin or cello. For Thomson it was a handful of leather. We shall not look upon his like again.

At least the name of John Thomson has stayed alive among subsequent generations of Celtic supporters, many of whom have made the pilgrimage to that cemetery in Bowhill, Cardenden. There are many good reasons why the name of John Thomson has stayed alive for so long. He was the Prince of Goalkeepers, the symbol of clean-living youth, the epitome of great talent unfulfilled and the young man who, in death, exposed the shallowness and futility of sectarianism in the name of sport. In short, he was the stuff of which legends are made.

The following Saturday there was a home game with Queen's Park, and the Celtic supporters had their opportunity to pay a last tribute in the stadium which Thomson had so often graced. Before the game, pipers played 'The Flowers of the Forest', a bugler sounded 'The Last Post', and a silver band 'in soft cadence and with exquisite sympathy played Newton's immortal hymn, 'Lead Kindly Light'. The *Glasgow Observer* reported:

With bowed heads, players and spectators heard the solemn strains die slowly away. It was a sign of mourning so touching and poignant that its memory will linger with us for years to come. There was grief for the bright young life cut off in its bloom; and oh, what a gap, what an aching void has Thomson's passing left in the place where he was wont to captivate all hearts with his magical personality – the lingering light of his boyhood's grace. No wonder the players seemed heavy-hearted and leaden-footed. Johnny's tragic death was a crushing blow.

# 9

# FIFTY YEARS OF CELTIC:
## *The Golden Jubilee and*
## *the Empire Exhibition*

HROUGHOUT the inter-war years, crowd trouble at Celtic–Rangers matches was commonplace, and the bitterness of emotions intense. Percy Sillitoe, who arrived in Glasgow as Chief Constable in 1933, was soon to threaten to ban the fixtures as part of his drive against violent crime in the city. The gangs which proliferated in Glasgow during the 1920s and 1930s tended to divide along sectarian lines and, for sociological, historical and political reasons which went far beyond football, quasi-religious hostility was established as an endemic feature of Scottish society. Celtic's origins and Rangers' policies ensured that football would continue to be used as a vehicle for these unhealthy emotions.

The *Glasgow Observer* occasionally carried appeals to the Celtic supporters to 'ignore the taunting challenges and silly flag-waving of the opposition' and to cut out 'chanting of childish ditties, varied – and this is the most objectionable feature – by verses of a hymn'. But such pleas fell on a significant number of deaf ears. The truth was that encounters between the two sides had, at their fringes, become thoroughly unpleasant occasions; the best which could be said for this aspect of Celtic–Rangers encounters was that they acted as safety-valves for prejudices which might otherwise have found expression outside football. On 3 October 1931, just two months after its latest admonition to supporters, the *Glasgow Observer* reported that – at the first Old Firm game since the death of John Thomson – 'not a vestige of colour was to be seen, hardly a sound heard . . . no singing, no flag-waving, no provocative challenges'. But it did not last long.

'The shock [of Thomson's death] had a tremendous effect on our players,' wrote Willie Maley, 'one which we firmly believe was responsible for many failures during the next few years.' Faced with the grim task of finding a successor, Maley remembered the performance of Joe Kennaway of Fall River during the close-season American tour. He was invited over, and made his first appearance on 31 October 1931 against Motherwell. Kennaway soon proved himself equal to the challenge and became a big Celtic favourite, staying in Glasgow until the outbreak of the Second World War took him back across the Atlantic. But the melancholy of Thomson's death was to hang over the remainder of that season and beyond. The club was hard hit by injuries, and Peter Scarff had to retire from football with an illness which soon ended his life. Celtic finished third in the League, and the only consolation lay in the preservation of a record – Motherwell took the title, thus preventing Rangers, who were in second place, from equalling the 'six in a row'.

As Celtic struggled to emerge from their slough of despond, a Scottish Cup triumph came as a surprise to even their warmest admirers. This was in the 1932/3 season, during which the new faces making their appearances included Malcolm MacDonald, signed from St Anthony's, and teenager Bobby Hogg from Royal Albert who took over at right-back when Cook moved to Everton in December 1932. Both were destined to have long careers at Celtic Park. The brothers Frank and Hugh O'Donnell, from Wellesley Juniors, and John Crum from Ashfield Juniors also entered upon the scene. There were clearly the makings of another very good homespun side, but consistency was lacking in League games and Celtic finished a modest fourth.

Their Cup form was more impressive. Dunfermline, Falkirk, Partick Thistle and Albion Rovers were disposed of before Hearts went down to goals from the extraordinarily prolific Jimmy McGrory and Alec Thomson in a semi-final replay, after a goalless draw. The Celtic team for the Final, in front of a 102,000 Hampden crowd, was: Kennaway, Hogg and McGonagle; Wilson, McStay and Geatons; R. Thomson, A. Thomson, McGrory, Napier and H. O'Donnell. In a game which lacked the drama of 1931, a goal from Jimmy McGrory took the Cup back to Celtic Park.

But this was still a troubled period for the club in these Depression years of poverty and mass unemployment. Bert Thomson, the popular winger, was transferred to Blackpool after breaches of training discipline. There were disputes about signing terms and familiar accusations that Celtic were not prepared to spend money to acquire or retain experienced players. Season 1933/4 saw another undistinguished League campaign and a Scottish Cup exit at home to St Mirren. Willie Maley was much affected by the death from tuberculosis of Peter Scarff on 9 December 1933, at the age of twenty-four – a reminder in this more prosperous age of how that terrible plague had ravaged the population until relatively recently. Maley later wrote that, at that time, 'we seemed doomed to continual misfortune'. He summed up the mood of the period in the handbook which preceded the 1934/5 campaign:

In reviewing the season that has gone, I regret to have to put it down as the most disappointing one that we have ever had . . . Since 1931 our lot has been one of trial and disappointment. We won the Cup in 1933 against all the odds but we have since failed badly in the League race where our consistency used to tell its tale and where we wore down all opposition for years. That spirit seems to have been lost by our team . . .

Though the shedding of experienced players appeared carelessly over-regular, credit had to be given to Maley for the way in which – even at this time – he continued to come up with outstanding new material, almost exclusively from the junior ranks. Jimmy Delaney, a youngster from Cleland who had played just a few games with Stoneyburn Juniors, was the outstanding acquisition of 1934. He had worked for two years in the Lanarkshire pits, but was by then unemployed. 'It was like now – there was no work.' Delaney recalls receiving £2 per week in wages as a 'provisional' Celtic signing, after Maley and chief scout Steve Callaghan had watched him in a trial match. John Divers, signed from Renfrew Juniors, was also ready to make his breakthrough, while Jimmy McStay's career with Celtic ended when he went to Hamilton on a free transfer. Alec Thomson and Peter Wilson were also soon to depart, and money was again a factor. The great Wilson, at Celtic Park for over a decade, was quoted as complaining: 'The boss expects you to play like a genius on Saturdays, and to think like a half-wit on pay-days.'

The bad start to the 1934/5 season proved to be a mixed blessing. Only nine points were taken from the first ten games, gates were falling and, in response, the five-man board took the unprecedented step of appointing a coach – 'Napoleon' himself, Jimmy McMenemy. This was to prove a vital appointment in generating a Celtic revival, and it immediately coincided with a dramatic improvement in form, as young players were drafted into the first team, which finished second to Rangers in the League Championship, and went out of the Scottish Cup to Aberdeen. The only consistent consolation for the Celtic supporters during these lean years was the performance of the reserve side, which dominated the honours and exuded promise for the future.

But the Celtic support was, by the middle of the decade, tired of waiting.

The last Scottish League title had been won in 1925/6, and the gap which had followed was easily the longest in the club's history. The intermittent Scottish Cup successes had staved off total embarrassment, but the reality was that Rangers had been the dominant club of the 1920s and 1930s, claiming no fewer than thirteen out of eighteen League titles since the end of the First World War – including eight out of nine since Celtic's last success. Even the Glasgow honours had become rare sights on the Celtic sideboard. Since the dawn of the thirties, there had not been a solitary Charity Cup success and the Glasgow Cup had been secured only in 1930/1 – the season which had held out so much promise before the dark days set in.

The prelude to the 1935/6 season included yet another clear-out of the experienced players. Napier went to Derby County, the O'Donnells to Preston North End and McGonagle to Dunfermline Athletic, where he joined Alec Thomson. Only Chic Geatons (signed in 1928 from Lochgelly Celtic) and Jimmy McGrory (signed back in 1923 from St Roch's) now remained of the 1931 Cup-winning team, with Joe Kennaway the only other 'veteran' from the 1933 side. The transition had been extremely rapid, and there was a general feeling that Celtic had thrown away their immediate prospects of success by releasing too many of their older players within such a short space of time. But into the team, soon to become captain, came centre-half Willie Lyon from Queen's Park, and the half-back line of Geatons, Lyon and Paterson was destined to become as legendary as Young, Loney and Hay.

A 3–1 defeat by Aberdeen in the opening League game seemed to endorse the pessimistic view, but then Celtic hit the kind of successful run which had long eluded them – sixteen games with the loss of only one point. When they beat Dunfermline Athletic on 16 September, Jimmy McGrory's hat-trick set a new Celtic and Scottish record of 351 goals in first-class football. The following week Rangers were beaten 2–1 at Ibrox – astonishingly, the first League victory for Celtic at the ground since 1920/1. These were portents which encouraged the long-suffering supporters to believe that there really was new hope at Celtic Park. A 4–3 defeat against Rangers on New Year's Day was one of the few setbacks as this newly moulded side raced to its first League title in a decade, with sixty-six points from thirty-eight games. Appropriately, Jimmy McGrory scored a hat-trick on the day the title was won at Ayr – his seventh of the season – but an injury ruled him out of the final game, against Partick Thistle, when he would have had the chance to improve his fifty goals in the season and perhaps even beat the Scottish record of fifty-two, held by Motherwell's MacFadyen.

A rather ignominious Scottish Cup exit to St Johnstone could be overlooked in the light of League success, and the Celtic supporters heaved a collective sigh of relief. This was reflected in the pre-season handbook for 1936/7, which looked back on the disappointing events since 'the tragic days of 1931' and reflected on 'the gleam of hope if our lads get going properly' which had sustained the Celtic support. Three players were singled out for praise: Joe Kennaway, who, the handbook complained, was 'despised and rejected of the Scotland selectors'; Jimmy McGrory, who had confirmed his status as 'one of the great Celts this club has been blessed with'; and Willie Lyon – 'strong as the proverbial Lion, he scorns to use the strength God gave him except in the straightest and fairest manner, and he has never lost anything by doing so'. McMenemy was praised for 'his influence with the younger generation'.

For good measure in 1935/6, the club won the Charity Cup ('for which trophy we have always had a special fondness') after a ten-year break. The club handbook, in this moment of long-awaited glory, also had a lofty – and surely ill-merited – word of chastisement for the club's followers:

It is good to know that our support has returned to us again. Our people roll up when the team does well, but are inclined to be ready to sit back when fortune does not follow us. This is not the real Celtic spirit nor the one which has brought the club to the position it holds. Never say die is our motto, and the followers of the club should learn that it is only by unswerving support that any club can hope to maintain a position such as they wish us to occupy.

The same publication contained a tribute to Tom E. Maley, the Celtic pioneer who had died in 1935. He had gone on to be a successful manager with Manchester City, Bradford and Southport, but on retiring to Glasgow, 'his strong and undying affection for Celtic FC was evinced in the quiet, unobtrusive but practical interest he took in all that appertained to its good'.

Season 1936/7 opened with the same team – a rare event in recent seasons. James Handley summed up their attributes thus:

Kennaway was superbly safe in goal, Hogg and Morrison were first-rate backs, the half-back line was as good as ever, Delaney had developed into a great winger, Buchan was a player in the Wilson mould with an easy, graceful, almost lazy style, and McGrory was playing with his usual sprightliness.

Crum and Murphy formed the equally exhilarating left-wing pairing. It was a great Celtic team, but surprisingly the League challenge fell away in the latter part of the season. However, there was steady progress towards the Final of the Scottish Cup after a close shave against Stenhousemuir in the first round, when a replay was required. Albion Rovers, East Fife, Motherwell and Clyde were disposed of before Celtic lined up at Hampden against Aberdeen in front of a British record crowd for a club match (a record which survives right up to the present day) of 146,433, with an estimated 30,000 locked outside. Willie Maley pondered on that great congregation and could not help recalling 'the struggles of our early days – days when nothing but great enthusiasm and dogged determination kept the flag flying'. The team on that historic day was one whose names would be revered by a whole generation: Kennaway, Hogg and Morrison; Geatons, Lyon and Paterson; Delaney, Buchan, Crum, Divers and Murphy. Jimmy Delaney – who the previous week had played in front of an even bigger crowd for Scotland against England – recalls the atmosphere as 'tremendous'. Crum gave Celtic an early lead, but Armstrong soon equalized. The winning goal came twenty minutes from the end, when McGrory set up a chance for Buchan – and so another milestone became Celtic's permanent (it can now be reasonably assumed) property: victory in front of that never-to-be-exceeded British club attendance.

There were high hopes that the League flag would be regained during the club's golden jubilee season of 1937/8, but there was a poor start, followed by some disappointing developments for the supporters. Willie Buchan was transferred to Blackpool for the large fee of £10,000. Jimmy McGrory retired from the playing side of the game in October 1937; in his final game, against Queen's Park, he scored a goal to bring his career tally to 550, spanning fifteen seasons. Robert Kelly wrote:

Nobody has ever excelled McGrory in the art of heading the ball; he had the extraordinary ability of diverting the strongest cross down towards the goal-line . . . equally well will Jimmy be remembered by older Celtic supporters as a man who time after time rallied the team with his unquenchable enthusiasm.

For James Handley, he had been 'the greatest menace to goalkeepers in the history of the game'. At the time of his retirement from playing, prompted by persistent injuries, he was 'wearing well – not so fast as of old, but still the greatest opportunist in Scottish football when he was on the field'. The supreme tribute came shortly afterwards from Willie Maley, McGrory's mentor throughout his playing career:

With all respect to the many other splendid Celts we have had and still have, I want to say this: We have never had, with one exception, a player whose prowess and o'erflowing enthusiasm have led us to so many brilliant victories. The exception is Paddy Gallagher. As a goal-getter McGrory stands supreme . . .

In December 1937, McGrory retired from playing on being offered the managership of Kilmarnock, a post for which he had not applied. In an article at that time, he looked back on his long and prolific career and selected his own choice of the best goal he had ever scored. Few of the fans who had seen the incredibly low, diving header against Aberdeen at Celtic Park on 21 December 1935 would have dissented from the choice. 'Johnny Crum sent the ball over from the left, and my directors told me later that they considered it an impossible ball for heading purposes. But I made a dive, and when I was in a horizontal position headed into the net.' Celtic had co-operated fully in allowing McGrory to accept the Rugby Park job, but there was no room for sentiment when Kilmarnock promptly eliminated Celtic from the Scottish Cup in the third round – an upset which came as a bitter blow in the jubilee year and, to Maley's considerable irritation, focused attention on the possibility of McGrory soon returning to Celtic Park as manager.

With McGrory's departure, the standard Celtic forward line had been rearranged into a notably skilful combination of Delaney, McDonald, Crum, Divers and Murphy, with Joe Carruth, a versatile signing from Petershill, and Matt Lynch from St Anthony's, who tended to come in for Delaney, as regular performers when injury struck. As the season wore on, the team's League form became steadily more impressive, but it seemed that the title might slip from their grasp when they went down 3–0 to Falkirk in the first game of April. However, there followed a 4–1 victory over Motherwell, and Dundee were overcome both home and away in the space of three days, after which on 23 April 1938, a 3–1 victory at Love Street secured the title, for the nineteenth time, in this eventful fiftieth season. The Charity Cup was also taken, and the coincidence of dates between Celtic's founding and the great Glasgow Exhibition of 1888 soon provided another memorable anniversary event to add to the celebrations of their own half-century as a club.

To mark the passing of fifty years since the original, another great exhibition was held, centred upon Bellahouston Park. This was the Empire Exhibition, which combined displays of the achievements of Scottish industry and enterprise with pavilions full of presentations from all countries of the Empire. King George attended the opening ceremony at Ibrox Park on 3 May 1938, and the event totally captured the imagination of the Glasgow people – pushing aside, at least temporarily, the grim prospect of war, which was intensifying each day as Hitler's conquests expanded and Franco edged the Spanish fascists towards power. 'In this pleasant Glasgow park,' wrote one commentator, 'a remarkable thing has been done. A microcosm of Empire, an enclave of sanity and order, has been created, in which it is possible to walk for a space almost forgetting that there are such things as crazy ambition and bomb-wrecked towns, shellfire and the clash of armies.'

A football tournament was included in the festivities, with Celtic, Rangers, Hearts and Aberdeen challenged by Sunderland, Chelsea,

Everton and Brentford from the south. The competition, like the Exhibition as a whole, drew a tremendous public response and there were 54,000 at Ibrox, where all the games were played, for Celtic's opening tie against Sunderland. It ended without score, but on the following evening two goals from Divers and one from Crum took Celtic through to meet Hearts. In that game Crum scored the only goal, and so Celtic were in the final against the mighty Everton, who had previously disposed of Rangers and Aberdeen, and who had ten internationalists from the four home countries to call on.

A crowd of 82,000 witnessed a great final, in which Lawton was of especial menace to Kennaway's goal. But ninety minutes were concluded without score and, seven minutes into extra time, John Crum shot home the goal which took the trophy – 'the replica in silver of the Tower of Empire' – to a permanent home at Celtic Park. The Empire Exhibition competition stimulated a great interest in the idea of a regular competition which would bring together the best in Scotland and England, and this might well have come into being had war not soon intervened.

Jimmy Delaney recalls the Exhibition Trophy-winning side as the best he had ever played in, and Malcolm MacDonald as 'the finest all-round player I've seen'. Delaney's recollections give an insight into life at Celtic Park in the 1930s.

The directors left everything about the running of the club to Maley. There was very little coaching or anything like that. Five minutes before we went out, he would put his head round the dressing-room door and say 'good luck, boys'. That was it. If someone didn't play well, he would call him into his office on a Monday morning. He would ask if there was anything wrong at home; anything worrying the player – questions like that. The thinking was that if you had been signed to play for Celtic, they expected you to be a good footballer without being told how to play. It was left to you to read the game and, if you'd played against the opposition before, you knew their weaknesses. There really weren't any tactic talks. We weren't told to run here or run there. During the week, the trainer got us fit – most of the training was running round the track and short sprints. The discipline was strict. If you were five minutes late, you were told very firmly to get there in time. But the atmosphere was terrific. Kennaway and Crum were the two comedians – they kept the spirits up.

For a young man in these days, being asked to play for Rangers or Celtic was the greatest thing that could happen to him. The biggest occasions for us were when we were playing against Rangers. We were always on a big bonus against them. Relations between the players were very good though you always had a couple of nags on the park. Off the field, if you saw a Rangers player, you would walk over and have a drink with him. I remember my first international in 1935 when we met in an hotel and the first man who came to me was Bob McPhail. He told me just to play the way I did for Celtic. That was pretty typical. The religious thing didn't really enter into it among the players – in the '30s, of course, half the Celtic team wasn't Catholic. Maley was a great man, and Celtic all his days. He and the directors were very strict on drink – they didn't like to hear of you being seen in a pub during the week. We went to Maley's Bank Restaurant before and after a game. A lot of supporters would go there for a drink, and to have a word with the players. That was where we were to report – nowhere else.

Throughout this period, all Celtic publications carried an invitation to wine and dine at 'The Bank' in Queen Street: 'There are two places you can dine in comfort – at home and here.'

Celtic's golden jubilee was celebrated at a dinner on 16 June 1938, when representatives of football interests in Scotland, England and Ireland were present. On display were the Exhibition Cup of 1901, which Celtic had captured from Rangers the following year, the Exhibition Trophy won the previous week, the shield presented by the SFA in recognition of the 'six in a row', and the Glasgow Charity Cup. Tom White presided, and a cheque for 2500 guineas – 50 guineas for each year of service – was presented to Willie Maley. The toast to the Celtic club was proposed by Sir John T. Cargill, honorary president of Rangers and of the Glasgow Merchants' Charity Cup Committee, who recalled that he had performed the same task at Rangers' jubilee dinner. Rangers and Celtic had been great rivals, said Sir John, but they were also great friends.

Celtic Football Club is an Irish club, and one of the great characteristics of the Irish race is not only their generosity and large-heartedness but they are the greatest sportsmen in the world. They take an interest in every sport, and played every sport magnificently as only Irishmen could.

Turning to the management of the club, Sir John noted that Tom White had also been president of the SFA.

He brought to the football world a delightfully breezy manner which made him and his club so popular . . . Then they had Mr Maley, who answered the description, in a way, of the strong but not silent man. He was a strong man with strong views, but one needed that to succeed as manager of a football club.

Sir John's tribute was certainly unstinting, and before Tom White – always in great demand as an after-dinner speaker – replied, the company sang 'The Dear Little Shamrock'. It was an occasion to disappoint sectarians – though the more radical members of the audience must have had mixed feelings about the words of Sir John Cargill, described by Patrick Dollan in *Forward* as 'the patron saint of Tory capitalism in the West of Scotland'. In administrative circles, if not on the terraces, the Celtic and Rangers clubs co-existed quite happily and to their mutual financial benefit.

There was no indication at the jubilee dinner of events which were soon to follow, when Tom White declared that 'the triumphs of the Celtic club are the triumphs of Mr [Willie] Maley, whose life has been indissolubly allied to Celtic . . . The name of Maley is synonymous with the Celtic club and almost with the name of soccer.' Maley, who had just turned seventy, thanked Almighty God for his guidance and goodness. His work for Celtic, he said, had been a labour of love. He listed the club's achievements on and off the field of play, recalling in particular the crucial role of Brother Walfrid and John Glass in ensuring the club's survival when 'funds were low and the opposition of a section of the public very strong', and noting that only John Madden, who had been in Prague as a coach for thirty years, and he himself survived of the first Celtic side. When his own enthusiasm had led him into 'some indiscretions', the board knew all the time that it was 'just his old Irish heart beating too fast, and that it was all meant for the best'. Maley expressed pride in the fact that 'never has there been any club manager with such complete liberty of action or fullness of power as the Celtic management has accorded to me, and in all my years with them, I have never betrayed that faith'.

The triumphant Celtic team entered the new season with a 9–1 victory over McGrory's Kilmarnock, and the Glasgow Cup was soon won. But injuries set in and the high hopes of continuing glory evaporated. The most serious of these injuries befell Jimmy Delaney on 1 April 1939 at Arbroath, when he was pushed to the ground as he challenged for the ball from a corner kick. He fell awkwardly and sustained an arm injury which was to keep him out of the game for two years and three months. Delaney recalls: 'The professor said the arm was just like a jigsaw puzzle. If it had been an industrial injury, they would have taken the arm off.' Celtic went out of the Scottish Cup to Motherwell and finished with forty-eight league points from thirty-eight games. Maley characterized it as 'one of the most disappointing, if not *the* most disappointing, in our fifty-one years of existence'. As usual, in his annual report, Maley complained a great deal about referees, but concluded:

With the yearly leaven of youth, we go forward to 1939/40 with that confident optimism which has carried us over the long years, and I sincerely hope that the new season will see us regain our poise and bring to Celtic Park the old form and real good football which is indelibly associated with the name of our club the world over.

He had, however, reckoned without Adolf Hitler, whose long shadow was eventually to fall over the whole of Europe.

# 10

## AT WAR AGAIN
### *Apathy and Unrest at Celtic Park*

T HE 1939/40 season opened as Europe drifted rapidly towards war. When Celtic met Clyde on 2 September and won by a Divers goal, the thoughts of the Shawfield crowd were elsewhere. That weekend, the Government was putting into effect the scheme to evacuate children from the cities, and the Saturday newspapers announced the start of conscription. Parliament was sitting that afternoon; the black-out had begun, and before the weekend was out, Britain was at war with Germany. Monday's reports were of the sinking of the *Athenia*, most of whose crew were Glaswegians.

Once again, sport became a marginal activity as society adjusted to the rigorous demands of war. But whereas aeroplanes had been 'more of a curiosity than the deadly menace they are today' in 1914–18, the threat of aerial bombing was now a strong factor in making the Government apprehensive about allowing large crowds to gather in confined spaces. At first, this high level of expectation that the outbreak of war would quickly lead to regular air raids on our cities led to a complete ban on sport and entertainment. Scottish football administrators were very active in lobbying the Government for a relaxation of the ban, and they appear to have been influential in securing a change in attitude. Football matches – at first friendlies only – would be allowed on Saturdays and public holidays, with crowds at big grounds like Celtic Park limited to 15,000.

Within a few weeks, guidelines had been drawn up for the return of competitive football; as in 1914, the Government had concluded that the game's beneficial impact on morale outweighed the arguments in favour of banning it. But there was no reason for footballers to be exempted from war duties, and the ruling which emerged was that players would be allowed to appear for whichever club was convenient, according to their location at any given time. Some English clubs simply closed down for the war years, and their Scottish players returned home. Restrictions on travel added further complications, and at first, the Scottish League decided to operate two regional divisions, East and West. As James Handley recalled:

The demands of wartime industry with its heavy and prolonged hours of labour, the difficulties engendered by curtailed transport and multiplied when petrol rationing was introduced served, without the necessity of official interference, to diminish the crowds at First Division football matches generally to three or four thousand; and the players themselves often arrived at the pavilion straight from work, with blackened faces and tired limbs.

Celtic's first game under this set-up was on 21 October 1939 against Hamilton Academicals, who had three Anglo-Scottish 'guests' in their team, while Celtic had just one, Willie Buchan, who had transferred to Blackpool in 1937. They lost 4–3, and the pattern was set for the club's miserable wartime record. Unlike other clubs, notably Rangers, Celtic did not take wartime football too seriously. They made little effort to attract big-name guests, and went into a period of lethargy from which it subsequently proved difficult to emerge.

The arctic winter of 1939/40 was a particularly miserable one for those who sought to draw comfort from the diversion of supporting Celtic, and matters came to a head when the club's board took the plunge and decided to part company with Willie Maley – by then in his seventy-second year and his fifty-second of intimate involvement with the affairs of the club. The astonishing longevity of his reign, and the fact that he had only recently recovered from a long illness, did not prevent him from reacting with great bitterness when his resignation was finally sought.

Maley, largely on the strength of his football connections, had become a substantial businessman in his own right, and Celtic had dealt generously with him at the time of the jubilee. A substantial ex-gratia payment was also made on his retirement. In retrospect, the need to initiate change when a manager is over seventy years of age appears self-evident. But Maley took umbrage, an undignified row developed over who should pay the tax on his 'golden handshake', and the parting left wounds which were never really healed. The Celtic directors, particularly chairman Tom White, had simply had enough of Maley's autocratic and increasingly secretive style, and his reaction to their decision to retire him hints at the correctness of their conclusion. For an old man, steeped in football, it was nevertheless a bitter blow. A few months later he wrote:

My thoughts go back to August 1939 when we started off in what we well imagined would be another successful season and which I did not think would be my last year in football management . . . It has been to me the end of my football career and has robbed me of the very tang of life. Football has been my thoughts morning, noon and night for all the 52 years I have been in it, and it has been hard to drop out of my regular ways.

The circumstances of the parting were not conducive to handsome financial tributes, and Celtic were criticized for not acknowledging Maley's long and generally distinguished service more formally. A programme note briefly announced his departure, which 'cannot fail to cause widespread regret, and to Mr Maley probably most of all, as the club and all it stands for has been his life's work. May his leisure be long and full of happiness is the prayer of every true Celt!' For some years thereafter Maley would not enter Celtic Park, but this was remedied during the last years of his life. When Maley died in July 1958, chairman Robert Kelly – whose father had played alongside Maley in the very first Celtic team – paid tribute at a board meeting to 'that grand old man of the game' and added that he had 'visited the park up to six months prior to his death'.

Maley had been a disciplinarian, an outstanding judge of young players, and a reasonable tactician in an era when management generally had little to do with on-field tactics. He was also an assiduous worker for charity, and the leading figure in that school of thought which has always maintained that Celtic do not receive fair treatment at the hands of football officialdom, on and off the park. Robert Kelly recalled Maley's approach:

The best way, he said, to ensure that a referee did not affect a Celtic result was to hit so many goals into the opposing team's net that the referee could hardly knock most of them off. That was especially the case, he used to insist, if the opponents were Rangers. My father and he once decided that they would congratulate our great rivals when they won the League by a minimum of five points; that was the start, they reckoned, that Rangers had over the other clubs.

After Maley's departure, Jimmy McStay was appointed in his place, but the suspicion persisted that the proprietor of the Bank Restaurant continued to wield considerable influence – a perception which, in turn, helped to undermine the new manager's authority. McStay, the great centre-half of the thirties, had gone on to obtain some managerial experience in Ireland and with Alloa Athletic. But his five-year tenure as Celtic manager was not a particularly happy one. It is doubtful whether McStay was aware of the fact that he was looked upon only as a stop-gap manager, but this was subsequently made clear by Robert Kelly – at that time the rising star of the Celtic board – who wrote:

Jimmy never had the chance to become a famous manager such as Maley. In the first place, his appointment came in time of war when football was at sixes and sevens and Celtic were having a doleful period. In any case, we had already earmarked the man who we hoped would become Celtic manager. He was Jimmy McGrory.

It was perhaps scarcely surprising, in the light of that revelation, combined with their tendency to produce unpredictable line-ups, that Celtic drifted aimlessly through the war years with only a minimal contribution to public morale, at least among their own supporters. The first wartime season was already dead for Celtic when McStay took over in February 1940, and they finished in a miserable thirteenth place in the League, having won only nine of their thirty games. But as James Handley wrote:

No matter what the SFA might determine to give the impression of business pretty much as usual in the prevailing conditions, the man who paid his humble bob at the turnstile was not deceived. He handed over his money to see in action the team he had come to know and he was not going to be fobbed off by a weekly frolic of permutations and combinations on the part of the management.

After one season of the unsatisfactory arrangement of the Scottish League being split into two regions, the official body gave up and left it to the clubs to organize themselves into competitions. A new Southern League was formed with sixteen clubs, and wages continued to be fixed at a £2 maximum – though the clubs which had 'guests' on their books certainly made additional payments to them. This was equally certainly a factor in persuading Celtic to rely largely on players from the junior and Boys' Guild ranks. There was a substantial public, eager for wartime football of a reasonably serious variety, and – crowd restrictions having been further relaxed – 50,000 turned out to see Celtic and Rangers contest a goalless draw on 7 September 1940.

But decline soon set in, and Celtic finished fifth in this second season of war. As many who were looking for some relief from the privations of these days still recall, Celtic supporters were frustrated by the club's exceedingly modest ambitions during this period. The Celtic handbook complained lamely of 'how unlucky we were on the whole, due to draws and defeats by the odd goal results, due in no small measure to the old fault of our players' poor finishing'. The only encouraging news was that, after more than two years out of the game with his arm injury, Jimmy Delaney was ready to return for the start of the 1941/2 season.

The first Old Firm encounter of this season was marred by crowd trouble at Ibrox Park, after both Delaney and Crum had been carried from the field on stretchers. There were five arrests, and the SFA made the extraordinary decision to close not Ibrox but Celtic Park for a month – one of the occasional episodes, scattered throughout the club's history, which have given credibility to conspiracy theorists. This time, Celtic managed third place in the League, while Rangers continued to rule the wartime roost.

Prior to the start of the 1942/3 season, the Celtic guide noted: 'The departure of Willie Corbett to the Royal Navy deprives the club of the most brilliant young centre-half discovered in Scotland since the war. His going will provide an opportunity for young John McPhail.' The eighteen-year-old McPhail, who was to become one of the outstanding Celtic personalities of the generally bleak forties and fifties, had been signed after only a few junior games with Strathclyde, having played most of his football for St Mungo's Academy. By this time, Celtic had only six players from before the war on their books – Crum, Hogg, Delaney, Malcolm MacDonald, Lynch and Murphy. The 1942/3 guide also included a poem, 'The Faithful in Arms', which provided the quite famous lines: 'And the question slips from Celtic lips/ How did "the boys" get on?' The poem continued somewhat fancifully, given the on-field reality at that time.

> Tho' seas divide they think with pride of the team that they left behind,
> They are faithful still, through good and ill, they bear the Celts in mind;
> So memory clings in their wanderings to lighten a trooper's load –
> The tramp of feet down Janefield Street or a vision of London Road.

The load of Celtic-supporting troopers must, however, have felt a good deal heavier during the ensuing season. Not only were the directors uninterested in bringing players of reputation into the side, they apparently made little effort to hang on to those who were already there. In 1942/3, Celtic fielded six players who had been in Boys' Guild sides a few months earlier, while Crum followed Divers to Morton as the outflow of experienced players continued. They finished tenth in the League, and the depths of ignominy were plumbed in the New Year's Day fixture when a team in Celtic colours lost 8–1 at Ibrox after both Malcolm MacDonald and Lynch had been sent off for arguing with the referee. Whatever the exonerating circumstances, it was by far the club's worst result in the long history of the fixture. The club policy, if it existed, was difficult to discern. The decision not to pursue big-name guests extended even to Matt Busby of Manchester City and United fame, who – having returned to his native Lanarkshire – was desperate to play for Celtic. The directors turned down McStay's request to field him and he went to Hibs instead, doing much good work at Easter Road in the fostering of young talent.

There was considerable improvement in the 1943/4 season, with Divers returning from Morton and Delaney to something like his best form. Celtic finished second in the Southern League with forty-three points from thirty games – seven behind Rangers. The most promising portents came from John McPhail who, having switched positions, made a strong impression as partner to Jimmy Delaney, and Willie Miller, a fine goalkeeper signed from Maryhill Harp. With the course of the war turning in the Allies' favour, enthusiasm for diversions such as football increased, and the first all-ticket League game in Scotland attracted 75,000 to Celtic Park on New Year's Day 1944.

But the circumstances under which the competition was conducted continued to be extremely difficult. The Celtic handbook reported: 'On the question of transport the matter is serious. On various occasions last season the Celtic players had to travel in hopelessly overcrowded trains, even in the guard's van, with first-class tickets in their pockets.' Players found it difficult to reach the ground for evening training, 'and even to arrive in time for the kick-off on match days'. Jimmy Delaney recalls that his inside partner was, quite often, someone he had never previously met! But another youngster who was to become a Celtic 'great' was signed from St Anthony's in 1944 – Bobby Evans. He was to make his debut, as a forward, against Albion Rovers in the second game of the new season.

Celtic made an indifferent start to this season, and though they rallied with a run of seventeen undefeated games, this was not enough to catch Rangers. James Handley neatly summarized the Celtic condition as the war drew to a close:

At this stage the team had physique and power, but the old guile and polish were pretty much confined to Malcolm MacDonald and Delaney. McDonald was a useful coach for the younger players. Mallan, who had come from Pollok in 1942, was a sound centre-half, and the team as a whole had at last evolved into a satisfactory combination considering the conditions of the time, but they were far from being in the old Parkhead tradition and still had the unhappy wartime knack of giving the occasional performance that played tricks with the blood pressure of their followers.

The Glasgow Cup in 1940/1 and the Charity Cup in 1942/3 had been Celtic's only wartime honours, but the managership of Jimmy McStay did at least conclude on a high note with the Victory in Europe Cup coming to Celtic

Park on 9 May 1945. This trophy had been put up by the Glasgow Charity Cup committee, to raise money for war charities, with Celtic and Rangers invited to meet. Rangers declined, however, and Queen's Park provided the opposition at Hampden. In these days, corners were sometimes used to separate the teams for 'sudden-death' purposes, and Celtic had a single corner advantage when the game ended 1–1. That was enough to secure the presence of another of these magnificent 'once and for all' trophies which adorn Celtic Park. The Celtic team for the occasion was: Miller, Hogg and P. McDonald; Lynch, Mallan and McPhail; Paton and M. MacDonald; Gallacher, Evans and McLaughlin. Only Bobby Hogg and Malcolm MacDonald had been members of the Exhibition Cup-winning side of 1938.

Two months later, Jimmy McStay was asked to resign in order to make way for Jimmy McGrory. He did so with considerable resentment over the way in which he had been treated – the final insult being that he learned of his impending departure from a newspaper billboard, as he returned home from a holiday in Ayr. But McStay was later to return to Celtic Park as chief scout under McGrory, in which role he played a significant part during the 1950s in building for future glory. The Celtic handbook announced, more than a little disingenuously:

No more acceptable appointment to the managerial chair could be made than that of Mr James McGrory, which took place during the close season. The indifferent achievements of the team last season provided the need, and the resignation of Jimmy McStay gave the opportunity, of making a change. It is 22 years since Jimmy McGrory joined the Celtic.

He faced an uphill struggle. The few remaining players who had been alongside him in pre-war teams were sceptical about his managerial potential, because they doubted whether he was sufficiently firm or decisive for the job. Although the war in Europe was over, normality could not yet return as call-up intensified for the continuing struggle against Japan. As Celtic faced the 1945/6 season, thirteen of their players were still on active service – including Willie Lyon, a captain in the Royal Artillery, who had been awarded the Military Cross for bravery.

By this time, the Celtic Supporters' Association had been brought into existence. The initiative was taken in September 1944 when a newspaper announcement attracted just fourteen supporters to a meeting. It was none the less decided to hold a further meeting at the AOH Hall, Alexandria Parade, and this time large crowds turned up. By the end of the war, the Association had grown into a large network of branches, the first being founded in Coatbridge. The old 'brake clubs' tradition had been revived, and adapted to modern conditions. In his message to all Celtic supporters, contained in the first magazine produced by the Association in 1946, its president, Joe Regan, reflected:

The war years have not brought much glory to our team. It has to be admitted that they don't get many breaks – Fate and 'other elements' seem to take a hand just when things look best . . . Our team has not reached the standards one associates with the name of Celtic, but now that we are back to pre-war conditions we are looking forward to the future for much better results than has been our lot in recent years.

# 11

## TURMOIL AND TRAVEL
### *The Quest for Divine Inspiration?*

T SOON became clear that Celtic's wasted war years would be paid for dearly, as the new 'A' division was formed from the clubs with greatest drawing power. Along with McGrory, Chic Geatons had been brought back to Celtic Park as coach. The supporters' hopes of changed fortunes were enhanced by the signing of Kiernan, a former Albion Rovers inside-forward who had been in the forces for five years, and Bogan from Hibs. (The latter was signed to replace Jackie Gallacher, the popular centre-forward who had been called up to the RAF.) But Malcolm MacDonald had departed for Kilmarnock, and in January 1945, Jimmy Delaney – now aged thirty-one and anxious to obtain a more secure future for himself after losing the best of his career to the war years – played his last game, against Falkirk, before joining Manchester United. This move reflected his dissatisfaction with the wages offered by Celtic at this time, and dismayed the by now long-suffering supporters, some of whom even volunteered to 'top up' his earnings. Delaney declined with thanks, believing that it was the club which should be giving him a better reward – particularly since he and other top players had been held to £2 a week during the war while knowing that guests were being more handsomely remunerated.

Celtic could do no better than finish fourth in the League, with thirty-five points from thirty games. They also failed to take the Victory Cup – one of those one-off competitions in which they had traditionally excelled – as the result of a notorious semi-final replay with Rangers. Two Celtic players, Mallan and Paterson, were suspended for three months after being sent off for disputing a penalty award. Another, Lynch, was suspended for a month, although he had not been sent off and Duncanson, his immediate opponent in the Rangers side, testified to his innocence. Celtic were fined and censured for scathing references to the referee in the club's handbook. Jimmy McGrory, in his report on the season, wrote: 'History will surely record that indiscretions in refereeing and harshness of punishment have imposed an undeserved penalty on club and players alike.' Another writer went further, complaining that 'the referee's peculiar interpretation of the laws of football reduced the contest to a farce', and reproduced a six-year-old match report of a game between Rangers and St Mirren in which the referee was alleged to have discriminated heavily in Rangers' favour! Celtic were also ordered to post warning notices against crowd trouble. It was yet another of these episodes which soured relationships between Celtic and Scottish football officialdom.

Things went from bad to worse in the next two seasons. Starting the 1946/7 campaign without the suspended players and with John McPhail recuperating from illness, they took only four points from their first ten games, and eventually finished seventh. They failed to qualify for their League Cup section, and made an immediate exit from the Scottish Cup at the hands of Dundee. In March 1947, the *Evening Citizen* opined: 'Celtic have been going through a bad time for several years. At no other time in their illustrious history have they slipped so low.'

After the initial euphoria surrounding McGrory's return, the supporters soon started asking the questions which were never to be far away from Celtic Park throughout his twenty years as manager: Who was really in charge? Who picked the team? How much say did Jimmy McGrory have? There were demonstrations in the second post-war season which called for the resignation of chairman Tom White, who was by now an old man in failing health. Increasingly since Maley's departure, power at Celtic Park had moved towards Robert Kelly, a director since his father's death in 1931 and a stockbroker by profession. The enigmatic figure of Kelly, who became the sixth Celtic chairman upon Tom White's death on 4 March 1947, was to dominate the next quarter-century of Celtic's history.

Kelly and his family were part of the Celtic fabric. His father, James, had become a successful businessman on the strength of his football fame. He and his wife, Margaret McErlean, daughter of another Celtic founder, had had six sons (of whom Robert was the fourth) and four daughters. James Kelly – 'the finest man I have known' – was the dominant influence on Robert's life. The doctrines of the Kelly household were sportsmanship, hard work and, above all, the Celtic tradition – a term which, according to Robert Kelly's writings, encompassed a respect for the club's origins, a determination that it should remain non-sectarian, and a devotion to attacking football.

Like many successful Catholics, James Kelly had been encouraged to send his sons to be educated at St Joseph's, Dumfries, one of the new fee-paying schools which had been opened to further the development of a professional Catholic middle class in Scotland. It was an education which ensured that Robert would have little in common, in social terms, with most of the lads who played for Celtic. His upbringing also left him an extremely devout Catholic all his days. It was Robert Kelly's great regret that he had not played for Celtic himself. Having sustained permanent damage to his right arm in an early traffic accident, his playing days were restricted to the junior grade. But with his elevation to the board in 1932, he was able to devote a greater proportion of his time to the club he had been brought up to love.

Kelly was far more interested in the club's traditions than in its balance sheet, although it is true that the former largely ensured the health of the latter. He certainly never amassed personal wealth from the club's success, as became apparent at the time of his death. There was never any likelihood of Celtic buying their way out of trouble as long as Kelly was in control, though the signing of occasional experienced players was acceptable. He found his delight in giving youngsters the opportunity to better themselves in the Celtic colours. Normally, these were Catholic youngsters, because it was overwhelmingly footballers from that background who aspired to play for Celtic. Whilst acknowledging that reality, Kelly none the less dealt firmly with any suggestion of turning Celtic into a 'Catholic club'. But it was central to his philosophy that Celtic's success should be a powerful vehicle for improving the morale and status of the community from which it drew the great bulk of its support.

Kelly's background and attitudes became extremely relevant to the story of Celtic, because there is not the slightest doubt that he dominated every aspect of the club's affairs and outlook throughout the managership of Jimmy McGrory. From the late 1940s onwards, his direct involvement in team affairs seemed like a distinctly dubious blessing to the increasingly restless supporters.

Kelly's first full season as chairman took Celtic closer than ever before or since to relegation. By the time Rangers won the New Year fixture 4–0, Celtic had played eighteen games, won six, drawn three and lost nine. They continued to struggle in the League, though they reached the semi-final of the Scottish Cup before going down to Morton. Facing their last game of the season at Dundee, they had taken only twenty-three points from twenty-nine games and were thus one of four clubs who could join Queen's Park in relegation. Only by overcoming Dundee at Dens Park on 17 April could they be sure of avoiding that fate – though defeat, it must be said, would not

*Brother Walfrid, the Marist Brother from Ballymote, County Sligo who was a key figure in Celtic's founding*

*The inaugural team picture from 1888. Left to right (back row) J. Anderson (trainer), J. Quillan, D. Malloy, J. Glass, J. McDonald (officials); (middle row) W. Groves, T. Maley, P. Gallacher, J. O'Hara (official), W. Dunning, W. McKillop (official), W. Maley, M. Dunbar; (front row) J. Coleman, J. McLaren, J. Kelly, N. McCallum, M. McKeown*

*The medal won by Neil McCallum when Celtic were losing Scottish Cup finalists to Third Lanark in their first season of existence, 1888/9*

*McCallum, who joined the club from Renton, was the scorer of Celtic's only goal in that Final*

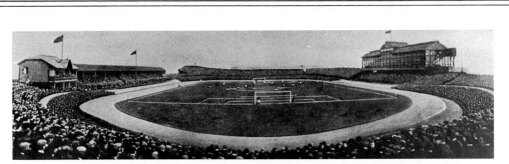

*Celtic Park in 1900, showing the impressive looking but ill-conceived Grant Stand on the right*

*It wasn't long before Celtic were regularly winning trophies and this team picture from 1908 shows them with the Charity, Scottish and Glasgow Cups. Left to right (back row) T. White, J. Kelly, T. Colgan, J. McKillop, J. Grant, M. Dunbar (directors); (middle row) W. Maley (secretary), J. Young, P. Somers, J. McMenemy, D. Adams, J. Mitchell, J. Weir, R. Davis (trainer); (front row) D. Hamilton, D. McLeod, W. Loney, J. Hay, J. Quinn, W. McNair*

*The medal struck to commemorate a game against Southampton, played in Bucharest during Celtic's first ever European tour in 1906*

*In 1923, Celtic visited Cologne to play against troops still serving in Germany*

*Jimmy McGrory holding the Scottish Cup in Detroit during the club's North American tour of 1931*

JAMES QUINN    ALEC McNAIR

JAMES YOUNG    J. McMENEMY

*ABOVE LEFT: A tour of a different kind. Willie Maley (middle row, far right) and his brother Tom (holding banner) on a pilgrimage to Lourdes in 1935*
*ABOVE RIGHT: Four Celtic stalwarts from the early part of the century*

W. MALEY. SECY.    W. McSTEY.    P. SHEVLIN.    H. HILLEY.    Mr. T. WHITE. CHAIRMAN.

P. WILSON.    J. McSTEY.    J. MACFARLANE.    A. McLEAN.

The CELTIC FOOTBALL CLUB CUP-TIE and LEAGUE TEAM
SCOTTISH CUP WINNERS. 1924-25. RECORD HOLDERS. WON THE SCOTTISH CUP ELEVEN TIMES.

P. CONNOLLY.    P. GALLACHER.    J. McGRORY.    A. THOMSON.

*The Celtic team that celebrated winning the Scottish Cup a record eleven times in 1924/5*

*Jock Stein inspired a Celtic revival by captaining the side to a League and Cup double in 1953/4, the first since 1913/14. Left to right (back row) F. Meechan, M. Haughney, J. Bonnar, R. Evans, J. Walsh; (front row) N. Mochan, W. Fernie, B. Peacock, J. Stein, S. Fallon, R. Collins*

*Forever to be remembered as the '7–1 team' who beat Rangers by that margin in the 1957 League Cup Final. Left to right (back row) J. Donnelly, R. Evans, S. Fallon, R. Beattie, J. McPhail, W. Fernie; (front row) J. McGrory (manager), C. Tully, R. Collins, B. Peacock, S. Wilson, N. Mochan, W. Johnstone (trainer)*

have ensured it. The men who carried the responsibility that day were: Miller, Hogg and Mallan; Evans, Corbett and McAuley; Weir and McPhail; Lavery, Gallacher and Paton. Robert Kelly later described it as 'the greatest ordeal I experienced in watching football in well over fifty years'. He vowed that 'we would never again, whatever the circumstances, reach the depths of 1948'. Jimmy McGrory was ready to resign if Celtic lost.

In the game's early stages, John McPhail had the ball in the net twice, but both were disallowed. Jock Weir – signed earlier in the season from Blackburn Rovers in a desperate attempt to obtain a goal-scorer – scrambled the ball home, but Dundee equalized before the interval. Then, after an hour's play, Dundee took the lead and Celtic hearts sank. But Weir brought the score back to 2–2 and then, with just two minutes remaining, completed his hat-trick to save the honour of his new club. Never had a transfer fee been more handsomely repaid in the space of ninety minutes, and Jock Weir's place in Celtic mythology was ensured. There were 31,000 at Dens Park that day, and it was some consolation for Kelly that 'Celtic in adversity were tremendously well supported'.

The directors were stung into action, and before the start of the 1948/9 season, Jimmy Hogan, the former Burnley player who had helped to develop the game in Hungary but was now nearing seventy, was appointed as coach. He had been the English FA's coach for six years and had also managed Aston Villa. It was an imaginative appointment for the time. Celtic also set their sights on three players from Belfast Celtic, but secured only one – the immortal Charles Patrick Tully – for the fee of £8000, in the face of stiff English competition. They also pipped Everton for the signature of Bobby Collins, an eighteen-year-old from Pollok Juniors. In spite of the SFA upholding a claim by the English club that Collins had agreed to join them, he refused to go, and Celtic gained a valuable recruit. Celtic had even signed a Polish left-winger who caused some short-lived excitement with his reserve-team performances – Konrad Kapler had been 'spotted' while playing with the Polish Army at Johnstone.

There was some promise in all of this, and in an entertainment-starved era of huge football crowds there were 55,000 at Celtic Park for the opening game of the 1948/9 season, with high hopes of something better transpiring. Charlie Tully made a disappointing debut, and the game ended in a goalless draw. The promise soon evaporated, and Celtic finished joint seventh in the League, their solitary trophy for the season being the Glasgow Cup. 'We have the players, but it appears we haven't got a team', said Robert Kelly, though Hogan's coaching was producing signs of a more constructive approach. Nevertheless, the attendances that the club continued to draw were, by present-day standards, truly astonishing: 43,000 at Celtic Park for a first-round Glasgow Cup tie with Partick Thistle; 87,000 for the Final with Third Lanark; and 105,000 for a League Cup game at Ibrox.

If the Celtic legions could not yet be rewarded with success, the least they deserved was entertainment. Tully quickly demonstrated that he was the man to provide it. His previous career had been with exotically named clubs such as Forth River and Ballyclare Comrades, as well as Belfast Celtic where he was 'the bane of manager Elisha Scott's life', according to a recent history of Irish football. He was first spotted by Jimmy McGrory playing in five-a-sides at the RUC sports in Belfast, a comfortable arena for what Tully described as his 'tricks' with the ball. He was persuaded to board the *Royal Ulsterman*, which he was to keep regularly entertained for some years to come, and head for the Broomielaw. It took him six games in 1948 to make an impression, but his breakthrough came against Rangers – 'the game that put Charlie Tully on the map', said the Celtic handbook – and that made it all the more welcome in the eyes of the Celtic supporters. John Rafferty later wrote: 'Celtic fans immediately canonised him. This was the prophet they had waited for through many long, barren years. He did lead them to the promised land, kept the country talking. He was good for the game.'

This season also saw the departure of Bobby Hogg, who left after being at Celtic Park since 1931 to become manager of Alloa Athletic.

The handbook which appeared at the start of the 1949/50 season contained for the first time 'A Message from the Chairman', in which Kelly denied that 'the old glory has departed for ever' and expressed confidence that 'we shall soon begin to recover some of our former greatness'. The choice of language is an indication of just how depressed things had become by this time. Celtic finished fifth in the League in 1949/50, and went out of the Scottish Cup in the first round to then lowly Dundee United. The main encouragement came from the performances of Tully, Bobby Collins – a dynamic workhorse in midfield – and Bobby Evans, who had grown indispensable in the right-half position. Among the other late-1940s signings which offered some of the promise for the future on which Celtic supporters were perennially asked to rely, were those of Bertie Peacock, a nineteen-year-old amateur from Glentoran, Willie Fernie from the Fife junior club Kinglassie, and Jimmy Walsh from Bo'ness Juniors.

The grim relationship which had developed between the SFA and Celtic was further exacerbated by the 'Tully–Cox incident' in a League Cup tie early in the 1949/50 season, when the Rangers back appeared to kick the new darling of the green-and-white battalions but went unpunished. This led to crowd trouble, and eventually to an enquiry by the SFA Referees' Committee – soon to be an even bigger tormentor of Celtic. The Committee reached the extraordinary conclusion that both clubs should post warning notices at their grounds, and that both players should be severely reprimanded – Cox for kicking, and Tully for having 'simulated any slight injury he might have received'. The SFA council upheld this wildly illogical outcome, and Celtic's appeals for a further enquiry were turned down. Once more, Celtic faith in the neutrality of the game's rulers was shaken.

Over twenty years later, Robert Kelly felt the episode important enough to devote a full chapter to it in his book of recollections. Whether or not such memories are selective and accorded an importance out of proportion to their true significance must remain a matter of judgement. But it is important to an understanding of Celtic's history that any tendency towards a persecution complex that may exist has been generously fuelled at regular intervals.

Indeed, relations quickly went from bad to worse when Celtic exited from the Glasgow Cup to a controversial goal by Findlay of Rangers, with the Celtic players protesting that the ball had not been 'dead' when Willie Waddell took a free kick. This modestly important source of indignation led the Celtic board into what was probably the club's only attempt at encouraging a crowd boycott. Jimmy McGrory explained:

The incident, coming so soon after the Cox affair at Ibrox, caused a great deal of controversy and it was felt that some protest should be made by the club. It was difficult to know just what to do, because our request to have a special enquiry into the Ibrox match had been turned down by the Scottish Football Association. It was therefore decided to ask the Scottish Football League to allow us to withdraw from the two League fixtures with Rangers. The League turned down this request and ordered us to play these matches, and our next meeting took place at Ibrox on 24 September. This day will go down in history as 'boycott Saturday', as the Celtic supporters showed their approval of the directors' action by staying away from the match.

This proved to have been a good piece of judgement on the part of the Celtic supporters, irrespective of the high principles involved, since the team – without Tully – put on an appalling show and lost 4–0. This season of feuds between the two clubs did end on a higher note, however, with Celtic. beating Rangers 3–2 in the Glasgow Charity Cup Final – a game that is remembered as the 'Danny Kaye Final', because of the American comedian's presence to kick off. This helped to swell the gate to the 81,000 who saw the old trophy secured by two goals from John McPhail and a deflection off Cox. The Celtic team was: Bonnar, Haughney and Milne; Evans, McGrory and Baillie; Collins, Fernie, McPhail, Peacock and Tully.

Jimmy Hogan's valuable two-year stint with Celtic ended after the 1949/50 season, as the supporters wondered aloud if good times were ever going to return to Celtic Park. A League Championship had not been won since 1937/8, nor the Scottish Cup – which had, of course, been in abeyance during the war years – since 1936/7.

In 1950, Sean Fallon signed from Glenavon. For the Sligo man it was the start of an involvement that lasted over thirty years, yet the initial financial arrangements were inauspicious. Jimmy McGrory offered him £10 per week, falling to £8 in the close season, plus £1 towards digs money. At that time he was earning £6 with Glenavon and £8 at his trade as a confectioner. However, since learning as a boy of the role of another County Sligo man – Brother Walfrid – in the Celtic history, there was no other club he wanted to play for. 'What Mr McGrory offered me was much less than would have been expected from other clubs of the same status. But signing for Celtic was realizing a boyhood dream.'

In spite of the uncertain fortunes on the field of play it was, he recalls, a fine time to be a Celtic player in terms of good comradeship and exciting experiences. As soon as the season ended in 1950 – Holy Year – the club embarked on a tour which had as its highlight a meeting with the Pope. 'Everyone was making their way to Rome that year, and our chairman was very much that way inclined,' Fallon recalls. 'Wherever we went, even in eastern Europe, the first place he would look for would be the church.'

Fourteen players, along with McGrory, Hogan and four directors (including Tom Devlin, who had joined the board) set out on 24 May 1950 for this epic tour. It got off to a flying start when Bing Crosby appeared as one of their fellow passengers on the SS *Royal Albert* to Brussels. 'We looked into the bar and John McPhail and Charlie Tully were already having a beer with him,' recalls Fallon. 'Trust Tully!' By the time Brussels was reached, Crosby had been prevailed upon to give his version of 'I Belong to Glasgow'.

A three-day train journey, with overnight stops at Lucerne and Milan, took the party to Rome, where Monsignor Flannigan of Baillieston and the Scots College became their 'guide, philosopher and interpreter'. Bobby Evans and trainer Alex Dowdells joined the party from Paris, where they had been with the Scotland team. The idyllic nature of the trip altered, however, when Celtic played Lazio of Rome. John McPhail was sent off in the course of a torrid game, and the players were in fear of attack as they left the stadium.

The following day the Celtic party had a more sedate appointment when they made their way to St Peter's Basilica, 'where, through the good offices of Monsignor Flannigan, we obtained a privileged spot in this huge edifice'. The Celtic team was by no means entirely Catholic at this time, but all the players joined in the visit. Having given a general blessing, the Pope went on to greet various groups in the Basilica – including the Celtic party. 'He thought we were Irish and greeted us in Gaelic', Fallon recalls. The Celtic handbook account of the event states:

Now, the Celtic Club have been the initiators in many things, and in being called out in St Peter's, they rank as the only football club to have that honour. The whole scene baffled description . . . We left St Peter's inspired and thrilled by this wonderful experience, and thankful that we had been privileged to be present at such an august ceremony.

The only other football of the tour was played against the student priests of the Scots College, and after ten days in Rome the party journeyed home-wards via Dijon and Paris. It was, to put it mildly, an unusual close-season expedition for a football club to undertake, but it was very much in the Kelly mould, and would long be remembered with affection by all who took part in it.

Peacock and Fernie became regulars in the 1950/1 season. George Hunter, a nineteen-year-old signed from Neilston Juniors, succeeded Miller in goal after he transferred to Clyde, and Evans, Boden and Baillie emerged as Celtic's best half-back line in a generation. This also proved to be John McPhail's finest season. James Handley described him thus:

He was not cast in the mould of previous successful Celtic centre-forwards. He was not a dasher, darter, juggler, dribbler or wizard with the head. Rather, he moved through the game with the ambling ease of a great St Bernard, but he had height and weight to brush aside physical challenge with insouciance and a swerve that threw many an opponent on the wrong foot. His shot was a strong one and within range of goal his extra inches were particularly effective, for he could rise high in the air to a cross and send it into the net with a skilful flick of the head.

The long dearth of major honours came to an end, with the winning of the Scottish Cup. It was a famous campaign in which East Fife and Duns were disposed of in the early rounds. Hunter gave a memorable goal-keeping performance as Hearts were defeated in front of a capacity Tynecastle crowd. There were 75,000 at Celtic Park for the quarter-final tie with Aberdeen, which finished with a 3–0 scoreline. Raith Rovers fell by the odd goal in five in the semi-final, and Celtic lined up against Motherwell in the Final. It was a remarkable case of history repeating itself, as Handley noted:

Twenty years before, the teams had met in such a final and Celtic, anxious to take the Scottish Cup with them on the American tour planned for the close season, saw their wishes fulfilled. Once more they were off to the States and once more they hoped to take the Scottish Cup with them.

In front of a 134,000 crowd, John McPhail scored a first-half goal, and Celtic hung on to this lead to take the Cup. The team was: Hunter, Fallon and

Rollo; Evans, Boden and Baillie; Weir, Collins, McPhail, Peacock and Tully.

The club's second expedition to America was launched with another mass send-off, this time from Central Station. Lasting seven weeks, it began with a transatlantic crossing on board the *Queen Mary*. 'The last dinner on board,' reported the Celtic handbook, 'was notable for the thoughtful gesture of the crew in giving us a wonderful cake, the decoration of which depicted Hampden Park, with the two teams lined up for the start of the final. It was a work of art and every detail was carried out in the correct colours.' Who can fail to mourn the passing of those days of civilized travel? The tour itself proved, like its predecessor of 1931, to be an exhausting round of receptions, public dinners and sightseeing with nine games in between – three of them against Fulham, with honours ending even. The defeat by Fulham in Montreal and the draw in Toronto were the only setbacks of the tour. There were victories over New York Stars, Fulham and Eintracht in New York, Philadelphia Stars, National League in Toronto, Chicago Polish Eagles in Detroit, and Kearny Select in the New Jersey home of large Scottish and Irish communities. In Toronto there was a nostalgic reunion with Bobby Muir – outside-right in the Scottish Cup-winning team of 1904! The disappointment of losing their unbeaten record to Fulham in the last game of the tour was soon overcome as the party sailed back to Liverpool on board the RMS *Parthia*. Another highly successful tour, in ambassadorial terms, had been completed.

On their return, Celtic were soon playing in the St Mungo Cup, run by Glasgow Corporation and the SFA as part of the 'Festival of Britain' celebrations. All sixteen First Division clubs were involved, and Celtic duly qualified to meet Aberdeen in the final. The team was: Hunter, Haughney and Rollo; Evans, Mallan and Baillie; Collins, Walsh, Fallon, Peacock and Tully. After going two goals down, Celtic fought back in the second half with goals from Walsh, Fallon and Tully. Thus Celtic added yet another one-off trophy to their collection, and therein lies a story.

The salmon features in Glasgow's coat of arms, and the cup's handles took the shape of that noble fish. When one salmon came away in the hand of a Celtic official, it transpired that the cup had been made in 1894 and previously competed for in 1912 when Provan Gasworks had won it by defeating the Glasgow Police. The Corporation, it transpired, had had it spruced up and re-inscribed to serve as the St Mungo Cup! The Lord Provost turned down Celtic's request for a new trophy with a pedigree more in keeping with the dignity of the occasion – and so the 'second-hand' object took, and retains, its place in the Celtic trophy room. In this period, it might be thought, Celtic were not in much of a position to be fussy about the calibre of the trophies they collected!

After the promise of the 1950/1 season, and the euphoria of the close-season activities, the following campaign came as another disappointment. In the League Celtic took just twenty-eight points from their thirty games, while they departed from the Scottish Cup in a first-round replay against Third Lanark – the first time in more than fifty years that they had lost in a Scottish Cup replay. Following the American tour, Celtic brought Giles Heron – a Jamaican whom they had seen in action in Detroit – to Glasgow, but the 'Black Flash', as he inevitably became known, did not prove to be a lasting success. Infinitely more significant was the arrival from Llanelli of one Jock Stein.

# 12

## CONFRONTATION
### *Flying the Flag*

N EPISODE which occurred in 1952 is worthy of detailed recall, since it went to the heart of the Celtic psyche and briefly threatened the club's place in Scottish football. Celtic supporters of that generation, and those to whom they have handed it down, recall the affair in straight-forward – and generally accurate – terms. The stark fact is that an attempt was made to force Celtic out of business if they would not agree to remove the Irish flag from their home ground. Celtic, in the person of Robert Kelly, stood firm and lived to tell the tale. But the fact that such an effort was made, on the basis of such an issue, reinforced the instinctive suspicion that there were many in Scottish football and wider society who would have been pleased to see the back of Celtic Football Club. (The fact that Belfast Celtic had been forced into oblivion for sectarian reasons in the late 1940s was a matter of quite recent memory.) The strong suspicion that the Scottish football hierarchy is not, in general, composed of people who have much affection for Celtic Football Club persists to the present day – perhaps to an irrational degree. But the vindictive attitudes which came to the fore in those early months of 1952 encouraged over-reaction, and long memories.

The incidents which sparked off the flag controversy arose at the Celtic–Rangers match of 1 January 1952. It was an extremely unhappy day for the home side. With thirty minutes remaining, they were trailing 2–1 when Shaw, the Rangers right-back, was carried off injured. Far from improving Celtic's prospects, this led to Rangers reorganizing successfully and scoring two more goals. In frustration over this humiliation, sections of the Celtic support started to fight and throw bottles, resulting in eleven arrests. It was not a particularly serious incident, but it attracted disproportionate attention because it was the latest in a number of flare-ups involving Celtic supporters.

The first to react were the members of the Magistrates' Committee of Glasgow Corporation. In 1949 control of the city had passed to the Progressives, who had not held office for fifteen years. They were relatively inexperienced in these matters, but had a record of castigating the previous Labour administration for being soft on crowd trouble at football matches. They wanted to be seen to act, and promptly arranged a meeting with the SFA and Scottish League. The Magistrates' Committee then made four proposals, none of which at first seemed very contentious. Their call upon the two clubs to avoid displaying flags which might incite feeling among the spectators seemed fairly innocuous, and the press criticized them for not doing enough, and demanded stiffer sentences. It was only when the recommendations of the Magistrates' Committee went before the SFA Referees' Committee on 11 February 1952 that warning bells began to sound for Robert Kelly.

The Referees' Committee decided that they would recommend to the full council of the SFA that Celtic should be instructed 'to refrain from displaying in their ground on match days, any flag or emblem which has no association with this country or the game'. Such an interpretation of the original magistrates' recommendation was extremely one-sided and, as Celtic argued, punitive. If the committee's interest was in stopping crowd trouble, as a result of what had transpired at the New Year's Day game, then they could scarcely argue that lowering the tricolour of Ireland would have this effect. The flag was unlikely to incite the Celtic support to violence, but Celtic were being asked to take it down. Kelly quickly realized what was happening. The report by the magistrates was being used by a powerful combination of anti-Celtic interests to pursue greater ends. Some of these, for ideological reasons, wished to see Celtic's links with Ireland severed, and others supported this aim for their own commercial reasons.

The leading forces in this combination were Mr Harry Swan, chairman of Hibernian Football Club and president of the SFA, and Mr George Graham, the Association's secretary. Swan had risen to prominence in Scottish football over the previous twenty years. In 1931 he had become the first non-Catholic to hold shares in Hibs, and three years later he became the chairman. He was an ambitious, far-sighted man who was to lead Hibs to their greatest period of success. But his first set of actions as chairman had been aimed at severing the Hibs' connection with things Irish: the harp which adorned the main entrance to Easter Road was removed; the right of priests to attend free of charge was abolished; there was talk of changing the club's name and colours. Such activities meant that Swan was credited with anti-Catholic attitudes which, according to some who knew him well, he did not hold.

The trick which he was trying to pull off was aimed at retaining the Hibs' traditional support while opening up the club to a wider cross-section of the populace. Celtic's ability to attract support from succeeding generations who belonged to the Catholic-Irish tradition, throughout Scotland, was a source of constant irritation to him, and his frustration was at its height in the late forties and early fifties when Hibs had had an outstanding run of success on the field of play without quite breaking into the top bracket in terms of support. When the flag issue arose, Swan was eagerly encouraged to turn it into a matter of high principle by Graham, who had enjoyed a close relationship with Willie Maley but who (perhaps as a consequence) was hostile to Celtic under Kelly. (The claim, carried in several books, that Graham was a prominent Orangeman appears to be mythological, though he was certainly an active Freemason.)

Kelly reckoned that there were only a few on the SFA council who wished to see Celtic humiliated to the point at which they would close down, but he suspected that equally few fully understood the strength of the club's feelings on the matter, the majority probably believing that Celtic would take the flag down if confronted with an SFA council decision to that effect. It was up to Kelly to convince them that Celtic weren't bluffing, and that they would accept suspension rather than have the flag removed. This assurance began to seep out through the press. The 'Waverley' column in the *Daily Record* reported on 18 February:

I have the unhappy feeling that there are many associates and adherents of the club who would be prepared to take such drastic action rather than submit to what they consider to be a grave indignity. During conversations I have had over the weekend with men who have been ardent supporters of the club for ever so long, men of good standing and a high sense of sportsmanship, I find among them the feeling that they would support a closed door decision.

Realizing that he would have to persuade the SFA council of the genuineness of this threat, Kelly also had to ensure that he had the opinion of the Irish-Catholic community firmly behind him. Celtic's enemies would look upon any dissension in these quarters as a green light to press their attack.

On 22 February the *Glasgow Observer* took the highly unusual step of printing a speech by Robert Kelly on its front page. Significantly, it was delivered to the Glasgow Province of the Knights of St Columbus, at their annual reunion, and its subject matter went far beyond the immediate problem faced by Celtic Football Club. It was about a more general threat to the standing of the Catholic community in the west of Scotland. Kelly declared:

It is necessary that Catholics should become more and more organized, because at present in the west of Scotland they are not making their presence sufficiently felt in proportion to their number. We are not wielding the same influence as our fathers and grandfathers did. In such societies as the Knights of St Columbus, it is one of our duties to make sure that Catholic laymen, in whatever profession they have been called, exert their influence to the fullest possible extent.

The flag had indeed become a symbol, and the message to west of Scotland Catholics was simple: 'We are under threat.' The right to fly whatever flag they pleased, in commemoration of their club's origins, was a litmus test of their ability to resist the erosion of their status.

In football circles, Kelly's efforts were having their effect – but not quickly enough. The full SFA council met on Monday 25 February, later described as 'a sorry day in Scottish football administration'. Before the debate started it was moved that the representatives of Celtic and Rangers should leave the meeting. This was defeated, but it was agreed that they should be excluded from the vote. Since Celtic were the movers and Rangers the seconders of the amendment calling for the Referees' Committee recommendation to be set aside, this was surely a unique piece of procedure! But Swan, Graham and their cohorts were in no mood to have the outcome put into doubt. In insisting on his right to put the Celtic case, Kelly quietly declared: 'It may be my swan-song, but I am determined to say what I have to say.'

Mr John Robbie of Aberdeen then moved the adoption of the Referees' Committee report, accusing Celtic of not having done 'everything possible' to counter the activities of hooligans. Indeed, by organizing resistance to the Referees' Committee decision, he claimed, 'Celtic gave the impression to the hooligans that they were being supported in their disgraceful behaviour'. He was supported by Mr Terris of Hibs. Robert Kelly moved that the Referees' Committee report should be accepted except for the section calling on Celtic to take down the flag. He outlined the links between Celtic and the flag of Ireland.

It has always had a strong association with Celtic where the game of football was concerned. No one previously has blamed the flag for causing trouble and I do not believe it is even remotely concerned with such. Surely it cannot be said that the flag causes trouble among Celtic supporters.

He was of the opinion (fortified by legal advice) that the SFA would be exceeding its powers by seeking to have the flag removed. Kelly pointed out that there was no rule in existence under which the flag could be barred and that 'the committee or the council cannot go beyond its own rules'. He was seconded by John F. Wilson, chairman of Rangers, who stated that his club was not in the least troubled by the flag. After Kelly and Wilson had left the SFA council chamber, the Referees' Committee recommendation was carried by 26 votes to 7.

Robert Kelly left the meeting bewildered and angry. He had shown the council that they did not have the authority to take the action they were proposing, yet they had voted to go ahead. Kelly and his fellow board members – in common with the vast majority of Celtic supporters – were now convinced that they were dealing with something much more than a rational attempt to minimize hooliganism. Some members of the SFA council were out to humiliate Celtic, and the SFA secretary, George Graham, was widely held to be the architect of this strategy. Robert Kelly later described him as 'a more powerful man in Scottish football than he had any right to be'.

Celtic remained convinced that their legal case was unassailable, and that the majority of clubs would not press the action if they were convinced that Celtic would accept closure rather than take down the flag. Kelly continued to rally the club's traditional support behind him. In another impassioned address to the Knights of St Columbus, he declared: 'We have no need to be ashamed of our fathers, nor have we any cause to be ashamed that those founders [of Celtic] came from that country that has provided protagonists for liberty wherever they have settled.'

On Sunday 2 March the Celtic Supporters Association called a special conference and over 500 delegates met for two hours in the St Mungo Hall, Glasgow. They were addressed by Robert Kelly, who explained what had happened at the SFA council meeting. After he had spoken, a motion was passed supporting the board in whatever action they took regarding the flying of the Irish Republic's flag at Celtic Park. The issue reached Parliament when John McGovern, the Labour MP for Shettleston, asked the Secretary of State for Scotland to intervene. The SFA's action, he suggested, was 'an insult to a friendly nation'. Was the Secretary aware that the flag was a personal gift from Mr de Valera, at that time Prime Minister of Ireland?

The day after the supporters' rally, the SFA council met again in a highly-charged atmosphere. The message that Celtic would, like their Belfast counterparts, go out of business before bowing the knee to their detractors was beginning to penetrate some cash-conscious minds. The ring-leaders changed their ground, and sought to make Celtic's refusal to comply with an SFA ruling the primary issue. Harry Swan declared:

We have gone far enough. This is a question of government or anarchy. No club, no matter how powerful, can be a law unto itself. If Celtic were not happy with the council's previous demand to take down the flag, their correct course would have been to accept the decision and to debate the matter afterwards. There seems to have been a misunderstanding in the minds of Celtic that they were punished for the behaviour of a section of their supporters and that one of the penalties under Article 114 should have been applied. They were not being punished at all. These hooligans must be got before they start trouble. Celtic have challenged the authority of the Association. To submit to such would lead to chaos in the management of the sport.

Swan then moved that 'unless Celtic give notice of their acceptance of the Association's order to remove the cause of the controversy within three days, the club and its directors be suspended'. Mr Robbie of Aberdeen seconded. 'I am a strong upholder of democratic government, and this Association is a democratic body. When a minority defies a decision of the majority, then law and order disappear.' But when Dundee United's representative, Mr McIntosh, moved that Celtic should be given until 30 April to comply, the Celtic chairman sensed that the united front was breaking up. Too many of the clubs depended on Celtic and knew that the three-day ultimatum could just as quickly backfire upon them. Now was not the time to step back, and Kelly, visibly moved, addressed the council.

My club has been in existence for sixty-four years. We have been loyal, very loyal, members of the Scottish Football Association and the Scottish League. In our long history, we have added to the fame of Scottish football, not only here but all over Europe and America. I am surprised at this motion. There have been suspensions on individuals and clubs before, but these suspensions have always been for breaking the Association rules. I hold that we have broken no rules. It has been said that this is only a trivial thing. Gentlemen, it is not a trivial thing.

It had been said, Kelly continued, that the ruling was not intended as a penalty, yet 'no penalty they might have imposed could have had the same repercussions that the lowering of this flag will have on my club. If you decide to suspend us, no good can be served for Scottish football.' The hush of the meeting was broken by desk-thumping and foot-stamping. It was noted that Mr Wilson of Rangers was among those who applauded most loudly. Kelly realized that victory was within his grasp.

It was clear that a majority on the council was looking for a token gesture by Celtic which would recognize the SFA's authority. The amendment giving Celtic until 30 April to take the flag down was passed by 16 votes to 15 – but the menace had now gone out of the situation. Kelly knew it, and merely noted the council's decision, stating: 'I cannot accede here and now

99

to take the flag down. A decision of this sort cannot be a personal one. I will report back to my club.'

Celtic were anxious now to make it as easy as possible for the SFA to complete the retreat. They agreed to write, accepting the SFA's authority and agreeing to take the flag down at the end of the season – as would normally have happened anyway. Behind the scenes, an agreement was made that a special SFA meeting would be called before the start of the 1952/3 season at which the March decision could be rescinded.

The new season duly commenced, with the flag of Ireland (as well as those of the United Kingdom and Scotland) in its familiar place. At best, the whole affair had been a case of maladministration by the SFA. At worst, it had been a blundering display of anti-Irish, anti-Catholic sentiment. Its most profound effects were on the Celtic club and the perceptions of the community from which it drew much of its support.

Whatever complex motives or complicated circumstances had caused the flag furore, the conclusions to be drawn from it were, in the eyes of many, clear. Scotland in the 1950s was still a place which harboured hostility towards the Catholic community and its Irish connections. Despite the progress that had been made in education, political representation and employment, forces still existed which would nullify it if at all possible. The one man who had stood up to these forces, winning the endorsement of Celtic supporters and sympathizers in the process, was Robert Kelly. The expert manner in which he had led Celtic through this crisis, and stood out for the club's traditions, bestowed on him an authority and position of respect which he retained for the rest of his life. It was a fund of good will upon which he would have to draw heavily in the course of the next dozen years. For his own part, Kelly's devotion to the cause of Celtic and the roots from which the club had sprung was reinforced by his experiences during this short period of adversity. If ever there had been a possibility of Celtic merging into the scenery of Scottish football by attempting to shed their traditional identity, it evaporated during those early months of 1952.

The flag issue was periodically to raise its head in the years that followed, though never again accompanied by such drama. Sections of the Scottish press, occasionally finding it necessary to demonstrate 'even-handedness' by criticizing Celtic and Rangers with equal force, have found it convenient to present the flying of the flag as a social evil on a par with the Ibrox club's sectarian employment policy – a ludicrous comparison, as its originators well knew. On several occasions during the 1970s, Celtic did remove the Irish flag for their own reasons – not least for the admirable purpose of displaying the nine successive League flags which were won during that glorious period in the club's history. Needless to say, there was no reciprocal 'gesture' from Ibrox, and the supposed balancing act between the clubs, as presented in the media, was revealed for the nonsense it was.

An extract from the minutes of Celtic's annual general meeting of shareholders in 1972, with seven of these League titles safely secured, provides a postscript to those dramatic days twenty years earlier. The new enclosure to replace the 'Jungle' was in hand, and one of the shareholders wondered if the Irish flag would fly from it.

Mr White replied that the flag would fly again at Celtic Park, not in the old place but among the other flags of the nations. The old place where the Eire flag now flew would be given to the flag with the large 'seven' on it. Provocation had been mentioned relative to flags, and he felt that this flag with the large seven on it would cause most displeasure in certain quarters. Mr Dempsey mentioned that it was a pity that the original flag of the yellow harp on the green background had been removed. Mr White stated that he definitely had a point, but that the flag with the yellow harp on the green background was the flag of United Ireland which, possibly, it could rightly be claimed, would cause provocation.

A knowledge of Irish history's subtleties has always been an asset in a Celtic chairman.

# 13

# ENTER JOCK STEIN
## *The Playing Days*

OCK Stein – or John, as he was known during his youth and early career – was a miner and the son of a miner. Born on 5 October 1922, he grew up in the Burnbank district of Hamilton and, like most of his fellows, went down the pit soon after leaving school at fourteen. He played amateur and juvenile football before turning out briefly for the junior Blantyre Victoria, of which his father was a committee member. In 1942, with wartime football struggling to survive and miners exempt from military call-up, he attracted the interest of Albion Rovers. Stein played three trials in the centre-half position – the first against Celtic, who were pulled back to a 4–4 draw after holding a 3–0 lead. Two heavy defeats followed for Rovers, but none the less Stein was offered signing terms which – after waiting a few weeks for the better offer which did not appear – he accepted. In 1948, when Albion Rovers won promotion from the Second Division, Stein was described in a publication to mark the occasion as 'the best capture the club ever made'.

By the start of the 1950/1 season, as his twenty-eighth birthday drew near, Stein was ready for a move. He had fallen out with the Coatbridge club over the parsimony of payment. Kilmarnock showed an interest but, curiously, it was a Welsh non-League club that was able to offer more favourable terms to Stein who, for the first time, was to make his full-time livelihood out of football. Llanelly would pay him a basic £12 per week – half as much again as at Cliftonhill. He left behind his wife and young daughter in a Hamilton council house – a valuable asset in those days of great housing scarcity, of which one did not lightly let go – but the Llanelly venture must have been a fairly miserable one, aggravated by news reaching him that the house in Hamilton had twice been broken into in his absence. It must, indeed, have seemed like the hand of fate reaching out when Stein learned of Celtic's interest. He had no particular affinity for the club, but was later to say that, at that time, he would have played for anyone who offered him a release from South Wales.

Celtic's need was inspired by a spate of injuries, and the reserve-team trainer, Jimmy Gribben, is given the credit for having put forward the name of Stein as a back-up possibility. A transfer fee of £1200 was agreed and he made his first appearance at Celtic Park on 8 December 1951, against St Mirren. At this time there were three centre-halves on the books – Jimmy Mallan, Alex Boden and John McGrory – and in those days of strict demarcation, Stein had at first been consigned to the reserve-team dressing room at training. Having gained entry to the first team, Stein held his place for a month before Boden returned. However, he made the position his own from mid February, and wore the number five shirt almost continuously until injury ended his playing career four years later.

As well as losing 3–0 to Rangers in the League Cup semi-final and taking only twenty-eight points from the thirty League games in 1951/2, Celtic went out of the Scottish Cup to Third Lanark in a first-round replay. This left them short of fixtures by April, and a brief tour of Ireland was undertaken during which the Celtic party met Mr de Valera in Dublin. The club returned to Belfast the following month to play in a charity match against ex-Belfast Celtic players for the funds of the De La Salle Brothers Orphans' Home, in front of a 28,000 crowd.

The great flag controversy which dominated the early months of 1952 provided Stein with ample opportunity in the first half-year of his career with the club to become familiar with the distinctive Celtic identity, which he was subsequently to emphasize with and enhance to an extraordinary degree.

Interestingly, the Celtic handbook which preceded the season of 1952/3 did not give Stein a single mention – he had already become a steady, if perhaps unspectacular part of the green-and-white scenery. But he was soon to become the club captain, and to lead it to its finest hour since the war. Sean Fallon, the iron man from Sligo, was appointed captain at the start of the season and (as was his right in those days) nominated the mature Stein as his vice-captain. Just before Christmas, however, Fallon broke an arm in a clash (ironically) with Jimmy Delaney, who was by this time with Falkirk. (Typically, Fallon finished the game at full-back before learning that the arm was broken in two places.) Fallon was injury-prone during this season, and the full captaincy soon passed to Stein. This was undoubtedly a crucial factor in allowing his talent for reading the game to develop.

Celtic had started the season without the services of Bobby Collins, who had broken an arm during the tour of Ireland in the spring. There had also been tragedy when a twenty-two-year-old player, John Millsop, had died after a short illness – signed in 1948 from Blantyre Celtic, he had been an occasional first-team performer. In November – 'always a bad month for the Celtic', wrote McGrory somewhat unconvincingly – the trail of injuries started, and the League title challenge rapidly evaporated.

The Scottish Cup campaign was characterized by one of Charlie Tully's most celebrated feats, but not much else. This occurred in a third-round tie at Brockville, against a Falkirk team which included Jimmy Delaney and which was two goals up at the interval. Two minutes after the restart, Tully took a corner kick, which curled in on goal and finished up in the back of the net without another player touching the ball. The celebrations were short-lived, as the referee instructed that the kick must be taken again – probably on the grounds that the ball had been outside the marked area. Tully promptly repeated his achievement, and the crowd went wild to such an extent that some crush barriers gave way. Willie Fernie equalized, and John McGrory scored a winner, provoking an invasion of the field by a section of the Celtic supporters. The team hustled the invaders off just in time to prevent the referee from declaring the game abandoned. Unfortunately, the following round proved something of an anti-climax, Celtic going down by 2–0 at Ibrox.

Just in time for the Glasgow Charity Cup Final, Celtic signed Neil Mochan from Middlesborough for £8000. A centre-forward with a savage shot, who hailed originally from Falkirk, Mochan had previously played for Morton. His connection with Celtic, which has since spanned thirty-five years, opened in stirring fashion when he scored two of the goals which beat Queen's Park 3–1 in the Charity Final.

It was a testimony to the club's reputation and drawing power, rather than to their League standing at the time, that they were included in the Coronation Cup competition of 1953 along with the top clubs in Scotland and England. Even then, Celtic came close to not participating, because of a dressing-room rebellion over money when it became known that Rangers players were looking for £100 a man to win the competition – not the kind of reward that Celtic were in the business of contemplating. Chairman Kelly called a meeting of players, and only four held out for better terms. When Kelly said that he would field a side anyway, the rebellion collapsed. Then Celtic quite unexpectedly beat mighty Arsenal 1–0 in the first round and, just as remarkably, Manchester United – who had disposed of Rangers – 2–1 in the semi-final. Hibs had overcome Newcastle United 4–0, and so it was an all-Scottish Final in front of 117,000 on

30 May. Fernie took over from the injured Tully on the left wing, but otherwise the team was as in the two previous games: Bonnar, Haughney and Rollo; Evans, Stein and McPhail; Collins, Walsh, Mochan, Peacock and Fernie.

The Final provided a fast and thrilling game worthy of the occasion. A characteristic thirty-yard shot from Neil Mochan, from Fernie's pass, gave Celtic the lead after twenty-eight minutes. Hibs dominated most of the remaining play, but Johnny Bonnar played the game of his life, Stein marshalled his defence against an onslaught led by Johnstone, Reilly and Turnbull, and Evans – dominant in midfield and capable of defence-splitting passes – enjoyed one of his finest hours. It was appropriate that, three minutes from the end, it was an interception and pass by Evans which triggered the move from which Walsh scored Celtic's second goal. McGrory described it in the Celtic handbook as 'one of the best finals seen at Hampden for many years', and observed hopefully that the future would be 'very bright' if the Coronation Cup form was maintained.

The Celtic board was by now reduced to three men through the death of Colonel John Shaughnessy after forty-one years as a director. For many years, he had taken a particular interest in the reserves, and served for a long period on the council of the Scottish Football Association. The Shaughnessy connection went back to the club's earliest days, but no member of his family was to succeed him on the board – which would now be made up of only Kelly, White and Devlin for more than a decade. Fallon recalls:

Bob Kelly was the boss. He was always responsible for picking the team. There were no great tactics then, though players worked out their own moves. I built up an understanding with Bertie Peacock, my wing-half. Anything coming down our right defensive side, I would come in behind the centre-half and Peacock would drop back to cover the square ball. If Charlie [Tully] said before the game, 'I was out last night', we knew we were in trouble.

It really was as simple as that, but more sophisticated methods were gradually developing elsewhere in the football world. Stein was becoming an increasingly interested learner, and Kelly's policy of taking the Celtic party south to see games of significance proved to be far-sighted. This was particularly true of the Hungarian national team's visit to Wembley in 1953, when they trounced England, introduced to an astonished public the concept of the deep-lying centre-forward, and really set Stein thinking in a new way about the tactics of football.

The season of 1953/4 saw Celtic start slowly but then race to their first League and Cup double since 1913/14. The hero of the season was Neil

Mochan, now playing on the left wing, and possessed of one of the fiercest whip-crack shots in football. He scored twenty-six goals in total as Celtic eventually eased their way to a five-point superiority over Hearts in the title race, with forty-three points from thirty games. In the Scottish Cup, Celtic won away ties against Falkirk, Stirling and Hamilton before facing Mother-well in the semi-final. There was a 102,000 crowd at Hampden to witness a 2–2 draw, but Celtic won the replay 3–1 in front of over 90,000 spectators. Aberdeen had beaten Rangers to reach the Final, and started as favourites to take the trophy. They had a vintage team which included Fred Martin in goal, Graham Leggat on the right wing and Paddy Buckley at centre-forward.

The Final attracted tremendous interest and, incredibly, demand out-stripped supply for the 134,000 tickets. The game lived up to expectations, with Celtic emerging as 2–1 winners. A diverted shot from Neil Mochan put them ahead early in the second half, but Buckley quickly equalized, and it fell to Sean Fallon to clinch Celtic's seventeenth Scottish Cup success when he shot past Martin after Fernie had set up the chance with a characteristi-cally skilful run. The Celtic team that day was: Bonnar, Haughney and Meechan; Evans, Stein and Peacock; Higgins, Fernie, Fallon, Tully and Mochan.

Celtic, at this time, seemed to be placing reliance on Ireland as a source of young talent – the only 'new players' described in the handbook published in 1954 being three young Irishmen of whom only Vincent Ryan would make even a modest subsequent impression at Celtic Park. The main claim to fame of another member of the trio, Eamon McMahon by name, was that he had played for Armagh in the All-Ireland Gaelic Football finals! The Kelly influence, in taking a somewhat starry-eyed view of Ireland as a Celtic breeding-ground, had undoubtedly been at work. But Kelly must also be credited for repeatedly exposing the Celtic management and players to the major footballing influences of the day.

In the summer of 1954 the club undertook a very significant trip to the World Cup finals in Switzerland, for which Scotland had qualified. This was the moment of truth for British football, when it was confirmed that continental superiority was absolute. Scotland were beaten 1–0 by Austria and humiliated 7–0 by Uruguay, who then went on to beat England 4–2 in the quarter-finals. But the great Hungarians beat Uruguay in the semi-finals, before going down 3–2 to West Germany in a memorable Final. While most of the Celtic party simply enjoyed the holiday, and sympathized with Evans, Fernie and Mochan who were in the Scotland squad, Jock Stein watched and learned – about the amateurish shambles of Scotland's preparations, and about the continental tactics, particularly from the Hungarians, which were revolutionizing the game.

The 1954/5 season proved to be an anti-climax, with the League slipping away to Aberdeen who held a three-point lead at the end over Celtic. Even more disappointing was the failure to retain the Scottish Cup. Alloa, Kilmarnock and Hamilton were overcome before Airdrie provided the semi-final opposition. (This was the first 'big game' which your author witnessed, at the tender age of seven, and it was a most distressing experience for me when Bonnar had to pick the ball out of the net within thirty seconds of the start, without a Celtic player having touched the ball!) Celtic eventually secured a draw, and won the replay through two goals from the recently restored John McPhail.

The Final against Clyde will be especially remembered by many of that generation who were not among the 106,234 Hampden crowd – for it was the first Scottish Cup Final to be televised live by the BBC. The Celtic defence was as in the previous year's Final, but – at the end of a season marked by the constant rearranging of the forward line – the attack selected was Collins, Fernie, McPhail, Walsh and Tully. Celtic led at half-time through a Jimmy Walsh goal, but were unable to add to this score, in spite of clear superiority. Then, with only two minutes left, Clyde won a corner on the right and Archie Robertson claimed a famous Hampden goal by scoring 'direct' – the goal-mouth 'swirl' for which the ground was at that time notorious among goalkeepers apparently deceiving Bonnar.

The Celtic forward line was shuffled once again for the replay, with the often inspirational Bobby Collins dropping out, apparently for some disciplinary reason, and Sean Fallon entering the attack. This was the kind of eccentric selection in which Kelly specialized on big occasions – and it was fiercely criticized by the Celtic supporters after Tommy Ring had scored the goal which gave Clyde the Scottish Cup. This defeat can be seen as the dividing line between that brief period of success which brought the Coronation Cup and the double to Celtic Park and the prolonged period of darkness which (apart from one very notable shaft of light) was to hang over Celtic Park for a decade.

The most notable feature of the 1955/6 campaign was the ending of Jock Stein's playing career after a series of ankle injuries. When Jimmy McGrory reported to the annual general meeting of shareholders at the end of the season, he highlighted the injury to Stein in the New Year's Day match at Celtic Park, as 'the turning of the tide against us' in the season. The half-back line of Evans, Stein and Peacock had been one of the great trios in the club's history.

The number of clubs in the top Scottish League increased in this season from sixteen to eighteen, and Celtic achieved a modest points total of forty-one from thirty-four games. The Glasgow Cup was won for the first time since 1948/9 in a 5–3 replay victory over Rangers – at this time a toiling and extremely physical side. But the major disappointment of the season was the second successive defeat in a Scottish Cup Final, this time at the hands of Hearts – who featured, at this time, Dave MacKay in midfield and the famous forward trio of Conn, Bauld and Wardhaugh.

Bobby Evans had become centre-half and captain, following Stein's departure from the side, and the team he led out on to the Hampden pitch in front of a 133,000 crowd was: Beattie, Meechan and Fallon; Smith, Evans and Peacock; Craig, Haughney, Mochan, Fernie and Tully. In short, Kelly had made another of his odd Cup Final selections, bringing in young Billy Craig on the right wing for his first cup-tie, and – to the even greater astonishment of the Celtic support – moving Mike Haughney up from his perennial right-back position to inside-forward. (In fairness, it should be pointed out that Collins was unavailable through injury on this occasion.) Hearts coasted to a 3–1 victory, and the frustration of the Celtic supporters over the backroom goings-on reached new heights.

It is worthy of mention that Celtic were not at this time a particularly wealthy organization. When they went to a building society in 1956 to fund a £90,000 programme of ground improvements, they were turned down for a loan 'due to present government credit measures', and had to sell 4500 savings certificates to help meet the cost. Nor was Robert Kelly anxious to see the business scale of football grow too large. He warned the 1956 annual general meeting that care must be taken with legislation on matters such as floodlighting and international club football – or 'the big clubs will grow bigger and the middle and small clubs smaller, with the possible weakening of the whole structure'.

# 14

# FLEETING GLORY
## *The Wilderness Years*

HE League Cup had been a post-war innovation, based on four-team mini-leagues, with the winner of each qualifying for the quarter-finals. The competition had soon become established as the third major tournament of the Scottish season, at the expense of traditional local trophies such as the Glasgow Cup. But it had not been a happy competition for Celtic who had never, in ten years of trying, reached the Final. That omission was remedied during the early stages of the 1956/7 season, in spite of Celtic having been drawn in a tough section with Rangers, Aberdeen and East Fife. Three points from the games against Rangers helped them to qualify, and Dunfermline Athletic and Clyde were then disposed of, taking Celtic through to a Hampden Final against Partick Thistle. The two semi-final goals against Clyde were scored by Billy McPhail – some recompense for the 1955 Scottish Cup Final disappointment against his old club. After a poor goalless Final against Thistle on the last Saturday in October, Celtic beat them in the replay and thus held the League Cup for the first time, thanks to three goals within a six-minute spell early in the second half; two came from Billy McPhail and the other from Bobby Collins.

But the rest of the season was an anti-climax for Celtic, with only thirty-eight points collected from thirty-four games in the League and a semi-final replay defeat from Kilmarnock in the Scottish Cup, after Rangers had been vanquished at an earlier stage. It was Celtic's first Scottish Cup victory at Ibrox since 1908, and was achieved through goals from John Higgins and Neil Mochan. The newspapers, always on the lookout for portents, pointed out that Celtic had gone on to win the Cup Final against St Mirren by 5–1 in that earlier season. But there was to be no repeat performance.

The European Cup had come into existence in 1955/6, due largely to the persistent efforts of the French sports newspaper *L'Equipe*, as part of the movement to build bridges in Europe in the post-war era. Failure on the domestic front would henceforth carry the price of exclusion from the increasingly glamorous prospect of competing with the Europeans – a frustration which the Celtic supporters would have to endure for some time to come.

But, though the process was neither systematic nor always apparent, the seeds of future glory were already being sown behind the scenes at Celtic Park. Robert Kelly, a great admirer of Jock Stein's influence on his fellow players and his growing interest in the tactical side of the game, had offered him a job as coach to the Celtic youngsters. The annual general meeting of shareholders on 6 September 1957 was dominated by excitement at the promise which this initiative held. Jimmy McGrory reported that the past season's highlight had been 'the policy on youth, with Jock Stein taking young boys from school and juvenile teams under his wing'. He was certain that some of them would one day play for Scotland. Kelly waxed eloquent upon the same theme, according to the minutes of the meeting:

The misfortune to Jock Stein has in a certain way been good fortune for us. Jock Stein is the ideal person to take on these boys and create a training school which could easily be the nucleus of our teams of the future. There has been a great crop of young Catholic boys from the schools and we wish to bridge the gap between leaving school and junior football, still retaining our live interest during this uncertain period. McNeill and Crerand are outstanding examples of this scheme. [Both had been signed on the same day.]

Billy McNeill went to Celtic as a seventeen-year-old part-timer, from Our Lady's High School in Hamilton. There were three promising centre-halves in Catholic schools football at that time, and he believes that it was the personal intervention of Stein which pointed Celtic in his particular direction. In Stein's early days, says McNeill, there was no great emphasis on tactics or ball-play in the junior side, any more than there was with the first team.

It was more that he took an interest in youngsters. He was prepared to sit down and talk to us and, maybe because I was a centre-half, he was particularly interested in my progress. Suddenly, the whole thing became much more than just reading your name up on the list in the dressing room. John Clark, Jim Conway and I were particularly lucky because, like him, we lived in Lanarkshire and we used to get his company home, listening and talking. The first steak I had in my life was when Jock Stein took the young lads down to Seamill Hydro for a weekend, and let us horse around and enjoy ourselves. He always tried to open up people's imaginations. Celtic at that time used to have lunch every day in Ferrari's Restaurant. Experienced players like Neilly Mochan, Sean Fallon and Bertie Peacock were great for us. They did nothing but talk about football.

The same AGM minutes reflect the fact that a less progressive school of thought was also present, with its own views as to the reasons for Celtic's shortcomings of recent seasons. One shareholder asked, did the chairman not think it would be better to have more Catholics in the team – 9, 10, 11? But Kelly vigorously reasserted the founding fathers' doctrine on that matter. It had always been the club's policy to field 'the best possible team regardless of denomination', the chairman declared. Non-Catholics, he added, had throughout the club's history played their hearts out for Celtic, and the same policy would continue. ' "With the new school of youngsters, Catholic youth will undoubtedly show up very strongly and have every opportunity to show its worth. The principle is, however, the same as always." The meeting concurred in his remarks.'

A few weeks later, Celtic celebrated one of their most famous victories in the never-to-be-forgotten League Cup Final of Saturday 19 October 1957. The talking-point of the season so far had been the partnership established by Sammy Wilson, picked up on a free transfer from St Mirren, and Billy McPhail. Once again Clyde were the semi-final victims, and the first ever Celtic–Rangers League Cup Final was then in prospect. The teams which lined up in front of 102,000 at Hampden were, Celtic: Beattie, Donnelly and Fallon; Fernie, Evans and Peacock; Tully, Collins, McPhail, Wilson and Mochan. Rangers: Niven, Shearer and Caldow; McColl, Valentine and Davis; Scott, Simpson, Murray, Baird and Hubbard. Valentine was a centre-half signed a few months earlier from Queen's Park, and the informal tactical decision arrived at by the Celtic players before the game was that they should 'play through the middle'. Never has a tactic been more fully vindicated. Celtic streaked to an astonishing 7–1 victory, and to this day that result is commemorated in the graffiti of Glasgow. For Celtic supporters who had grown accustomed to disappointments, and particularly to the all-too-regular failure of green-and-white guiles in the face of the more physical Ibrox approach, the match rekindled in a single afternoon all the pride and delight of earlier years. In his report of the match, the distinguished *Glasgow Herald* sports writer Cyril Horne – who was generally sympathetic to the Celtic point of view – opened on this point.

Eleven players of Celtic Football Club did more in 90 minutes at Hampden Park on Saturday for the good of the game than officialdom, in whose hands the destiny of the game lies, has done in years and years. For with a display of such grandeur as has rarely graced the great, vast ground they proved conclusively the value of concentration on discipline and on the arts and crafts of the game to the exclusion of the so-called power play which has indeed been a disfiguring weakness in the sport but which has frequently been accredited through the awarding of international honours to the 'strong' men.

So devastating an effect had Fernie, the forward turned wing-half, on Rangers who before the rout of Saturday were still considered as difficult opposition as could be found in the length and breadth of the football land, that the Scottish international selectors must surely now be considering whether they should destroy forthwith the impression that certain players are indispensable for future internationals, and build their sides round this wonderful footballer who achieves his purpose without the merest suggestion of relying on physique and who suffers the crude, unfair attempts of opponents to stop him without a thought of retaliation.

Though Rangers Football Club may not immediately be in a mood to agree, they cannot surely in the near future but decide to change their policy on the field. I am not one who is going to charge their players of Saturday with the ultimate responsibility for the club's humiliation, badly as most of them performed. The culprits are those who have, encouraged by results at the expense of method, not discouraged the he-man type of game that has become typical of the side in recent years.

Not since 'a slightly corpulent John McPhail' had played havoc with his opponents in the Coronation Cup had Celtic played football of such quality, opined Horne, and:

. . . how the younger, slimmer Billy McPhail has joined Fernie, Tully and company in the bewildering of Rangers by the same admirable methods. Valentine, not long ago a commanding figure on this same ground, was a forlorn, bewitched centre-half on Saturday, repeatedly beaten in the air and on the ground in a variety of ways, and the disintegration of Rangers' defence undoubtedly stemmed from McPhail's mastery.

Another major factor in Celtic's dominance lay in Mochan's superiority over Shearer, the Rangers right-back. Wilson and Mochan had achieved a modest 2–0 scoreline at half-time. McPhail headed a third, before Simpson made it 3–1. But before the end, McPhail completed his hat-trick, Mochan scored again and Fernie finished the rout with a last-minute penalty to make it 7–1. 'Never have I seen Rangers so outclassed in half-back play; Fernie, Evans and Peacock were, each in his own distinguished way, tremendous players in everything but brawn and bulk', wrote Horne. The Celtic support's joy was unconfined, and the following week's board meeting minuted recognition of 'the wonderful 7–1 victory over Rangers in the League Cup Final, a record score for the final of a major competition. A very happy evening was spent at Ferrari's Restaurant after the match.'

Serious injuries to Fernie and McPhail in a League game against Partick Thistle a few days before Christmas 1957 imposed a severe handicap on Celtic's League title pursuit, which had until then seemed promising. McPhail never fully recovered, and this was a particular disappointment since Wilson, with whom he had formed such a devastating partnership, faded away once it was broken. There were also injuries to Tully and Collins and it became increasingly apparent that several distinguished Celtic careers were now drawing to a close, while the youngsters were not yet ready to take over. The memory of that 7–1 result would keep the Celtic supporters buoyant for a while, but a distant second place in the League, which was won by Hearts, and a disappointing third-round exit in the Scottish Cup to Clyde, who went on to win the competition, had turned the season into another anti-climax. This marked the start of a grim five-year spell.

The relationship between directors and manager at this time was summed up at a board meeting when, after the team had been chosen as usual for a game with Rangers, 'the secretary intimated that a band was necessary at half-time according to our agreement with the magistrates of Glasgow. Mr McGrory was to take up this matter.'

There is another well-vouched-for story which testifies to Kelly's control over affairs. The Celtic first-team bus was on its way to a game against Airdrie when the chairman spotted the reserve goalkeeper, Willie Goldie, standing at a bus-stop. He ordered the driver to pull in and, when Goldie revealed that he was on his way to watch the game, he was taken on board. Kelly enthused over the spirit of the player, who was prepared to make his own way to Airdrie in order to see Celtic play, and by the time the bus reached Broomfield, Goldie was in the team!

In August 1958, the directors were shocked to receive a transfer request from Bobby Collins, 'for domestic reasons'. When he remained adamant that he wanted to leave, he was sold to Everton for £23,550. This was a major loss to Celtic, who would desperately lack the steadying influence of a shrewd, Collins-style inside-forward during the next few transitional seasons. Sean Fallon, whose playing days had ended with a pre-season injury, was added to the coaching staff and there was press speculation that he had leap-frogged over Jock Stein in the line of succession. The directors agreed that Stein 'should make a statement to the press intimating that he himself had asked the directors that Fallon be employed as coach under his scheme. The statement was to settle beyond all doubt who was in charge of the coaching scheme at Celtic Park.'

The break-up of the experienced team continued, however, with the transfer of Willie Fernie to Middlesbrough in December and the retirement of Charlie Tully the following spring. (Tully returned to Northern Ireland, where he managed Bangor, and he died in 1973.) Bobby Evans had missed four months of the season due to a back injury. All of this meant that the youngsters whom Stein had been coaching were drafted into the first team out of urgent necessity. Frank Haffey would soon become the regular goalkeeper in place of Dick Beattie, whose habit of losing inexplicable goals had become unacceptable. Haffey and the seventeen-year-old Billy McNeill, signed from Blantyre Victoria, made their first-team debuts on 23 August 1958, in a League Cup tie against Clyde at Celtic Park. Initially, the instantly impressive McNeill was deputizing for Evans at centre-half, and later in the season he also played in the right-back and right-half positions. Crerand, Auld, Conway, Divers and Colrain were other names with which the Celtic supporters now became familiar.

The 1958/9 season yielded no honours. Celtic went out of the League Cup and Scottish Cup at the semi-final stage to Partick Thistle and St Mirren (who went on to win the trophy) respectively.

The sale of Collins and Fernie did have one beneficial side-effect. Desmond White reported to the board early in 1959 that 'if there was any intention of establishing floodlighting at Celtic Park within the next five years, the present accounting period was the obvious time to embark on this venture', because of the very large profit to which the sale of the two players had contributed. It was agreed to proceed with a scheme costing £33,000. Celtic were regularly in profit during this unproductive period, but they were not noted as high payers in the football world. First-team players were on around £16 per week, and the lure of higher salaries certainly contributed to the determination of Collins and Fernie to export their considerable skills to England.

Jock Stein's first recorded appearance at a board meeting was in November 1958 when he successfully pleaded for a wage increase on behalf of some of his young players, including Bertie Auld and Pat Crerand. He also took the opportunity to obtain a £1-per-week increase for himself! The following May, the board agreed to increase Jimmy McGrory's annual salary to £1500 plus £250 for each competition won, Stein's to £1000 and Fallon's to £780. The directors noted with satisfaction that Celtic was the first club in Scotland to establish a provident fund for the players – 'in excess of the scheme at present in operation in England under the auspices of the English League'.

At the 1959 annual general meeting, Bob Kelly declared that the club was 'in a more promising position' than at any time in the thirty years he had been connected with it. They had 'reverted to the original conception of the club' by rearing their own players and this policy, declared Kelly, would 'achieve results, if not immediately, in the reasonable future'. Large amounts of money had been ploughed into ground improvements, and the investment in floodlights would soon pay off.

The competitive side of the season which followed provided little immediate encouragement for the support. Celtic failed to qualify from a weak section for the League Cup quarter-finals. Their League form yielded thirty-three points from thirty-four games – only the fifth time in their history that they had failed to average a point a game. Hearts won both of these competitions, while in the Scottish Cup, Celtic went down 4–1 in a semi-final replay to Rangers, who then won the trophy. During that Scottish Cup run, Celtic came within six minutes of the most embarrassing result in their history. Against Elgin City at Boroughbriggs Park, they were a goal behind until John Divers and Eric Smith salvaged their dignity at the last minute.

It was a dreadful season for Celtic, but perhaps the worst news of all was that Jock Stein was to depart, to take over the managership of Dunfermline Athletic. There is no evidence to suggest that Celtic 'farmed him out', as has sometimes been suggested, to gain managerial experience. 'It might have been in the minds of the directors that if I made the grade I should be asked back, but if this was the case I knew nothing about it', Stein later wrote in the *Celtic View*.

On Sunday 13 March 1960, Stein broke the news of an approach for his services from Dunfermline to Bob Kelly, Desmond White and Jimmy McGrory at Celtic Park. He was immediately offered an increase of £250 per year if he would stay, but Stein insisted that this was an opportunity which he should accept. He then asked for permission to leave Celtic Park immediately so that he could assume command of Dunfermline's struggle against relegation, and this request was reluctantly granted. The following Saturday at East End Park, Dunfermline played their first game under Stein's managership, beating Celtic 3–2 after taking the lead only ten seconds into the match. It was a fitting start to the greatest of all Scottish managerial careers, and Dunfermline duly avoided relegation. If he can do this for Dunfermline, wondered the Celtic supporters, what could he have done for us? Twelve years later, in the course of a BBC television interview, Stein said that he had talked over his position at Celtic Park with Kelly, who 'thought that I had gone as far as I could expect to go with a club like Celtic; I was a non-Catholic and maybe they felt that I wouldn't achieve the job as manager, but I moved out to try and prove that I could be a manager.'

Before the end of the season, Celtic were looking positively incident-prone when they became involved in an unseemly quarrel with the long-serving, much-praised Bobby Evans. During the course of the season, the Celtic board had agreed to the player's request for a new house. They had bought him one in Dumbreck, 'and made a special arrangement with him concerning his house should he finish his career with Celtic'. The minutes of Kelly's report to the annual general meeting stated:

It was in consequence with some astonishment that we heard from the manager that he wished a transfer, as we had all hoped that this great servant of the club would finish his days with Celtic. We agreed to let him go but feel assured in our own minds that he could not get a better deal anywhere than with Celtic. It was also with great regret and astonishment that we found he had consented to sign his name to articles which appeared in the *Daily Express*, stating among other things that he had virtually been cheated by the club . . .

Evans went to Chelsea, where he lasted only a season, and Celtic eventually won £500 damages plus costs from the *Daily Express*, but the whole affair did no good for the club's public image at a time when the supporters were already accusing them of parsimony and small-time thinking.

Bertie Peacock was next to retire, home to Ireland, and there were no new signings for 1960/1 as Kelly persevered with the youth policy. Celtic went straight out of the League Cup, having been drawn in the same qualifying section as Rangers. They lost 5–1 to Rangers at Celtic Park in the League, promptly followed by defeats from Third Lanark and Airdrie. There was a note of desperation – although no mistaking the source of decision-making power – at the first board meeting of October 1960 when 'Mr Kelly considered that it was advisable to secure the services of W. Fernie from Middlesbrough for our match with St Mirren. The manager was instructed to contact Middlesbrough immediately and arrange a transfer, a figure in the region of £10,000 having been previously agreed.' The deed was done, and things picked up for a few weeks, though Fernie's second stint at Celtic Park did not last long.

After losing the New Year fixture to Rangers, the directors engaged in serious contemplation of the club's position. In a long overdue realization that the players' training was inadequate, Bob Rooney was recruited by Kelly from Cambuslang Rangers and gradually, with Fallon, introduced ball-play into the routines. The directors repeatedly discussed the scouting system and came up with the remarkable conclusion that 'a card index system should be introduced, which would indicate how good the scouts were and how good the players observed were' – scarcely an adequate response to a critical situation.

By the end of the season, Celtic were once again nowhere in the title race with thirty-nine points from thirty-four games, and the irony of Stein's departure was reinforced when the Scottish Cup brought Dunfermline Athletic to Hampden for the Final. Scottish football was in a state of shock at this time, following the unprecedented 9–3 defeat of the international side at Wembley. It had been Frank Haffey's misfortune to be brought into the side two days before that game and, inevitably, he had borne the brunt of the ridicule for what had transpired. It was not the ideal preparation for a Scottish Cup Final. But, notwithstanding Celtic's erratic form, few could take seriously the possibility that they would not overwhelm the unfashionable Fife club, which would surely be intimidated by the vast Hampden audience. On the day, the crowd numbered 113,328. The wily Jim Rodger, writing in the *Daily Record*, was one of the few who thought it worthwhile to warn:

I know this game will be no walkover for Celtic. This may be Dunfermline's first time in the final. But they have behind them the inspiration of that solid man, that sometimes underrated man, Jock Stein, who now has his team playing the blend of soccer that wins cups.

Dunfermline duly declined to be overawed, and forced a goalless draw. For the replay, Stein made a couple of shrewd tactical switches, goalkeeper Connachan had the game of a lifetime, and the Celtic supporters were once again left to mourn when Haffey dropped the ball with two minutes left, allowing Dickson an easy chance to score.

At the end of the season, centre-forward Conway – an early product of the youth policy – was sold to Norwich for £10,000 and Bertie Auld to Birmingham for £15,000. A few weeks earlier, the Celtic board had decided to fix the first-team wage level for the coming season at the 'greatly increased terms' of £26 per week, but to cut out lunches on match-days and expenses unless there were 'most exceptional circumstances'. This was an attempt to compete with the lures of England where, much to Bob Kelly's irritation, the maximum wage had been abolished. The Celtic chairman, who was also president of the SFA, deplored the 'extraordinary weakness' of the English League in meeting the players' demands. It would have 'great repercussions in Scottish football', he feared.

In spite of the conspicuous lack of playing success, Celtic were still making money and the directors agreed at the close of this singularly unproductive season that 'from the point of view of publicity, the profit should be cut down to a figure in the region of £10,000' by writing off part of it to depreciation of assets. There is no evidence that any of the Celtic directors or shareholders were making much out of the club, since the 20 per cent dividend paid annually did not add up to a lot when applied to the relatively small number of shares, while the director's fee of £150 per annum had remained unchanged for twenty-five years and was scarcely exorbitant. But there was no way that Celtic were going to lurch voluntarily into a bigger financial league – as Rangers seemed prepared to do, particularly with their willingness to reinforce their ranks by buying established players. Sean Fallon recalls that Kelly was 'always talking about Sunderland' as an example of how paying big money for players did not guarantee success.

Between 1960 and 1964, Rangers were once again the dominant force in Scottish football, with one of their greatest sides. They won three out of four League titles, the exception being in 1961/2 when the memorable Dundee team of that era registered its solitary triumph. The Scottish Cup went three times in a row to Ibrox, following Dunfermline's success, while only Hearts' triumph in 1962/3 disturbed a Rangers monopoly over the League Cup. The contrast in fortunes was hard for Celtic supporters to take. In the Celtic handbook for the season of 1961/2, Kelly chided the support for criticism of the team. 'We ask that young players on the threshold of their careers be not ruined by ill-advised attacks on them while they are doing their best.' His promise of 'much to delight us' in the future was taking on a tediously unconvincing ring, and in any case the criticism was far more of the management than of the young players.

Over this period Celtic's performances were often entertaining, they obviously had brilliant players in the likes of Crerand and MacNeill, and they won considerably more games than they lost – but somehow they could not get their act together to turn all this into success. In retrospect it seems astonishingly obvious that what was required was a change of manager, in style as well as personality.

Early in the 1961/2 season, a slight youngster called Jimmy Johnstone was brought along to Celtic Park by his headmaster. He was signed on a provisional basis and farmed out to Blantyre Celtic. Tommy Gemmell, from Coltness United, and Bobby Lennox, from Ardeer Recreation, were recruited from the junior ranks. The new 'Celtic Song', recorded by Glen Daly, was issued in October 1961 – but it would still be a while before there was much to sing about. Celtic failed to qualify from their League Cup section, secured a modest forty-six points from their thirty-four League games, and lost 3–1 in the Scottish Cup semi-final to St Mirren, a game marred by a pitch invasion from Celtic supporters. John McPhail, by then a journalist with the *Daily Record*, offered some unwelcome advice to the club after this defeat. The young players like Chalmers, Carroll, Byrne and Gallacher had not developed as expected, he said, because of the lack of an experienced player behind them. Celtic bought Price from Falkirk in an effort to remedy that omission, but this was hardly sufficient to rectify the situation.

There was an early highlight to the season of 1962/3 when Real Madrid came to Glasgow for a charity game. The Spanish club had dominated the European Cup during its early years, and all Scotland remembered the Hampden Final of 1960 when they had defeated Eintracht Frankfurt 7–3 in a game which further opened the eyes of the football public to the progress that had been made on the Continent. Although Celtic lost 3–1 to a side which included di Stefano, Puskas, Santamaria and Gento, the quality of play of the 'Kelly Kids' offered the supporters a glimpse of what was possible. One observer, Malcolm Munro of the *Evening Citizen*, wrote in advance of the game: 'Celtic can play well up to the 18 yard line. After that – bedlam. It's all right a team being inspired by its support. What's wrong with Celts is that they don't get so much inspired as excited.' But the following day he joined in the praise and opined: 'In his form in the last 45 minutes, Pat Crerand must go down in the same book as Puskas and di Stefano.'

At a time when laps of honour were a novelty, the Celtic supporters demanded one from the defeated side – as well as from the victors. Little did they know the unorthodox manner in which the Celtic players had learned of their selection that night. Twenty minutes before kick-off, trainer Rooney had read out the defence and told them to get changed. The forward line could not be revealed, however, as Mr Kelly had not yet arrived at the ground. Ten minutes before the start, the chairman arrived – and the team list was finalized!

Celtic had finally staggered into the Fairs Cities Cup (forerunner of the UEFA Cup) of 1962/3, as reward for coming fourth in the League. They were drawn against Valencia in the first round, lost 4–2 away and then drawing 2–2 at Celtic Park. The following week's board meeting was agitated about the way in which the newspapers had 'written down the value of the Valencia team . . . it was felt that if Rangers had been playing Valencia, the press's comments would have been very different'.

But the supporters were no longer interested in such trivial grouses. Around this time, insurrection in 'The Jungle' was accompanied by moves to challenge the power of the Celtic board, either through takeover or even by forming an alternative club. The man chiefly associated with these moves was a Glasgow councillor, Bailie James F. Reilly. Eventually, they petered out, but this was the only time in the club's modern history when some serious calculations took place about where shareholding power lay, in preparation for a challenge which might have posed a threat to the dominant factions.

# 15

# THE RETURN OF STEIN
## *Back on the Road to Greatness*

 LOW point in Celtic's fortunes came on 15 May 1963, when Rangers gave them a terrible beating in the Scottish Cup Final replay at Hampden Park. Ralph Brand and Davy Wilson put Rangers two ahead at the interval, and Celtic were in tatters long before Brand scored the third. All the unease, the feeling of foreboding which had suffused the Celtic support in the run-up to the Final, was fully vindicated. There had been just one real glimmer of hope at the end of the first match, eleven days earlier, when almost 130,000 spectators had witnessed a 1–1 draw. Then, for some obscure reason, in the continuing tradition of eccentric Cup Final selections, the highly promising Jimmy Johnstone was dropped for the replay, along with Jim Brogan. The teams which lined up at this sharply contrasting moment in the two clubs' fortunes were, Rangers: Ritchie, Shearer and Provan; Greig, MacKinnon and Baxter; Henderson, MacMillan, Millar, Brand and Wilson. Celtic: Haffey, MacKay and Kennedy; McNamee, McNeill and Price; Craig, Murdoch, Divers, Chalmers and Hughes. The replay attendance was 120,273, with the huge Celtic contingent attending more in hope than optimism. And, as so often in the recent past, the hopes turned to dust.

The 3–0 scoreline was bad enough, but there was also the knowledge that even that was an inadequate reflection of the gulf which had developed between the rival clubs. Rangers had been so far ahead in every department

of the game that, a full twenty-five minutes from the end, thousands of Celtic fans were streaming from the stadium. Some of them burned their scarves, while most angrily proclaimed their disaffection with the club and, in particular, its chairman. This humiliation of their side at the hands of the arch-enemy was the final straw after the disappointment and frustration endured by Celtic supporters through most of the preceding decade. By this time things were so bad that even recalling the 7–1 game was something of an embarrassment – a hollow attempt, drawn from the increasingly distant past, at retaliation in the face of taunts from followers of the ascendant Rangers. On the evidence of the Cup Final replay it was difficult to see much cause for optimism about the future.

In the League, Rangers took the flag with Celtic in fourth place, a distant thirteen points behind. For a campaign which lasted for only thirty-four matches, it was a huge differential. The annual general meeting heard from Bob Kelly that Celtic appeared to be 'one of the few clubs in Scottish football that are showing a definite profit each year'. If the long-suffering supporters had been privy to this sentiment, the mood of insurrection might have been accelerated. But there was no word of cheer in the manager's report.

Mr McGrory stated that once again he had to admit great disappointment in not making the grade in winning one of the major trophies. He went over the season's results culminating in the Scottish Cup Final replay with Rangers, where the real issue lay not so much in defeat but in the lack of fight of the team.

One shareholder sought to apportion the blame for failure on religious grounds, stating that there had been only Catholics in the Cup Final team. Was it the policy of the club to try to play an all-Catholic team? This was strongly denied by Kelly, who declared that in recent years the Catholic teams had been very successful in schools football and were almost un-challenged at the top of the leagues. This was why they had secured the services of more young Catholic players than usual. 'We have at the moment one very promising young player who is not a Catholic and he should go far – Tommy Gemmell. We hope he will be joined by others.'

There was no doubt, indeed, that a pool of considerable promise had formed at Celtic Park. But it all seemed far too unplanned, and the breakneck pace of the 'Kelly Kids' cried out for the introduction of experienced heads, which might cost money to purchase. The youth policy had now been offered for several years to the supporters as the guarantee of better things to come. They were running out of patience, and the anger levelled against Bob Kelly intensified. Those who sat in the directors' box at that time recall the stoicism with which he sat through torrents of abuse from the supporters in the enclosure, just in front of the stand. Demonstrations at the entrance to Celtic Park became commonplace, in the wake of fresh disappointments. When Kelly did choose to reply, it was to tell those who were unhappy with his stewardship to stay away from Celtic Park and come back when they had a winning side.

This was intended as a chastisement to the disloyal, but many faithful Celtic supporters began to take Kelly at his word. In those days of even bigger gates than today's, Celtic's attractiveness was rapidly on the wane. They played Rangers five times in the following season, and never did better than a single-goal defeat. In League Cup section qualifiers Rangers twice repeated the 3–0 scoreline. Steve Chalmers broke the scoring duck in the first League game at Ibrox, but it still ended in 2–1 defeat. On New Year's Day, Celtic went down 1–0. In the Scottish Cup quarter-final, goals by Jim Forrest and Willie Henderson just before and just after the interval ensured another unproductive season. Celtic finished the League in third place, eight points behind treble-winners Rangers. By mid March of 1964, the week after the Scottish Cup exit, the normally attractive visit of Hibs could draw only 11,000 to Celtic Park, and interest in the remainder of the season was sustained only by the novelty of the first European run.

During the 1963/4 season, there was at least the consolation of this entertaining and unexpected progress in the European Cup Winners' Cup, even if qualification had been only by dint of the fact that Rangers were engaged in the League champions' competition. The youthful enthusiasm and undoubted skills of the Celtic team flourished for the first time in the European arena, and they reached the semi-final by beating Basle of Switzerland, Dinamo Zagreb of Yugoslavia and – most impressively – Slovan Bratislava of Czechoslovakia, with 1–0 scorelines in Celtic's favour both home and away. Players such as Billy McNeill and Jimmy Johnstone gained precious experience from this run, and important lessons were learned in ultimate defeat.

Celtic achieved a splendid 3–0 victory over MTK of Budapest at Celtic Park on 15 April 1964, with Jimmy Johnstone scoring his first European goal and Steve Chalmers the other two. Anti-climax was, however, to follow, for Celtic went to Budapest two weeks later, suffered from tactical naïvety and lost the game 4–0. In considering the disappointing outcome, the Celtic board bemoaned the quality of refereeing and displayed an unusual appreciation of history. 'It was not thought correct that a referee from Austria should have controlled this match. Austro-Hungary used to be one country and as far as they were concerned, it was to all intents and purposes a home referee.'

Celtic had previously played in the short-lived Friendship Cup against Sedan in 1960/1 and against Valencia in the Fairs Cities Cup in 1962/3. The Cup Winners' Cup run was, however, their first serious foray, and in Bob

Kelly's post-Budapest view, it should have been their last. In a pronounce-
ment notably lacking in foresight, Kelly told the Celtic shareholders at the
annual general meeting on 28 May 1964:

For the future, surely a better competition would be a British Cup for the top eight
clubs in English and Scottish Leagues. This, as well as being an excellent competition in itself, would revitalize the Leagues, where every team would be playing for a
place in this lucrative competition.

The club's financial position remained healthy in spite of the suffering
League gates, due to the European success and the previous season's
progress to the replayed Scottish Cup Final. But Jimmy McGrory could find
no consolation when offering his eighteenth report to shareholders as
manager of Celtic.

Mr McGrory stated that once again he could not find words to express his
disappointment at not having won a major trophy. He then dealt with the playing
season. With full maturity in the team, he hoped that he would have something
positive to report on next meeting.

Indeed, the 1964/5 season opened quite promisingly following the failure of
an improbable errand aimed at securing the transfer of the great, but ageing,
Alfredo di Stefano of Real Madrid. Jimmy McGrory and John Cushley, the
reserve centre-half who had the advantage of being a fluent Spanish speaker,
were despatched to Spain for negotiations but failed to lure the player to
Celtic Park. While there was a tinge of desperation about the initiative, it
did at least indicate that Celtic were ready to deviate from their long-held
policy of patiently waiting for youth to fulfil its potential.

A free-scoring start to the 1964/5 season, including a 3–1 win over
Rangers, offered hope that the corner might at last have been turned. But a
familiar pattern then began to develop. The League Cup was lost by a single
goal to Rangers. On the following Saturday, there was an embarrassing 5–2
defeat at Kilmarnock, and further League defeats from St Johnstone and
Dundee quickly followed. Early in December Celtic were ousted from the
Fairs Cities Cup by Barcelona. On New Year's Day at Ibrox, there was yet
another 1–0 win for Rangers. By this time, even Billy McNeill was on the
verge of asking for a move. He recalls:

I was coming on for twenty-five and had been at Celtic Park since I was seventeen.
Nothing significant had happened throughout that period and nothing significant

looked like happening. There were clubs biting my ear, and I was an internationalist. It is an indication of how bad things were that I was getting to the stage where I was ready for shifting.

In the Celtic board-room, too, the pressure for action was growing. A new director, James Farrell, had been co-opted to the board in mid December, ending a lengthy period during which the club was presided over by the triumvirate of Kelly, White and Devlin. He recalls a clear mood of 'something has got to be done', with Desmond White and himself most anxious for change. Celtic had long been caught in a dilemma over the position of manager. Such was the bond between Kelly and McGrory, and indeed the whole club's loyalty to the latter, that the question never arose of him being removed from office at the cost of his dignity. It must also be said that the presence of McGrory in the manager's chair fitted in well with Kelly's enthusiasm for controlling the club's fortunes. The Celtic supporters recognized the true nature of the relationship by directing their discontent almost exclusively towards Kelly. It had been widely speculated that Sean Fallon, McGrory's assistant who had been responsible for signing the bulk of the 1964/5 team, might eventually succeed him. On the other hand, the name of Jock Stein was never far from the lips of Celtic supporters and Kelly had maintained contact with him since his departure for Dunfermline. The New Year's Day defeat and reports that Wolves were interested in securing Stein's services may have been two more factors that finally prompted Kelly to take the action which was to transform the nature of Celtic as an organization, as well as the club's fortunes on the field.

The curriculum vitae which determined Kelly's eventual response to mounting crisis had grown ever more formidable. It was fourteen years since Stein had arrived at Celtic Park from Llanelly, and throughout that period he had demonstrated an uncommon capacity for leading others to success on various fronts. Sean Fallon's injuries had given him the opportunity to flourish as captain of a successful Celtic side. The testimony of his contemporaries is that he was already miles ahead of everyone else in his understanding of the game, and in studying how the investment of energy could be tailored to maximum effect. While the rest simply 'went out and played', Stein was immersing himself in the nuances of the game's structure. The whole concept of a youth policy at Celtic Park – the hope to which Kelly had clung – had its origins in Stein's success as a coach following the end of his playing career.

Misgivings persisted about whether, starved of proper recognition at Celtic Park, he should ever have been allowed to depart for Dunfermline, where his success at East End Park had been both immediate and lasting in its effect. Not only had they avoided relegation and won the Scottish Cup;

henceforth Dunfermline would regard themselves as a big club. Through Stein's astuteness in the transfer market, they were able to afford a new stand and a ground commensurate with their transformed status. But Stein's days at East End Park were numbered almost from the moment he first touched the Fife club with success. Hibs were struggling to regain past glories, and saw him as their ideal man. He joined them in 1964 and led them to the short-lived Summer Cup before the new season was properly under way. This modest triumph reinforced Stein's reputation as a man to rival Midas and run him very close.

It was an astonishing fourteen-year record which pointed, with increasing strength, in only one logical direction. The possibility of Jock Stein returning to Celtic began to crop up informally in the private conversations of directors, as well as on the terracings. After the New Year's Day defeat, Celtic drew with Clyde and lost to Dundee United. John Fairgrieve wrote on 12 January 1965 in the *Scottish Daily Mail*: 'They are being left behind by provincial clubs with a fraction of their resources. They are being left so far behind by Rangers that it is no longer a race.' Also on that day, the four Celtic directors held a special board meeting in the North British Hotel. A formula had been found to release Jimmy McGrory from the managership without loss of face. The terse minutes of that meeting summarized the momentous steps which Kelly had, in effect, decided upon:

After much discussion, all have agreed our desire to obtain the services of J. Stein as manager. Mr Kelly was to approach Stein with a view to offering him the position. Fallon was to be offered an increased salary with increased status if Stein was secured. McGrory was to continue as public relations officer.

Two evenings later, the Celtic board held its normal weekly meeting, with Jimmy McGrory and Sean Fallon in attendance as usual. The minutes record:

The chairman stated that he had interviewed Stein and that he was willing to join the club as manager. He had asked however to be allowed to remain for a time with Hibs as they had a chance of winning the League, and that in any case he would require to give reasonable notice. This was agreed to.

Having heard this news, the directors proceeded to meet with anxious representatives of the Supporters' Association, who might have been in a happier frame of mind had they known of the bombshell that was soon to break on Scottish football. Celtic were remarkably successful in keeping the impending news out of the press, but speculative reports did begin to appear. On 28 January the board held their weekly meeting and 'in view of the leakage of information, it was considered necessary to make a statement to the press. This was to be arranged for Sunday.'

The day before the news of Stein's impending arrival was made public, Celtic ran riot in their home League game against Aberdeen. As if in salute to an era which, for all its disappointments, had spawned the makings of a world-beating side, they trounced Aberdeen 8–0 with John Hughes scoring five, and Lennox, Murdoch and Auld scoring the others from the penalty spot. These names hint at a very significant fact which, in the lauding of Stein's memory, should not be forgotten. It is simply that all but one member of the team which was later to win the European Cup, as well as most of the other key members of that pool, had been assembled by the time the managerial transition occurred.

Sean Fallon's role had been vital, particularly in the closing months of McGrory's reign. It was he who persuaded the manager and Kelly that he should travel south to bring Bertie Auld back from Birmingham City for a £11,000 transfer fee and, for the player himself, the deposit on a house in Glasgow. This was the signing that was to add crucial poise and experience to the side. Similarly, Celtic had long suffered from a goalkeeping problem. Frank Haffey, depending on his mood, could contribute either genius or farce. John Fallon was superbly gifted, but suffered from on-field nerves. Sean Fallon heard that Jock Stein was about to transfer the veteran Ronnie Simpson from Hibs to Berwick Rangers as player-manager. He was given permission to contact Stein and sign the keeper for £2000 and a signing-on fee of £1000.

Kelly spared a considerable amount of thought for Fallon's position, and was concerned that he might be affronted by the appointment of Stein. It was arranged that the two men should meet to discuss the new situation in Edinburgh, where Hibs were playing Aberdeen in a mid-week game. Having agreed that he could work as assistant to Stein, without a trace of hard feelings, Fallon rushed back to the North British Hotel in Glasgow. He had got wind of the fact that Tommy Docherty was there, trying to sign a youngster called David Hay for Manchester United. Fallon arrived in time, and secured that signature too for Celtic. It has been suggested that Kelly toyed with the idea of a joint managership between Stein and Fallon, but this appears improbable. Fallon himself states that he never heard of any such proposal and that it would have been 'laughable'.

Stein's first game as manager was at Broomfield in a mid-week League game against Airdrie. Celtic won 6–0 and Auld contributed five of the goals. The following evening, the new manager was at the weekly board meeting. Possibly for the first time in the club's history, team selection was not an item on the agenda. Henceforth, that would be the manager's prerogative. Though Stein was always happy to chat with directors and confidantes about the team's performance, and possible improvements, the right to select had firmly and finally been taken away from Kelly and his fellow directors.

The League title was already well out of Celtic's reach, and they were eventually to finish eighth, with Kilmarnock taking the title. But just before Stein arrived, Celtic had scraped through to the Scottish Cup semi-finals with a 3–2 win over that same Kilmarnock side. Winning the Cup was now Stein's immediate aim, and the supporters were revitalized by the prospect. But during the first game with Motherwell, Celtic twice had to equalize goals from a fellow called Joe McBride, who was wearing the claret and amber and assuming the entire workload up front. Bobby Lennox and Bertie Auld salvaged a replay, and the second match was a 3–0 canter with goals from Chalmers, Hughes and Lennox.

Celtic returned to Hampden on 24 April for the Final against Dunfermline. The team which, in front of a 108,000 crowd, took the Scottish Cup to Celtic Park for the first time since 1954 was: Fallon, Young and Gemmell; Murdoch, McNeill and Clark; Chalmers, Gallagher, Hughes, Lennox and Auld. Celtic twice fell behind, and twice Auld equalized. Then, in the final minute, Billy McNeill rose above the Dunfermline defence to head home a corner from Gallagher – a goal that continues to live in the memory of all Celtic supporters who witnessed it. There may never be another day like it in Scottish football, for at the same time, Kilmarnock were winning the League title showdown against Hearts, to take the flag on goal average.

But, for once, the Cup made bigger news – for Celtic's victory clearly heralded the birth of a new era in Scottish football. The supporters' faith in the manager's potential for greatness was reinforced. So too was the players' faltering belief in themselves. Many years later, Jock Stein reflected: 'It wouldn't have gone as well for Celtic had they not won this game.' Bobby Lennox recalls that the team bus couldn't move for the exultant throng as they left Hampden. 'Later, once they got used to us winning cups, that kind of thing didn't happen.'

There was nothing infallible about even Stein's judgement, however, as the minutes of a board meeting on 29 April 1965 illustrate. After six weeks as manager, and five days after the Scottish Cup success, he presented to the board a list of players he would like to buy (including Joe McBride), and another list of those he would consider selling. The latter category included John Hughes, Charlie Gallagher and Jimmy Johnstone! The minutes testify: 'It was agreed after discussion that we should accept Mr Stein's plans for the strengthening of the team.' Fortunately for the course of football history, subsequent sales policy was restricted to less conspicuous names! Celtic players of that period believe that Stein must, at that point, have been preoccupied with the need to develop teamwork, rather than give licence to individual skills. Ultimately, his greatest achievement would be to combine both – incorporating the extraordinary skills of Johnstone, in particular, into the team framework.

The annual general meeting, held on 5 August 1965, was a very different affair from its recent predecessors. Jock Stein told the small but exultant gathering that he 'would certainly not consider we had returned to past glories until the League was won'. But a more poignant contribution came from the man who had previously occupied the managerial chair and who, a year earlier, had expressed the hope that 'with full maturity in the team', he would have 'something positive to report on next meeting'. Now, he said, he addressed the gathering with considerable emotion. The minutes record that: 'He was delighted with our success last season. Had he himself been the chooser of his successor, it would have been Mr Stein. He wished Mr Stein every success.' Jimmy McGrory continued for many years to give Celtic valuable service as public relations officer, and Jock Stein went out of his way to show respect for his predecessor's experience and status within the Celtic hierarchy.

For some sections of the press, the footballing significance of Stein's appointment had scarcely been given greater prominence than the sensation of a non-Catholic being appointed as manager of Celtic. This was not a factor which had entered into Kelly's calculations. He had come to respect Stein in the aftermath of the Coronation Cup success, and never lost that personal affinity. 'They were compatible, maybe because they were both Lanarkshire men', Sean Fallon recalls. Their personal relationship was not particularly close, and Stein never deviated from the view that the best place for football club directors was in the background. But there was mutual respect, and a shared love of Celtic provided the basis for a productive working relationship. With one action, Celtic had confirmed the message that had been repeated throughout the decades – that, while proud of its origins and distinctive identity, the club had always eschewed sectarianism in its employment policies. The appointment of Jock Stein, and the great era which now ensued, impressed that message upon all who had ears to hear and eyes to see.

# 16

## LISBON MANIA
### *Champions of Europe*

 OCK Stein's first signing as Celtic manager was of Joe McBride, on 5 June 1965. Still five days short of his twenty-seventh birthday, McBride was a ten-year veteran of senior football who had given notable service and a steady flow of goals to five clubs – Kilmarnock, Wolves, Luton, Partick Thistle and Motherwell. It was largely on account of McBride's emotional attachment to Celtic that he accepted Stein's offer for his services, since, remarkably enough, there was a higher bid from the upwardly mobile Dunfermline Athletic. The new broom had arrived at Celtic Park, but the purse-strings were still well under control. McBride recalls:

Motherwell wanted me to go to East End Park because they would get a bigger transfer fee – £25,000 against Celtic's £22,500. So I told Dunfermline that I wanted a ridiculous amount of money, in the expectation that they would lose interest. But George Farm, their manager, came back and said they could meet the signing-on fee, though I would be on the same wages as everybody else. That gave me the get-out I needed because, of course, I could earn more at Parkhead in wages. The money had little to do with it – I wanted to play for Celtic. But the truth is that I got £1000 for joining big Jock and I could have had £5000 from Dunfermline!

McBride proved to be a remarkable bargain. Gifted with the great goal-scorer's instinctive grasp of how attacks will take shape and where the ball will be at the end of them, he completed his first Celtic season with forty-three goals – a post-war record for the club.

The *Celtic View*, edited by Jack McGinn, was launched at the start of the 1965/6 season, and immediately there was plenty to write about. It was an exhilarating season, with Celtic in all-out pursuit of four trophies. A glut of early scorelines served notice that, under Stein's management, the club's traditional emphasis on attacking play was to be reinforced with enthusiasm. There were twenty-four goals in the six League Cup qualifying games and thirty-two in the first eight League matches. Victories such as 8–1 at home to Raith Rovers, 7–1 when Aberdeen came to Glasgow, 4–0 away to Dundee United, 6–1 at home to Stirling Albion, 5–2 at home to Hearts and 4–3 away to Falkirk cluttered this opening burst. Suddenly, it was great to be a Celtic supporter. The only fly in the ointment was a 2–1 defeat at Ibrox in the first Old Firm game of the season, but even in that game the manner in which Celtic pursued an equalizer during the final thirty minutes was encouraging.

With Hibs crushed 4–0 in the League Cup semi-final replay the first acid test of the season was the League Cup Final on 23 October 1965, with Rangers as the opposition in front of a 107,609 crowd. It was Celtic's first League Cup Final since the 7–1 game, and the team was: Simpson, Young and Gemmell; Murdoch, McNeill and Clark; Johnstone, Gallagher, McBride, Lennox and Hughes. Two penalty goals by John Hughes put Celtic in the clear before John Greig reduced the margin near the end. The celebrations on the Hampden terracing were cut short, however, when the team's lap of honour was brought to a hasty conclusion by an invasion of the pitch from the Rangers end. It was an ugly incident, and it led to bans or curtailments on laps of honour in Scotland thereafter. The following week's meeting of the Celtic board recorded dissatisfaction with press coverage of the incident, which directed most of its criticism at Celtic, 'for allowing the players on to the field – only Aitken in the *Citizen* had come out strongly on our side'.

The Celtic goal-storm was the product of Stein's tactical approach to the game, as Billy McNeill recalls:

It was no accident that Celtic became such an attack-minded team. Jock believed fervently in forward play and that was why he paid so much attention in the early days to signing goal-scorers. His wisdom proved itself in the number of men in our squad who could find the net. Quite apart from the obvious team members like Joe McBride, Bobby Lennox and Stevie Chalmers, people like Bertie Auld and Bobby Murdoch – to say nothing of Tommy Gemmell – were encouraged to move up and do some damage. I remember specifically Jock telling us one day that a great deal of space could be found on the fringe of the penalty area for players moving forward from the back. That sounds old hat now, but twenty-odd years ago it was brand new.

Murdoch and Auld and Gemmell were all briefed to head for that area and see what they could pick up. And, of course, the recognized forwards were instructed, when they were faced with a packed defence, to look for the opportunity to cut the ball back to team-mates supporting from midfield and defence.

The tactic paid startling dividends.

On Christmas Day, Celtic limbered up with an 8–1 win over Morton, and 1966 was welcomed with a 3–1 stroll at Shawfield. The traditional New Year's Day fixture had been moved to a little after the high point of alcohol consumption, and took place at Celtic Park on 3 January, with the teams neck-and-neck at the top of the League, each having lost just one game. In the first minute David Wilson put Rangers ahead, and that was still the position at half-time. The Celtic support, which had waited so long, would now have found anti-climax hard to bear – but fortunately it was not to be imposed upon them. Five minutes into the second half, Tommy Gemmell carried the ball to the line and cut back for Steve Chalmers to score. It was the start of a rout, with Chalmers completing his hat-trick and Murdoch and Gallagher bringing the score to 5–1. Who could stop Celtic now?

Meanwhile, the European Cup Winners' Cup run was going well, Dutch and Danish opposition having been easily disposed of. The quarter-final draw brought Dinamo Kiev to Celtic Park on 12 January 1966, and a remarkable 3–0 win was achieved through two goals from Bobby Murdoch and the other from Gemmell. Never had the encouragement of attacking defenders been better rewarded. The return leg was to be in the relatively temperate Tbilisi a week later, because Kiev was in the grip of winter. It was Celtic's first experience of travelling to eastern Europe, and Desmond White was wont to recall, until his dying day, the complexities which had to be resolved in these pre-*glasnost* days.

First, when visas failed to arrive in time, the game was put back by a week. There were all sorts of difficulties in making the Aer Lingus charter flight acceptable to the Soviet authorities – the least they demanded was that it should be routed via Moscow. In the event, it also had to make an emergency stop at Copenhagen. The game was played and, with the aid of another Tommy Gemmell goal, an excellent 1–1 draw secured. But Celtic's travel difficulties continued when they were diverted on the return journey to Stockholm, where they were snowbound, finally returning to Glasgow on the Friday evening. The following day, in the absence of an offer from the Scottish League to postpone their fixture, they lost 3–2 at Tynecastle.

There were, indeed, three successive away defeats – to Aberdeen, Hearts and Stirling Albion. This tiring and nervous spell came dangerously close to losing Celtic that vital League title, since they allowed Rangers to stay in close contention. But the Stirling slip-up on 26 February proved to be the last, and Celtic were undefeated in the League from then until the end of the season. In the course of nine hectic April days, however, Celtic lost two of the trophies they were chasing. They went to Liverpool in the semi-final of the European Cup Winners' Cup, leading by a Bobby Lennox goal from the first leg. Bill Shankly's great side scored twice, but the game ended in bitter controversy when, with two minutes remaining, Lennox appeared to pull back the crucial aggregate goal – only to see it ruled off. He recalls: 'It was a disgraceful decision. Joe McBride jumped with Ron Yeats and got a touch on to me. One of the full-backs was in front of me, and I played it past him before rounding the goalkeeper.' Thus Celtic were denied their first European final, and the disappointment was all the greater because it was to be played at Hampden.

But Billy McNeill has no doubt that the 'bad experiences' of that campaign stood them in good stead for the next one. Four days later, Celtic played out a goalless Scottish Cup Final against Rangers – but the following Wednesday a famous Kai Johanssen goal took that trophy to Ibrox. It says much for the team's nerve that the three final League games against Morton (2–0), Dunfermline at East End Park (2–1) and Motherwell (1–0) were won, to secure by two points the first League title since 1954. The barren years were most definitely over.

The annual shareholders' meeting on 11 August 1966 heard that though the club had enjoyed 'easily record receipts', there had not been record profits because the wages bill was 'out of proportion' and still rising. Jock Stein, in his report, struck a more visionary note. He was still not satisfied with progress, according to the minutes of the meeting. 'The past was now history and tomorrow was the future of the club. We had many aims in view and, certainly, winning a European competition ranked very high.' It was astonishing that, after less than eighteen months at Celtic Park, he could talk in these terms and still be thought a realist. Increasingly, his profound belief that nothing was beyond the reach of this Celtic team was permeating the minds of those who were under his leadership. The club had just undertaken a long, unbeaten tour of North America, and Billy McNeill is convinced that the crucial breakthrough, in terms of self-belief, had taken place during these weeks of friendship, relaxation and further success. He recalls the excursion with natural fondness – and a deep understanding of its significance.

It began with a genuine break in Bermuda. That was just the thing to get us rested and re-charged after winning the Championship. Even during our stay there, in a couple of bounce games against locals, you could sense the strength of spirit that was developing. I remember quite clearly being conscious of the way things were taking shape. The confidence – at times it was downright cockiness – oozed out of us, and we really came to believe that we were the best in the business. We played Spurs three times on that trip, and won them all. They had some team at that time, and they got the shock of their lives. We played twelve matches in all, including a tournament in Los Angeles which we won.

Jock was like a breath of fresh air, knowing instinctively what was best for the players, and how to get them to respond as he wanted. It wasn't hard to believe that we were destined for very big things. We had already won three major tournaments since Jock took over. Then in America, everything came together. There was a bubbling enthusiasm about everything we did and an utter conviction that there wasn't another team on the planet as good as us. At the head of it all was Jock, frequently having to give us a hard time when he felt we needed it. There were an awful lot of good men in our company, but I don't recall bumping into any angels. We could play hard off the field, but we worked hard too. That was crucial to our success.

Bobby Lennox confirms: 'That was the greatest tour ever.'

The hurricane, having gathered its energy on the other side of the Atlantic, was ready to sweep all before it. The season opened with a crushing 4–1 victory over Manchester United, complete with their stars from England's World Cup success at Wembley, in a challenge match. Inside three August days, St Mirren and Clyde were crushed 8–2 and 6–0 respectively in the League Cup. The six qualifying games yielded twenty-three goals, of which thirteen came from Joe McBride. The League results were just as spectacular. It was 5 November before a single point was dropped, at home to St Mirren. Throughout the whole season, there were to be only two League defeats – both at the hands of Dundee United. The only other competitive defeat that season would be the away leg of the European Cup quarter-final against Vojvodina.

Of fifty-nine games played in the four major tournaments, forty-eight were won and eight drawn. Celtic amassed 184 goals – an average of more than three per game. The rewards for all this were the Scottish League title for the second season running; the Scottish Cup for the second time since Stein's arrival; the Scottish League Cup for the second season running; and the immortality that went with becoming the first British club to win the European Champions' Cup.

Celtic's form en route to the League Cup Final had been sensational. The free-scoring pattern set in the qualifying section was maintained with a 9–4 aggregate win over Dunfermline in the quarter-finals. Then Murdoch and McBride scored the goals which beat Airdrie in the semi-final. Once again, Rangers provided the final opposition – and Celtic already had the psychological advantages of a comfortable League win over them as well as a 4–0 trouncing in the Glasgow Cup. The side which lined up at Hampden on 29 October 1966 was: Simpson, Gemmell and O'Neill; Murdoch, McNeill and Clark; Johnstone, Lennox, McBride, Auld and Hughes (Chalmers). It turned out to be one of the more anxious games for the Celtic supporters to watch during the course of that season, since Rangers held the overwhelming territorial advantage. However, it was a measure of Celtic's capacity for winning at that time that they brilliantly took one of the very few chances which fell to them. In the nineteenth minute, Joe McBride headed the ball down, for Lennox to slam it home. Rangers, for all their relentless attacking, had failed to make the blood-letting incision.

The Scottish Cup that season was, for Celtic, almost like a rehearsal studio, to be used for firming up their act in advance of other more demanding events. Arbroath, Elgin City and Queen's Park were the early round 'extras', before Clyde caught Celtic in a mood of rare uncertainty in the semi-final, which ended in a no-score draw. Early goals by Auld and Lennox turned the replay into a formality, and the Final itself was not much more tense. Aberdeen were the opponents, and they were without the presence of manager Eddie Turnbull, who had become unwell just before the team left for Hampden. They then played as if in a daze, and goals from Willie Wallace, three minutes before and four minutes after the interval, made the rest of the task straightforward. Celtic's Cup-winning side that day, 6 April 1967, proved to be identical to the one which would, on 25 May, contest the European Cup Final.

The most surprising fact about the season was that Celtic's extraordinary League record had not pulled them far clear of tenacious Rangers. After thirty-one League games, Celtic had lost only once – 3–2 at Tannadice on Hogmanay. Yet, with three games left, they could still be overtaken. The remaining games were the return fixture with Dundee United, Rangers at Ibrox and Kilmarnock at home. Astonishingly, by the standards of that season, they again lost 3–2 to United. This meant that a point was required at Ibrox on 6 May if a nerve-racking last day of the domestic season was to be avoided. Two goals from Jimmy Johnstone duly secured a draw. 'It was a great way to win the title', says Bobby Lennox.

There had been one enforced personnel change during the course of the season. On 2 December 1966, Stein told the board that he wanted to buy Willie Wallace of Hearts, 'whom he considered was necessary to his pool of players. It was decided to secure his transfer if possible.' Four days later, 'Wispy' Wallace was acquired for a £30,000 fee. Billy McNeill says:

I remember big Jock telling me about his intention of buying Willie Wallace. He said: 'We're going for Wallace because I think he and Joe McBride could become the greatest striking partnership in the history of the Scottish game, maybe even in Europe too.' There was something very powerful about the way he said it, as though there was no point in anyone arguing otherwise. Mind you, when Jock was in that inspired form, there really was no point in taking any course of action other than believing him. It seemed, though, that Willie had only been at Celtic Park ten minutes when Joe had to go through his bad times. I know they did play together later, but that early pairing, when they were both absolutely at the top of their game, was lost. We'll never know just how deadly they might have been together but, looking back, I can't help thinking they would have made a terrifying partnership.

It was the cruellest of luck that prevented Joe McBride from going any further in that historic season than the League match against Aberdeen on Christmas Eve 1966. By then he had scored thirty-five goals in twenty-six games. The previous Saturday, Wallace, Chalmers and McBride had all featured on the score-sheet, in the course of a 6–2 victory over Partick Thistle. To say that he suffered a knee injury at Pittodrie is a mild understatement. After eleven years of hard wear and tear, the back wall of McBride's kneecap was starting to flake, and the floating pieces of bone left him in agony. In a highly complex operation, the surgeon managed to save the striker's career. But there was no possibility of him reappearing before the end of the season. Wallace became, effectively, the replacement for McBride alongside Steven Chalmers. McNeill says:

Stevie, the so-called quiet man, had his own hardness about him, that snapping tenacity which gives opponents no rest whatever. His contribution summed up what we were like then – full of enthusiasm, application and confidence. That's not to mention, of course, a barrowload of skill throughout the team.

The European Cup campaign had started at Celtic Park against Swiss champions Zurich on the evening of 28 September, with goals from Gemmell and McBride providing a satisfactory 2–0 cushion for the away trip. It was appropriate, perhaps, that the first goal in Celtic's European Cup career – an anxious sixty-four minutes into the game – was scored by the cavaliering Tommy Gemmell, a man who epitomized the attacking flair and excitement which, now more than ever, was the club's hallmark. Stein decided for the return leg that the European convention of defending the lead which had been established on home territory should be ignored. Celtic went on the attack in Switzerland, Gemmell was given full rein, and remarkably, the great full-back scored two more goals, with a third coming from Steve Chalmers to complete an outstanding result. In the second round, Celtic were drawn against Nantes of France, with the first leg away from home. Goals from McBride, Lennox and Auld helped to secure a 3–1 victory in that game, and the same result emerged from the Celtic Park return on 7 December when Johnstone, Chalmers and Lennox were the scorers. Celtic's form in these first two rounds, against quite substantial opposition, was sufficiently impressive to cause Europe to start taking notice, as the European Cup went into winter recess. The chant 'We're on our way to Lisbon' could be heard permeating the chill Parkhead air during those long winter months.

The first leg of the quarter-finals, which did not take place until 1 March, was eagerly awaited by the Celtic support. Celtic were drawn against Vojvodina, the Yugoslav champions, and in a most intelligent move, Stein arranged for a friendly match against Dinamo Zagreb early in February – 'this,' he told the directors, 'would give us an indication of the strength of Yugoslav football'. Stein indulged in some tactical experimentation, and Celtic lost to a last-minute goal. But the knowledge acquired may well have been crucial for Vojvodina, a powerful side from Novi Sad, proved to be formidable foes. Billy McNeill recalls:

They were one of the biggest sides we had ever played against, and they turned out to be the most difficult opponents we had to beat in Europe that season. They had power and skill, but we played so very well against them in Novi Sad. A wee mistake by Tommy Gemmell gave them a one-goal lead – and I remember missing a good chance. But by that time, we probably felt that we could give anyone a goal of a start, and beat them at Celtic Park.

Euphoric with the season's success, everyone in the 75,000 crowd at the return game shared the assumption that the one-goal deficit would quickly be cancelled out and the Yugoslavs overtaken. But it proved to be an extremely tense occasion. Eventually, in the fifty-eighth minute, the ever-attentive Steve Chalmers took advantage of a goalkeeping error to score an aggregate equalizer. The sense of relief was enormous, but still it seemed, as the match crept towards its finish, that the prearranged play-off in Brussels would be required. In a last great assault, Celtic forced a corner on the right. Charlie Gallagher struck the ball perfectly, and Billy McNeill cannoned it home with his head. 'With Charlie,' says McNeill, 'I always felt I had the chance of getting something. He was such a beautiful striker of the ball. If Vojvodina hadn't put the weest fellow in their team on the line, it might not have gone in.' There has probably never been a more marvellous climax to a game at Celtic Park.

Semi-finalists Dukla Prague had a fair pedigree to bring with them to Glasgow for the first leg on 12 April. Their stars included the great Josef Masopust, who had led his country to the World Cup Final – and for whom McNeill had a great deal of respect based on international encounters. Jimmy Johnstone put Celtic ahead, but the Czechs equalized just before half-time. However, Willie Wallace repaid his transfer fee and much more by scoring his first two European goals, to create a 3–1 lead.

For the second leg in Prague on 25 April, Stein took the painful decision to forsake temporarily his precious philosophy of attacking football. Celtic set themselves up for a siege. It was not pretty, but it worked and they secured the 0–0 draw which took them through to the Final. Lennox says: 'I spent most of that game standing next to Big Tam. We went out to play defensively, but not that defensively! We didn't have any choice.' McNeill recalls Masopust refusing to shake hands at the end, but later coming into the Celtic dressing room to apologize and telling them he had been so upset because he realized that he would now never get the chance to play in a European final. It was an emotional reaction from a great player which the young Celtic team could understand. Stein was almost apologetic about the manner of his team's achievement, and declared that such defensive tactics would never be adopted again. But nobody at home was about to hold it against the big man. Just this once, surely, the end justified the means. As Lisbon mania took hold of Glasgow, Celtic had to wait another week for a play-off to decide who their opponents would be. The answer turned out to be Internazionale of Milan, rather than CSKA of Sofia.

Four days after Prague, Celtic won the Scottish Cup Final and within the following week, the League title race was brought to a satisfactory conclusion. For four Celtic players – Simpson, Gemmell, Wallace and Lennox – this astonishing period also included participation in the memorable 3–2 victory over world champions England at Wembley. By the time the Celtic squad went to Lisbon, they were already assured the status of legends in their own lifetimes. During the build-up to the Final, says McNeill, 'we became aware of being important in football'. The Italian media followed them everywhere.

I wonder if they contributed to us winning it, just by the way they boosted our self-image. Then there was all the great excitement of people getting to Lisbon. By the time the official party arrived there, the fans had gone a long way towards winning the hearts of the Portuguese. The punters went there full of fun.

It was the perfect psychological backdrop against which to play the most momentous game in the club's history. An expeditionary force, around 12,000 in number, had joined in the joyous pilgrimage. McNeill emphasizes the carefree Celtic approach. The night before the game, the team went to the home of an expatriate Scot, to watch an England international on television.

Neilly Mochan said we would walk back to the hotel. Neilly's walks were legendary, and this one was no exception. We were climbing fences and clambering over rocks. What a way to prepare for a European Cup Final the next day. I don't know what

Inter would have made of it, if they could have seen it. But that was how it was – unbelievably relaxed and everyone really enjoying themselves.

Helenio Herrera, manager of Inter Milan, seemed to have the only gloomy face in the Portuguese capital. The inventor of *catenaccio*, the appallingly defensive system that he had instilled into Inter Milan, had met his match. Throughout the build-up to the game, the impression developed that Stein was capable of seeing right through everything that Herrera did and, consequently, was able to come up with the antidote. Stein also won his share of the psychological jousts. The Celtic manager was irritated by Herrera's breach of agreement at training the day before the game. Celtic, it had been agreed, should train first in the stadium – but the Italians arrived early, trained and then stayed to watch Celtic. It was a matter of no great importance, but Stein was determined not to let his rival away with anything else.

   The next point of conflict arose over Herrera's claiming of the home side's bench at the stadium, before the kick-off, in breach of the official allocation. This time Herrera's bluff was called. Stein, in his inimitable style, approached the disputed bench and said: 'Naw, you'll have to find another place.' That other place was a hundred yards away and Herrera, not used to being dictated to, had to make the lonely walk with dignity impaired. It was a neat little victory over people who set great store by pre-match intimidation. The greatest significance of the Celtic manager's obvious success in such peripheral jousting came from the effect it had on his own players. Jimmy Johnstone saw the entire bench incident and, twenty years later, recalls thinking: 'The big man has Herrera in his pocket.' That alone demonstrates that Stein was absolutely right in asserting himself as he did.

   It was part of Stein's gift that he could undermine the confidence of the enemy through strategies which also helped to reinforce his own men's belief in their own invincibility. The Celtic players that day took the field singing, laughing and generally giving their Italian opponents a unique psychological puzzle with which to contend. In the idyllic Lisbon setting on that historic Thursday, West German referee Kurt Tschenscher presided over the following teams:

Celtic: Simpson, Craig and Gemmell; Murdoch, McNeill and Clark; Johnstone, Wallace, Chalmers, Auld and Lennox.
Inter Milan: Sarti, Burgnich and Facchetti; Bedin, Guarneri and Picchi; Bicicli, Mazzola, Capellini, Corso and Domenghini.

At home in Scotland, work stopped and school-rooms emptied as the nation watched its television screens. In Lisbon and London Road the great Celtic roar was stilled after just seven minutes when Jim Craig conceded a penalty kick, which was converted by Sandro Mazzola. Celtic's response was to attack, attack, attack. Gemmell and Auld both shot against the crossbar. Sarti performed goalkeeping miracles. At half-time, says Billy McNeill, they went in still angry about the penalty award. Stein told them to settle down. 'We could have had three or four by half-time, but Sarti kept them in the game. Jock just told us to keep playing like that and it would come.' In the sixty-third minute, Jim Craig squared the ball across the eighteen-yard line to Tommy Gemmell, whose shot past Sarti was perfectly placed.

Now Celtic had all the advantage of the team which has come from behind and is buoyed by the optimism which that brings. A replay, had it been necessary, would have taken place in Lisbon three days later. But there was now an inevitability about the arrival of the winner, just five minutes from the end. Murdoch shot, Chalmers diverted and Sarti could not adjust quickly enough to the change in direction. The remaining seconds ticked away in a frenzy of excitement, before the final whistle sounded and Celtic were champions of Europe. Bill Shankly walked into the Celtic dressing room, stretched out a hand to Stein and uttered the peerless phrase: 'John, you're immortal.'

McNeill makes the point:

On and off the field, everybody made a contribution, some loudly, others quietly. Many people refer to the Lisbon Lions as the actual eleven who played that day. There were a lot more fine players than that involved in the all-round achievement. Consider players such as Joe McBride, Charlie Gallagher, John Fallon, John Hughes and Willie O'Neill and you will realize that it was a genuine squad effort. I was reminded of it all in May 1987 when we had a reunion at a supporters' function. They were all there, the entire gang, all still the same, all wise-cracking, ribbing each other, generally having the same kind of fun we had enjoyed twenty years earlier. It all came flooding back.

Celtic's return to Glasgow, and their procession through the streets of the East End, was an occasion of deep emotion. The club which had grown out of a poor community, and which had contributed so much to its sense of identity and pride, now returned to it with the highest honour in club football. It was not necessary ever to have seen a game of football in order to share fully and justly in the spirit of the celebration for a wonderful achievement.

Before the game, Stein had told Hugh McIlvanney of the *Observer*: 'We don't just want to win this cup. We want to win playing good football, to make neutrals glad we've won it, glad to remember how we did it.' His every wish had been fulfilled.

# 17

# A WORLD-CLASS SIDE
## *And the One that Got Away*

 T IS a curious fact that the Lisbon Lions only ever won one European match, and that was the great Final itself. Indeed, they were together for only three games in continental combat – the semi-final second leg in Prague, then in Lisbon, and finally for the opening game of their European Cup defence, at Celtic Park on 20 September 1967. It was only by mischance that Celtic were involved at this stage at all. Normally, there were thirty-three teams in the tournament and the previous season's winners were not included in the preliminary round. However, the Albanian champions withdrew – and so Celtic went into the draw with the rest. It gave them one of the toughest available tests, against Dinamo Kiev of the Soviet Union. On 20 September, the Celtic supporters looked on in shocked disbelief as their heroes displayed alarming unsteadiness in defence and went two goals down, before Bobby Lennox pulled one back after sixty-two minutes. So the European Cup-holders travelled to the Ukraine having to do what no other club had done in the history of the tournament – retrieve a tie after losing the first leg.

The improbable seemed to become the impossible when Bobby Murdoch was sent off after fifty-nine minutes – yet, three minutes later, Celtic were in the lead, thanks to the irrepressible Lennox. Heroic as the attempt was, however, there was to be no glory that afternoon. By this time, away goals counted double in the event of an aggregate draw; so Celtic had to pursue a decisive second. Kiev took advantage of Celtic's frenzied attacking efforts and snaked an equalizer literally seconds from the end, to progress on a 3–2 aggregate.

Apart from a 1–0 League defeat at Ibrox, Celtic had opened the season in the manner to which the supporters were becoming accustomed, with the team qualifying undefeated from a uniquely difficult League Cup section which also included Rangers, Dundee United and Aberdeen. The 3–1 win over Rangers at Celtic Park in the section decider should, the directors agreed, 'be minuted as one of our best ever results against Rangers' – the team had come from being a goal down to score in the final, exhilarating thirteen minutes through Wallace, Murdoch and Lennox.

Celtic were also looking forward to the so-called 'world club championship' play-off with Racing Club of Buenos Aires, the South American champions. With this in mind, a friendly match with Penarol of Uruguay had been arranged for Celtic Park early in September, and the following week's board meeting noted that it had been 'an excellent game with hardly a foul given; a match between a South American and Scottish side that did great credit to all concerned'. In the wake of all this, the European Cup exit came as an abrupt shock, and just two weeks later, Racing Club came to Celtic Park. Yet another dramatic winner from the head of Billy McNeill gave Celtic a slender first-leg lead – but not before the Argentinians had established their intention to pursue a regime of intimidation based on spitting, hacking and foul-mouthing their opponents.

There are those who argue to this day that the Scottish champions should not have travelled to South America for the return match; that if Racing Club wanted the title so badly that they were prepared to behave like thugs, they should have been conceded the tie and peace allowed to reign. With hindsight, that seems reasonable, but it fails to recognize Stein's burning ambition to lead Celtic to another pinnacle – and where would the club have been without Stein's sense of ambition? It must also be remembered that there were no shirkers in that Celtic squad when it came to a skirmish and the players, in general, shared the big man's determination to go all the way. Billy McNeill recalls:

I never doubted that we should go. It was essential. What happened in the stadium came as a complete surprise to us. I remember going to church shortly after we arrived. The people could not have been more friendly, as the Argentinians are. But the football crowd worked itself up into a frenzy, and the reception we got at the game was nothing short of horrific.

The worst fears were vindicated by an incident just before the kick-off in Buenos Aires when Ronnie Simpson had to be replaced by John Fallon after being felled by a missile from the crowd. Yet the 120,000 hostile home supporters saw Celtic take the lead with a Tommy Gemmell penalty before Racing Club came back to win 2–1. Once again, there was a case for pulling out and calling the semi-official 'world championship' a tie. Bob Kelly was strongly in favour of this course of action, but Stein successfully lobbied against it. McNeill says: 'I didn't think we should have gone to Montevideo. There was too much talk along the lines of "why are we going?". That was not the ideal preparation for players, because it put other worries in our heads.'

But Celtic pressed on to the Uruguayan capital for the play-off, and the Penarol players who had visited Glasgow a few weeks earlier came along to commiserate over the events in Buenos Aires, and to add their own horror stories about what the Argentinians are capable of. (No love is lost between these two peoples.) The game soon developed into the demeaning farce which many had feared all along. The provocation to the Celtic players was immense, and the performance of the Paraguayan referee appalling. But part of the problem, as McNeill recognizes, was that 'we went out like avenging angels'. The game should never have taken place, and Stein subsequently admitted frankly: 'Mr Kelly was swayed by our arguments and I now have to say that he was correct in the first place.' The club's dismay had almost nothing to do with the 1–0 defeat, as illustrated by the minutes of the board meeting held on 9 November 1967

The club was disappointed with the result of the second match in Montevideo but the directors were far more disappointed with the conduct of some of the players in that match. Three had been put off – Lennox, Johnstone and Hughes. Certainly, it was difficult to understand why Lennox and Johnstone were ordered off, but two other Celtic players [Gemmell and Auld] were most fortunate in not being ordered off. What worried the club was the break-down in control and discipline. We had built up an image of a top-class, well-disciplined side. That image was sadly tarnished. The players had had much to contend with, particularly in the Buenos Aires match . . . nerves had been strained to breaking point. A stance had, however, to be taken to rescue their good name. It was decided to fine the players – the whole team – £250 each.

Just prior to the South American trip, the League Cup had been won with a 5–3 victory over Dundee in the Final. Now Celtic had to put the Kiev and Montevideo experiences behind them and concentrate on the all-important business of qualifying again for the European Cup.

It was an epic race for the League title. Celtic had already dropped two points to Rangers and one in a home game against St Johnstone. On 2 December they drew at home with Dundee United, and on 2 January they shared four goals with Rangers at Celtic Park. They then won their remaining sixteen League games to finish with sixty-three points from a possible sixty-eight. But Rangers – who had invested heavily in the transfer market in an effort to break Celtic's supremacy – were doing just as well, and approached their last match of the season, at home to Aberdeen, still unbeaten. They had a favourite's chance of completing a League Championship without defeat for the first time this century. Celtic were idle that day, 20 April, and were confirmed as champions for the third successive season when Aberdeen won 3–2. Celtic had to play their final game against Dunfermline the following Tuesday but, already a distance ahead on goal difference, they could afford defeat. In the event they won 2–1, coming from behind with goals from Bobby Lennox in the forty-seventh and seventy-second minutes. In the big upset of the domestic season, the club Stein had taken into the 'big league' had knocked Celtic out of the Scottish Cup by coming to Glasgow and winning 2–0 in January.

Whatever the disappointments suffered by the Celtic fans at the early exits from the European and Scottish Cups, this was not reflected in the size of their support during those fraught matches on the run-in to the Championship. There were full houses at Tannadice, Tynecastle and Pittodrie. In the penultimate game, at home to Morton, a staggering 51,000 turned up. And there was a capacity 30,000 at East End Park for the grand finale to an unprecedented League campaign. Billy McNeill recalls that night in Dunfermline:

We knew that the title was already in our hands, and it would have been easy for us to treat the game as a lap of honour. But the troops were there in their thousands, and it was part of the character of Celtic players then to see to it that the business was done properly. We went behind, and then fought like demons to come back and win. There was little chance of us celebrating a League victory with defeat on the night. Dunfermline went on to win the Cup and deserved it, because they had beaten us on the way.

The 1968/9 season opened with a crowd of over 80,000 at Celtic Park for a friendly match with Leeds United. It then followed a similar pattern to most other Celtic seasons of that era. Another treble of Championship, Scottish Cup and League Cup was recorded in the ledger, and in Europe, the team beat St Etienne of France and Red Star of Yugoslavia before succumbing to AC Milan in the quarter-final. Having secured an excellent 0–0 draw in Italy, they went down to a single goal at Celtic Park. The original draw for the first round of the European Cup had paired Celtic with Ferencvaros of Hungary, but the competition was redrawn after Celtic had complained that no western European club should be 'forced to fulfil any football commitment' in any Warsaw Pact country, following the Soviet Union's intervention in Czechoslovakia. In the emotional atmosphere of the period, this initiative attracted considerable support from other western clubs in the competition. It was decided by UEFA to redraw the European competitions (though the practical difficulties of travelling between east and west at this time were quoted as the official explanation).

While it was very much in tune with international outrage over events in Czechoslovakia, Celtic's initiative raised a much wider question. Should international sporting contact, at club or national level, be conditional upon political judgements about the calibre of the other country's regime? Clearly, if many such adjudications were to occur, international sporting contact would quickly diminish. This was demonstrated when the eastern European clubs withdrew from that season's European tournaments in protest against the decision to redraw – even though, by that time, UEFA had decided that the zoning should apply for one round only.

During that season, significant changes were taking place. It is a measure of Jock Stein's ambition for Celtic that he was not prepared merely to consolidate domestic supremacy and bask in the glory of Lisbon memories. He had made the European Cup winnable and, as a result, believed that his ambition should not drop below that objective. This persuaded him to start changing personnel, in the search for a combination that would once again be good enough to go to the very top. There are players from that period who remain adamant that Stein began the break-up of the pool much too early. Joe McBride was allowed to join Hibs, Willie O'Neill left for Carlisle United and Charlie Gallagher was allowed to negotiate his own terms with Dumbarton. Tommy Callaghan was bought from Dunfermline and Harry Hood from Clyde.

The next great wave of talent which was bursting through at Celtic Park was, paradoxically, part of Stein's dilemma. Kenny Dalglish, George Connelly, Lou Macari, Danny McGrain and David Hay were already part of a second string which would surely itself have finished in the top half-dozen of the old First Division. These youngsters were showing the kind of form which would have won them a place in the first team of any other club in the country. If they were to be held back for the sake of prolonging a legend, could they be blamed for growing unsettled enough to seek their fortunes elsewhere? Stein's decision was to effect the introduction of new blood as painlessly as possible, and to allow some of the more experienced players to go their different ways while they still had something left of their playing careers. On another front, the Lisbon memory was honoured with the announcement of a knighthood for chairman Bob Kelly in the 1969 New Year's Honours List.

Celtic won the League by five points from Rangers in 1968/9. The League Cup campaign included a 10–0 scoreline against Hamilton, with five goals apiece coming from Lennox and Chalmers. Because of a fire at Hampden, the Final against Hibs was delayed until April 1969, when Celtic beat them 6–2. As a result, the three legs of the treble were tied up within a three-week period. The season was climaxed by goals from McNeill, Lennox, Connelly and Chalmers, which helped to beat Rangers 4–0 in a joyous Scottish Cup Final on 26 April, when the Celtic team was: Fallon, Craig, Gemmell, Murdoch, McNeill, Brogan (Clark), Connelly, Chalmers, Wallace, Lennox and Auld.

By the time Celtic reached their second European Cup Final in 1970, they had tucked away another League title and another League Cup, and had been runners-up to Aberdeen in the Scottish Cup Final. Rangers were again one of the teams eliminated in the League Cup qualifying section, but a game between the clubs at Celtic Park on 20 August 1969 yielded a most unusual episode. The referee, Jim Callaghan, booked John Hughes in the first half. Later, a linesman drew the referee's attention to a clash between Hughes and Johnston of Rangers. Mr Callaghan spoke to Hughes, but took no further action. Rangers complained to the SFA and after an enquiry, Mr Callaghan – a top official of previously unblemished reputation – was suspended for two months. This was surely the only occasion on which a referee has been suspended, in effect, for not sending a player off. It was difficult to imagine that a complaint on similar grounds from any other source would have met with the same outcome. Celtic met St Johnstone, at that time an exciting side under Willie Ormond, in the Final at Hampden, and won by a solitary goal scored by Bertie Auld in the second minute.

Goalkeeper Evan Williams, brought back to Scotland from Wolves, defenders Hay and Brogan, and midfielder George Connelly became first team regulars in the course of this eventful season. Kenny Dalglish's name would also appear on the first-team sheet for the first time (coming on as a second-half substitute at Hamilton in a League Cup tie). After collecting just three points from their first four League games, Celtic recovered more normal form and had the title won by twelve points from Rangers by the time they met Aberdeen in the Scottish Cup Final on 11 April 1970. All too often it is possible to reach the closing stages of the Scottish Cup without having been drawn against very substantial opposition. But on this occasion, Celtic had to overcome Dunfermline, Dundee United, Rangers and Dundee to earn their Hampden place in April.

It was a game awash with controversy, most of which surrounded the refereeing of Mr R. H. Davidson of Airdrie (who was not highly regarded in Celtic circles), during a crucial ten-minute spell. First he awarded a penalty kick against Bobby Murdoch for a 'hand-ball' offence which appeared wholly beyond the player's control. Lennox appeared to equalize after Clark, the Aberdeen keeper, had dropped the ball. The referee ruled that a foul had been committed by the Celtic player, and then added insult to injury by declining to award the most blatant of penalty kicks when Lennox was spreadeagled inside the box. Aberdeen eventually won 3–1 and left Stein, in his inimitable fashion, loudly discussing the referee's performance in the Hampden foyer in such carefully chosen language that he was able to make his dissatisfaction known without giving the SFA the chance to charge him with illegal remarks!

Throughout the season, Celtic's European Cup charge had been building up. Basle of Switzerland provided the opening opposition and, after a 0–0 draw, goals from Hood and Gemmell at Celtic Park took the team through. Drawn against mighty Benfica of Portugal, Celtic gained one of the best results in their history – a 3–0 home win, with goals from Gemmell (a memorable thirty-five-yard shot in the second minute), Wallace and Hood. But Celtic needed all of this lead for the second leg in Portugal. As half-time approached Benfica scored twice, and after Celtic appeared to have weathered a second-half storm, the equalizer came in injury time. Extra time was played, and Celtic did extremely well in such circumstances to hold out. There were no penalty shoot-outs at this time, and Celtic went through when Billy McNeill called correctly on the toss of a coin.

Celtic drew Fiorentina of Italy in the quarter-finals and, in March, secured another outstanding home result – 3–0, through goals from Auld, Carpenetti (og) and Wallace. A skilful containment job was done in Florence, and only one goal conceded. The semi-final draw brought together the champions of Scotland and England – Celtic v. Leeds. It would have been an ideal Final, and the whole build-up to the first meeting, in Leeds on 1 April, implied that this was indeed the apex of the competition.

George Connelly had made a sensational impact in his first season as a regular Celtic player. Possessed of astonishing ball skills, he had first become known to the Celtic faithful as the provider of pre-match entertainment. Prior to one European tie, Connelly went round every line on the park, keeping the ball in the air. Bob Rooney recalls Connelly as 'the best young player I ever saw at Celtic Park', with a devastating ability to turn defence into attack with a single, incisive pass. Now Connelly was at the centre of Stein's pre-match battle of tactics and nerves with his friend Don Revie, manager of Leeds. Would Stein risk fielding the youngster in a match of such pressure? Revie wrongly concluded that he would not, and planned accordingly. Connelly played, and scored the winning goal after just forty-five seconds of the match. The Leeds players then spent most of the evening trying to contain the magical Jimmy Johnstone, with little prospect of gaining control of the match. It was one of Stein's finest tactical successes.

Celtic's superiority in what, inevitably, had come to be regarded as the British championship was confirmed in the second leg, when John Hughes was pitted against Jack Charlton in a classic duel. The game was played at

Hampden Park, and a European Cup record crowd of 136,500 – not including those who scaled the walls to get in free – saw goals by Hughes and Bobby Murdoch overcome an early score by Billy Bremner to take Celtic into the Final. On this occasion, Celtic were permitted a lap of honour.

Much ink and many words have been expended on analysing why Celtic then lost the Final to Feyenoord of the Netherlands, who – though they were doubtless blissfully unaware of the fact – lined up in the San Siro Stadium, Milan on 6 May 1970 with Scottish bookmakers offering the ridiculous odds of 6–1 against them. Numerous excuses have been offered for Celtic's anti-climactic performance. Stein suffered criticism for supposedly underestimating the opposition. The players were accused of worrying too much about their commercial interests, which had been neglected completely prior to the Lisbon Final. But this implies that financial naïvety, once lost, can then be restored when the occasion demands without any further psychological price being paid, and that is surely itself naïve. For all the words and retrospective wisdom, too little attention had been paid to the fact that Feyenoord were an extremely good side, who played brilliantly on the night. The defeat came so unexpectedly because the pre-match assumptions, true to Scottish football tradition, had been so irrationally optimistic.

Celtic had been the innocent underdogs in Lisbon, with everything to play for. Had they lost to Inter Milan, the honour accorded to them would still have been great – the first British club in the European Cup Final, ambassadors of attacking football, and so on. This role, brilliantly exploited and turned to advantage by Stein, had been crucial to their psychology and ultimate victory. The circumstances of 1970 were very different, and it is idle to imagine that some sort of replica build-up could have been achieved. Jim Craig, who played in Lisbon and observed Milan at close quarters, is surely near to the mark when he says:

There is no doubt in my mind that we climbed our mountain against Leeds in the semi-final. We lulled ourselves into thinking that Feyenoord represented the other side of the peak, and that we were now coasting downhill. Of course, that means that we may have been complacent – but it is also human and understandable.

Billy McNeill admits frankly:

We totally underestimated them. We didn't recognize that Dutch football was on the ascendancy. In beating Leeds home and away, we allowed ourselves to get carried away. Our preparations for the Final were not good. Feyenoord were still in competitive action in Holland, while our season had finished. The full team only played one preparatory game, against Stenhousemuir. Half went to Gateshead to play a friendly; the other half went to Fraserburgh.

He also thinks the club was too preoccupied with arranging open-top buses and other details of the celebrations which were taken for granted. Bobby Lennox says simply: 'It was the low point in our careers and I'll never forget the feeling. Feyenoord were better than us, yet we were within four minutes of getting another game.'

The teams which lined up in front of a 53,000 crowd in the San Siro Stadium, Milan were:

Celtic: Williams, Hay, Gemmell, Murdoch, McNeill, Brogan, Johnstone, Wallace, Hughes, Auld (Connelly) and Lennox.
Feyenoord: Graafland, Romeyn (Haak), Israel, Laseroms, Van Duivenbode, Jansen, Van Hanegem, Hasil, Wery, Kindvall and Moulijin.

Celtic took the lead after thirty minutes with a typical Tommy Gemmell thundering shot from a short Murdoch free kick. But most of the Celtic followers realized that the team was not on top of its task and this was confirmed, within two minutes, when Israel equalized. Feyenoord were now filling precisely the role that Celtic had occupied in Lisbon. They had planned carefully and, encouraged by the equalizing goal, relentlessly pursued the winner for most of the time remaining. Celtic held out until the end of ninety minutes, and the game moved into extra time. With no penalty shoot-outs in these more civilized times, a replay would have taken place in Milan two days later. The Celtic fans prayed for this opportunity to regroup and fight again. But four minutes from the end Kindvall struck the winning goal. It was a bitter disappointment for everyone whose hopes were vested in Celtic, and the subsequent recriminations were bitter. 'The scoreline flattered us,' says Billy McNeill. 'Other than Evan Williams, who had a superb match, we did not play well at all.'

Immediately afterwards, Celtic went off on the North American tour to which they were committed. It had been planned as a celebration, evocative of past tours in the same territory, but turned into an unhappy and generally unwanted expedition. Jimmy Johnstone did not go on the tour, supposedly because of his fear of flying. Celtic were involved in a tournament with Manchester United, who promptly beat them 2–0, and an Italian club of no obvious distinction called Bari. Jock Stein abruptly departed for home, leaving Sean Fallon in charge of the team, and Desmond White flew out from Scotland to take overall control. It soon became apparent that, in part at least, Stein's return home was to deal with Johnstone, who was about to ask for a transfer on financial grounds. Then Gemmell and Auld were sent home from New York by Sean Fallon for disciplinary reasons. The full-back also asked for a transfer. Both he and Johnstone were told they could go, and although both affairs petered out, they contributed to an unhappy few months at Celtic Park.

By the time twenty-two shareholders gathered for their annual meeting on 4 September 1970, a proper sense of perspective had been restored. Sir Robert Kelly was already unwell and may well have known that this would be his valedictory address. The club, he declared, had never in its long and illustrious history been in a better position either in the playing sense or financially. He continued:

The name and fame of Celtic is now world-wide, and we are recognized as a top team in Europe . . . All this gives me great personal satisfaction because in achieving these wonderful triumphs, we have confounded the critics of not so many years ago who laughed to scorn any predictions that we could and would reach such levels. I take this opportunity of paying tribute to our great manager, Jock Stein.

For his part, Stein soberly assessed the European Cup disappointment. They had beaten Leeds both home and away 'in the greatest club matches ever' and, with Feyenoord now on their way to victory over their South American counterparts, 'being second to the top team in the world is no humiliation'.

# 18

## GLORY GLORY DAYS
### And the End of an Era

ELTIC's difficulties continued into the new season, and they lost the League Cup to Rangers through a goal by sixteen-year-old Derek Johnstone in the Final. After an inconsistent start to the League programme, however, something approaching normality was restored. By now Celtic had won five League titles in a row, and on each occasion Rangers had been runners-up. But in 1970/1, it was Cup-holders Aberdeen – with players such as Bobby Clark, Steve Murray, Martin Buchan and Joe Harper – who emerged as the principal challengers. Danny McGrain, who had signed for Celtic in 1967, entered the first team for the opening League game of the season against Morton, and made intermittent appearances thereafter. Kenny Dalglish made his first appearance of the season, replacing Jimmy Johnstone during a 3–1 victory at Broomfield on 17 October 1970. During that season, however, he was to make only one full appearance in the League. It was a neck-and-neck struggle, with Aberdeen heading the table for a long period. However, Celtic went to Pittodrie on 17 April leading by a point, and an early goal by Harry Hood earned them a vital draw. The sixth successive League title was tied up with a 2–0 win over Ayr twelve days later.

For the closing League game of the season, Stein urged the supporters to turn out in force. With a characteristic burst of showmanship, he had decided to lay on a last farewell by the entire Lisbon Lions team. Ronnie Simpson, now retired, led them out before an emotional crowd of 35,000 which witnessed a 6–1 victory in the old style, with John Fallon in goal as the only alteration from the Lisbon side. John Clark's move to Morton now took place, and Bertie Auld – carried from the field on the shoulders of his colleagues – was transferred to Hibs where he saw out his playing days. The double was completed when, after a 1–1 draw, Celtic beat Rangers 2–1 in the replayed Scottish Cup Final. The team that night, 12 May 1971, was: Williams, Craig, Brogan, Connelly, McNeill, Hay, Johnstone, Lennox, Macari, Callaghan and Hood. Macari, who had come in for Wallace following the first game, scored the opener and Hood's penalty goal put Celtic two up before an own goal by Jim Craig resulted in a scoreline that was perhaps closer than it should have been.

In Europe, Celtic made their exit at the quarter-final stage. After easy victories over Kokkola of Finland and Waterford of Ireland, they were drawn against Ajax, pride of Amsterdam. Celtic were learning at first hand one of the outstanding football lessons of the seventies – that Dutch football had become very good indeed. In their home leg, Ajax built up a three-goal lead and Celtic could pull back only one goal, through Jimmy Johnstone, in Glasgow.

Throughout this season, the board of directors did not meet on a regular basis because of Sir Robert Kelly's illness. However, on 29 February 1971, Messrs White, Devlin and Farrell came together in the North British Hotel to confront a potential crisis. It was not long since Manchester United had been desperate to secure Jock Stein's services, and now press reports were suggesting with too much consistency to be ignored that he was thinking of leaving for Leeds. It was agreed to point out to the manager that he was being paid a very high salary, that 'loyalty to the club should play a very important part' in his thinking, and that 'we were not prepared to enter into an auction'. The minutes of the meeting added: 'The chairman, who was not present, was very much in agreement and very disappointed that he [Stein] should be so tempted.' The Celtic directors heard of his decision to stay at a meeting on 22 March – the same meeting that accepted Sir Robert Kelly's retirement and decided to make him the club's first honorary president since it had been formed into a limited company. Though matters had been smoothed over with Jock Stein, possibly in deference to the chairman's feelings, the question of the manager's future intentions was now firmly on the agenda, and was regularly to recur.

The 1970/1 season had been memorable for another, tragic reason. On 2 January 1971, sixty-six spectators died in an accident on stairway 13 at Ibrox. When Jimmy Johnstone put Celtic ahead late in the game, Rangers supporters started to leave the ground. But when Colin Stein equalized with seconds left, some of those who had departed prematurely tried to return to join in the celebrations. The tragedy occurred when they met the tide of people now rushing away at the final whistle. The disaster had far-reaching implications for regulations on stadium construction, attendance limits and crowd control. But its immediate effects were to put football rivalries in perspective, to unite Scotland in grief, and the two clubs in mourning. Players and officials of both Celtic and Rangers attended memorial services in the St Andrew's and Glasgow Cathedrals. Celtic contributed £10,000 to the Ibrox Disaster Fund.

The fine new Celtic stand, financed through the Development Fund set up in the 1960s, was officially opened by Jimmy McGrory on 1 September 1971, and the supporters were treated to a show game against Nacional of Uruguay, the South American champions – an event which went a long way towards exorcizing the vile memory of Montevideo. Celtic opened their League programme with a 9–1 win over Clyde and the seventh successive League title was duly taken by ten clear points from Aberdeen in 1971/2, in spite of this being another season of substantial transition.

The League Cup had, however, provided one of the biggest upsets in post-war Scottish football – the kind of upset, indeed, that keeps the game interesting. Having disposed of Rangers in the qualifying section, Celtic progressed easily to the Final on 23 October 1971. With Partick Thistle providing the opposition, it was generally assumed that Celtic would win with ease, even with Billy McNeill out through injury. But Thistle attacked from the start, to sensational effect. Within thirty-seven minutes, they were 4–0 up. It was the kind of scoreline which teleprinters had to repeat in words as well as figures in order to avoid accusations of gross error. Celtic could pull back only one goal, through Dalglish, as young Alan Rough in the Thistle goal revelled in this unique occasion.

Evan Williams carried the can for this embarrassment, and Stein immediately signed Denis Connaghan from St Mirren. He then added the scoring power of John 'Dixie' Deans, a striker in the McBride mould bought from Motherwell at a modest price. Steve Chalmers joined John Clark at Cappielow; Tommy Gemmell was transferred to Nottingham Forest; and Willie Wallace and John Hughes departed for Crystal Palace.

The Scottish Cup was retained with a 6–1 Final victory over Hibs on 6 May 1972. The team was: Williams, Craig, Brogan, Murdoch, McNeill, Connelly, Johnstone, Deans, Macari, Dalglish and Callaghan. The score-line equalled Renton's record win in 1888, and Dixie Deans' hat-trick was the first in a Final since Jimmy Quinn in 1904 against Rangers. McNeill had opened the scoring and Lou Macari contributed two late goals.

With the League and Cup double tied up, it was a satisfactory season for Celtic on the domestic front. Easily its most exciting aspect was the emergence of Kenny Dalglish, who won instant acclaim by producing the skills which would eventually cause him to be numbered among the greatest players the British game has ever known. Following his handful of appearances in the previous two seasons, Dalglish played fifty first-team matches during 1971/2, including only one as substitute. He scored seventeen goals, runner-up to Dixie Deans. Perhaps, in retrospect, the most eloquent testimony to Dalglish's sensational impact that season could be seen in the fact that he was in the Scotland team against Holland on 1 December, within a few months of becoming an established first-team player.

Dalglish also helped Celtic to their fourth European semi-final within the space of seven magnificent seasons. Before Christmas they had beaten Boldklub Copenhagen of Denmark and Sliema Wanderers of Malta. But, for a team in transition, Ujpest Dozsa of Hungary seemed like a tough nut to crack. Danny McGrain made his European debut in Budapest, and Celtic established an outstanding 2–1 lead. An early own goal was helpful, but it was another splendid tactical performance, with Lennox and Macari pressurizing the Hungarian defence and preventing Ujpest from going all out for home goals. They did manage an equalizer, but five minutes from the end Macari scored the second. Celtic then conceded the opening goal of the home leg, but a Macari equalizer took them through to the semi-final against Inter Milan.

It was back to the San Siro Stadium, with a team which contained an extremely promising mix of the old guard and the first-class talent which had been confirmed since the last visit to that city. Both semi-final legs were tense, cat-and-mouse affairs and neither yielded a single, decisive goal. Infuriatingly, the issue was to be decided on penalty kicks – a marginal improvement, perhaps, on tossing a coin but still no way to decide which club should qualify for a place in the European Cup Final. Mazzola scored Inter's first – and then the unfortunate Dixie Deans cracked under the enormous strain, and sent his effort over the bar. The Italians took their other four kicks with confident ease, and so they went through. Deans had to be content with his hat-trick against Hibs in the Scottish Cup, which included a quite outstanding solo goal.

However, Desmond White looked on the bright side when giving his first report as chairman to the annual meeting of shareholders, and concentrated his remarks on the unprecedented 'seven in a row' which broke Celtic's own long-standing record. He asked: 'How many of us remember now that at the time Celtic won the first of the seven, in season 1965/6, the club had won only three in the previous forty years and only one, in 1953/4, since the Second World War?'

The eighth in a row, 1972/3, was a much tougher League title for Celtic and it was touch and go for them to lead Rangers by a single point at the end of it. This was achieved thanks to a run-in of seven successive wins, while Rangers – by now under Jock Wallace – dropped a crucial point at Pittodrie in the penultimate game of the season. This left Celtic requiring a draw from their final game against Hibs at Easter Road; in fact they won 3–0. On the credit side, Dalglish had another outstanding season, McGrain became fully established and George Connelly achieved the best form of his career, to be named Footballer of the Year by Scotland's sports writers. But there was bitter disappointment for Stein when Lou Macari found the bait of more money in England irresistible. He was transferred to Manchester United, and this must be seen as something of a watershed. It was the first time since Stein's arrival at Celtic Park that an important player had been released under such circumstances.

Ominously, and much more seriously, Stein was taken to hospital in January 1973 with a suspected heart attack and spent a short time recovering away from Celtic Park. The League title was Celtic's only honour in 1972/3 – they lost the League Cup Final to Hibs, the Scottish Cup semi-final to Rangers and their European Cup hopes to old rivals Ujpest Dozsa of Hungary, on a 4–2 aggregate in the second round.

Most of the club's home games during this season had to be played at Hampden Park, due to weaknesses having become apparent in the design of the Celtic Park stand. The club had good reason to be grateful to a supporter, an experienced steel erector, who was the first to draw attention to defects which might otherwise have had serious consequences. It was an issue which involved the club in legal wranglings for several years.

Although the season of 1973/4 duly yielded a ninth League title, it was marked by other disappointments and not a little cause for disillusionment. At the same time as Celtic had been touching the heights of 1967, something equally remarkable had been happening in the background: a crop of extraordinary talent was growing up at Celtic Park. If it had stayed together it should have ripened fully by the mid 1970s; but by 1973 a very different scenario was emerging. Macari was gone. David Hay was in dispute with the club over money and was suspended after staying away from training, before being transferred to Chelsea. George Connelly was in the process of turning his back on professional football altogether. Meanwhile, the last of the Lisbon Lions were passing their primes. Bobby Murdoch left for Middlesbrough, to be replaced by the valuable midfield signing of Steve Murray from Aberdeen. Jimmy Johnstone languished in the reserves for much of the season. Against this background, it was extraordinary that Celtic should again emerge from the long League programme as champions – though the fifty-three-point total which won them the title, by four points from Hibs, was the lowest of the sequence.

For good measure they also took the Scottish Cup, beating Dundee United 3–0 in the Tannadice club's first Final. The Celtic team on 4 May 1974 was: Connaghan, McGrain (Callaghan), Brogan, Murray, McNeill, McCluskey, Johnstone, Hood, Deans, Hay and Dalglish. Goals from Hood, Murray and Deans secured the trophy in an otherwise unmemorable Final, played in front of a 79,959 crowd. In the League Cup, however, Celtic had lost the Final to Dundee, after apparently doing the difficult part of the job by beating Rangers 3–1 in the semi-final. The Final will be remembered by more politically minded supporters as a symbol of the Heath Government's declining months. It was played in December with a 1.30 p.m. kick-off, because the restrictions on the use of electricity forbade the use of floodlights. A crowd of only 27,974 stood in the snow and, to their general astonishment, saw Celtic go down to a seventy-fifth-minute goal by Gordon Wallace.

In the European Cup of 1973/4, the early draw favoured Celtic. They easily disposed of Finnish opposition, but then struggled to beat the unheard-of Danish club Vejle BK by a single goal scored in the away leg. There were more signs of strain when Celtic needed extra time in the quarter-final second leg to defeat Basle of Switzerland 6–5 on aggregate. This put them through to yet another European Cup semi-final – this time, alas, against Atletico Madrid. The Spanish club's performance at Celtic Park will go down as one of the most disgraceful in European football annals. The aim was intimidation, and Jimmy Johnstone was the chief target for a succession of assaults. By the end of the night, three Spaniards had been sent off and another seven booked.

Atletico Madrid were fined £14,000 by UEFA, and six of their players were banned for the second leg. It was an inadequate punishment, because their coach – if that is not too dignified a word for Senor Juan Carlos Lorenzo – had planned to do without these individuals in the return anyway. They had been briefed simply to secure a 0–0 draw at Celtic Park by any means, and this they did. The return was a nightmare from the start, with Atletico supporters and the press joining in the intimidation process from the moment the Celtic party set foot in Spain. A Spanish government official was quoted as saying that 'there could very well be a death if somebody is crazy there'. With the team hotel, and the park, bristling with armed troops, it was not a possibility to be taken lightly. With that kind of build-up, it was scarcely surprising that Celtic went down 2–0, although they held out until thirteen minutes from the end. The whole experience disgusted Stein and soured the memory of the great European years.

George Connelly was by now irretrievably lost to Celtic and top-class football. A gifted, ball-playing defender after the manner of Beckenbauer, the quiet Fifer had never greatly cared for the hassle and publicity which accompanied being in the public eye. A few generations earlier, Jimmy Quinn might have drawn the same conclusion – that football really wasn't worth that kind of bother. Connelly responded by occasionally, and then less occasionally, not appearing where he was expected. A team-mate and friend, searching for Connelly's basic instincts, once asked him what, if he had the choice, he would really like to be. 'A long-distance lorry-driver' was the reply. He envied the freedom and the chance to be on his own, away from smothering influences and hangers-on which are part and parcel of being public property. Connelly remained at Celtic Park for a while longer, but his heart wasn't in it. Visits to Connelly's home by Stein, Sean Fallon and Dr Fitzsimons, the long-serving club doctor, were all to no avail. By the summer of 1974 the career around which Stein had once said he would rebuild Celtic was effectively at an end.

Stein spelled out the truth to the annual meeting of shareholders in September 1974. They had lost Hay by transfer, the promising Brian McLaughlin by injury and Connelly 'through his own decision'. No club could afford such losses, he warned, and building another team which could aspire to the European Cup would 'obviously take some time'. However, they had now equalled the world record, held by CSK Sofia, of nine successive domestic championships in succession – and 'God willing, we intend to make it a full decade of Celtic supremacy.'

The following season was Celtic's ninth in the European Cup, but they went out in the first round to Olympiakos of Greece. Jock Stein commented succinctly: 'The only consolation is that if we were not good enough for the competition it was better to get out the way quickly and let others who were get on with it.' It was the end, for the time being, of the club's automatic presence in the premier European competition, for whether by divine intervention or for more prosaic reasons, the dream of a tenth successive League title slipped away in the early months of 1975. Celtic finished in third place, eleven points behind Rangers.

There were the Scottish Cup and League Cup as substantial consolations, won in Finals against Airdrie and Hibs respectively. But everyone knew that an era had ended. Billy McNeill confirmed it when, at the age of thirty-five, he retired from playing football following the Cup Final victory over Airdrie and was carried from the field by his team-mates in salute to a wonderful career. He soon realized that his decision to leave not only Celtic but the whole football world had been premature. Jimmy Johnstone went off to play in the United States. Apart from Bobby Lennox, the Lisbon Lions were gone and the glorious 'nine-in-a-row' era was now merely a memory to savour, the stuff of folklore for all who had witnessed it. But for Jock Stein, and all who cared about him, there was something much worse to follow.

In the early hours of the first Sunday in July, Stein was driving a Mercedes car from Manchester Airport back to Glasgow. He had just returned from a holiday in Minorca and there were four other occupants of the car – his wife Jean, fellow-manager Bob Shankly and his wife, and the Glasgow bookmaker Tony Queen. The road was, and is, notorious for its toll of accidents – sometimes caused by drivers wandering on to a dual carriageway heading in the wrong direction. That was precisely what happened on this occasion: a head-on crash occurred at high speed. Stein was eventually to be awarded substantial damages against the other driver, who was fined for reckless driving, but it was a blow for which there could be no appropriate compensation. According to the testimony of those who knew him best, Stein never fully recovered from that terrible accident, in which Tony Queen was also very seriously injured.

Stein was rushed to hospital in Dumfries, scarcely able to breathe – a condition which had not deterred a policeman from administering a breathalyzer test as he lay at the roadside. He was operated on and, within a remarkably short space of time, was making light of his misfortune. The wounds, however, were more than superficial. Tony McGuinness, another friend of long standing, says:

He was never back to the man he was, after the crash. Apart from the physical wounds, it took a lot out of him mentally. He never had a proper night's sleep thereafter. I also believe that he came back to Celtic Park far too early, because of his love for the club. From within a very short time after the accident, he was continuing to act in an advisory capacity.

Billy McNeill recalls learning of the accident to the man who had become much more to him than a mere manager, on returning from his own cruising holiday. He rushed to the hospital in Dumfries, but identifies it as one of the great regrets of his career that he did not, at that point, cancel his decision to leave the game and return to the club in what was clearly an hour of need.

The directors, meeting on 17 July 1975, appointed Sean Fallon as acting manager. But a disappointing season followed – defeat in the League Cup Final by Rangers, an early exit from the Scottish Cup at the hands of Motherwell and a late collapse in the new ten-club Premier League after leading the table until well into the new year. In Europe, Celtic's return to the Cup Winners' Cup after their nine-year run in that supreme competition ended at the quarter-final stage at the hands of the East German side Sachsenring Zwickau. It was Celtic's first season since 1963/4 without a major honour. On the brighter side, Dalglish and McGrain both had outstanding seasons, and youngsters like Roy Aitken and Tommy Burns were coming through from Celtic Boys Club which had been founded in 1971 to bring talented youngsters under the Celtic wing. Johannes Edvaldsson, an Icelandic international defender, was brought to Celtic Park and became a personality in the eyes of the supporters. So too did John Doyle, a fast and direct winger signed from Ayr United late in the season to strengthen the title challenge, but to no avail.

As early as November 1975, the Celtic directors had been reappraising the position in the light of Stein's injuries. 'The question of whether we had lost forever that vital spark which made the man he was, was still a matter of considerable debate,' the board meeting minutes recorded. 'Time alone will tell.' Two months later, events took a curious twist when director Tom Devlin – Celtic's representative on the SFA – reported to his colleagues that Stein had approached that body to indicate that he was interested in the post of Scotland manager. At a meeting between the directors and Jock Stein at the Ambassador Restaurant on 3 February, the manager 'intimated that if Celtic wanted him, he would be only too happy to stay with the club'.

The following week, the directors considered the possibility of approaching Pat Crerand to return to Celtic Park in Sean Fallon's role, with Fallon taking charge of scouting, but this was not pursued. Instead, two months later, they settled on the name of David McParland – former player with Partick Thistle and now their manager – as the man who was to assist Stein as he returned to his full duties at Celtic Park. At his own request Stein took charge for the first time since the road accident when Celtic played Manchester United in a benefit match for Jimmy Johnstone and Bobby Lennox at the end of the competitive season.

Stein was not consulted about the appointment of David McParland, and was not particularly enthusiastic about it, feeling that the directors should have stayed within the Celtic family to bring in the man who, inevitably, would be looked upon as his own potential successor. But they worked well together during the 1976/7 season, with Stein watching from the touchline as McParland took charge of the physical training and practice games in which the Celtic manager had revelled for so long. In a masterly move, Pat Stanton was bought from Hibs. He had served the Edinburgh club for twelve seasons and had all the experience and midfield drive to make the difference to the transitional Celtic side. Another remarkable signing during this season was of Alfie Conn, from Tottenham Hotspur, though his previous club had been Rangers. Joe Craig, an efficient striker, was bought from Partick Thistle. Happy days returned for the time being to Celtic Park, with another League and Scottish Cup double to conclude (as it would soon transpire) Celtic's catalogue of major honours under Stein's management.

After a tense battle for the League title, Celtic finally triumphed when a Joe Craig volley beat Hibs at Easter Road on 16 April 1977. In the Scottish Cup the early draws favoured Celtic and they disposed of Airdrie, Ayr United and Queen of the South before two Joe Craig goals beat Dundee in the semi-final. The scene was set for a final against Rangers on 7 May, and the attendance figure of 54,252 serves as a reminder that this was a period when public interest in Scottish football had gone into some decline. A penalty goal by Andy Lynch gave Celtic victory in an otherwise disappointing Final. The team that day was: Latchford, McGrain, Lynch, Stanton, MacDonald, Aitken, Dalglish, Edvaldsson, Craig, Wilson and Conn.

The season of 1977/8 was Jock Stein's last as Celtic manager, and it was not a happy one. Even before it had begun, Kenny Dalglish's enormous talents had been transferred to Liverpool. Celtic went on a close-season tour of Australia, and Dalglish was left at home after expressing extreme reluctance to join the party. By now he was determined to leave Celtic Park to seek further fame and fortune in England. Liverpool were quick to spot his absence from the touring party, and moved in for his signature. Stein never tried so hard to keep a player at Celtic Park, and was still pleading with him to think again minutes before the deal was concluded for a £400,000 transfer fee.

On top of this blow, Pat Stanton suffered a knee injury which effectively ended his career – the beginning of a string of mishaps to key players. Danny McGrain dropped out for what was to prove over a year with an ankle injury. Celtic lost the League Cup Final to Rangers, went out of the European Cup in the second round to Innsbruck, departed from the Scottish Cup to non-Premier League Kilmarnock and languished in the League.

On 2 March 1978 the directors held a special 'crisis' meeting with Jock Stein in attendance to discuss the club's lack of success. It was recorded in the minutes:

The chairman mentioned that personnel and staff at Celtic Park was largely the same as it had been 12 years earlier. It was appreciated that long and loyal service had been given by some persons, but the welfare of the club should take priority over personal factors. Mr Stein suggested that David McParland should take control of the first team and that he [Stein] should go with the second team with a view to improving the standard of young players coming through.

The directors turned down this remarkable idea, as they were not prepared to vest that degree of confidence in McParland. But the decisive step had been taken and Celtic were now looking for a new manager – with Jock Stein's support and assistance. On 20 April the meeting reconvened in the North British Hotel and Stein declared that there was only one man who could fill the manager's position at Celtic Park – Billy McNeill. Furthermore, he warned, there was no time to lose as McNeill might very soon be tempted to England if no move was made!

Billy McNeill's absence from football had been brief. He had planned to break from the game and concentrate on developing business interests, particularly in the hotel and leisure industries. But after only a season, he succumbed to a request from Hugh Birt, a friend of long standing, to become involved with Celtic Boys' Club. He immediately discovered that he loved working with the youngsters, and the question of a management job quickly cropped up. He had turned down some good offers during his self-imposed exile, but midway through season 1976/7, Clyde approached him and he took the plunge. Within a few months, ambitious Aberdeen – looking for a replacement for Scotland manager Ally McLeod – came on the scene. McNeill was very happy during his one full season at Pittodrie and, long after he had left, retained a respect and affection for that club. But when Jock Stein eventually tapped him about the Celtic job, at a football writers' dinner in Glasgow, he knew that there was only one place he really wanted to go: 'My heart didn't let me think.' Celtic would start the 1978/9 campaign with a new manager, who had been reared and matured in the club's traditions; the man who had held aloft the European Cup.

At the same meeting at which it was agreed to pursue Jock Stein's recommendation of McNeill as manager – and to terminate with 'golden handshakes' the appointments of David McParland and Sean Fallon – an apparently handsome offer was made to the outgoing manager. The minutes record:

In view of Mr Stein's long and valued service with the club, it was agreed that at the time a new manager was appointed, Mr Stein be offered an executive directorship with the club as recognition and compensation by the club for these services. Mr Stein indicated that he would be very pleased to accept such a directorship which, presuming Mr Stein accepted the Celtic job, would take effect at the time of the club's next annual general meeting.

For whatever reason, it never did. Billy McNeill regrets that he 'did not make it easier' for Jock Stein to stay at Celtic Park by making it unmistakably clear that his advice, far from being resented, would be warmly welcomed and appreciated. Stein may simply have had second thoughts about accepting a 'working directorship' which would have taken him into the commercial side of the business. When, a few months later, he accepted the managership of Leeds United, he said: 'I did not want to stay with Celtic as a director. I felt I had too much to offer football and I wanted a closer involvement.' James Farrell, the only surviving director from that period, is in no doubt that Stein would have made 'an excellent director' and regrets that misunderstanding confused the initiative.

He had always been interested in the commercial side of the club and was very interested in ideas about raising finance. We felt that this was a job he could do very well, and without too much stress – but it was presented in the press as 'selling tickets', which was completely wrong. There was a feeling at that time that Manchester United's lack of success had something to do with Matt Busby staying on at Old Trafford after he had ceased to be manager. Personally, I felt that was a completely false analogy. Jock would have been a genuine father figure.

The sensational news did not break upon Scottish football for another month. On 25 May Celtic made their official move as McNeill was due to head for the United States on Aberdeen business. Three days later, the great Celtic Park transition was announced. Concluding his statement to the press, Desmond White stated: 'Today we go forward with confidence to our centenary ten years away.' An entirely wrong interpretation has been placed on these events, suggesting that Celtic were reacting to the move by Rangers – announced on 24 May – in bringing John Greig back to Ibrox as manager in place of Jock Wallace. The records prove that the Celtic initiative came, coincidentally, to a climax a few days later – but had its roots in the meetings of 2 March and 20 April. No action could be taken, however, until Aberdeen's season was at an end.

On 14 August 1978, Liverpool under Bill Shankly and with Kenny Dalglish in their line-up came to Celtic Park to play in Jock Stein's testimonial match – an emotional occasion, with 55,000 in attendance. Liverpool won the game 3–2. The following evening there was a dinner in the city chambers to salute the great manager, and next day Leeds United's chairman took the opportunity to make overtures to Stein. A week later it was announced that Stein would be moving to Elland Road as manager, and thus ended the most famous of all careers at Celtic Park. Forty-five days later, Stein left Leeds United to become Scotland's team manager in succession to Ally McLeod.

# 19

# SUCCESS UNDER McNEILL
## *And a Temporary Parting*

HE appointment of Billy McNeill as manager was massively popular with the Celtic support, but the team which he inherited was in urgent need of transfusions. Recent signings had been erratic, while the outflow of players since the mid-70s had been debilitating. McNeill quickly made it known to the directors that money would have to be spent, perhaps on a scale which Celtic had not been accustomed to in the past, if success was to be recaptured. At the same time, he took a close interest in the redevelopment of the youth policy which had been the club's pride and joy for so long, but which had faltered somewhat during the '70s. Davie Provan, the winger, was bought from Kilmarnock for £120,000 – a record fee between Scottish clubs – and Murdo MacLeod, a strong midfielder, from Dumbarton for £100,000. Bobby Lennox returned from the United States to the Parkhead fold, while Paul Wilson was sold to Motherwell and Joe Craig to Blackburn Rovers. McNeill told the annual general meeting of shareholders on 3 November 1978 – the day after the £100,000 MacLeod deal was completed – that further purchases would probably be necessary.

There was no instant transformation, however, with early League form uncertain and defeat by Rangers in extra-time of the League Cup semi-final. Out of Europe for the first time since the mid-60s, Celtic were ignominiously removed from the short-lived Anglo-Scottish Cup by Burnley. To Celtic's great advantage, however, an extraordinarily severe winter ensued and League fixtures piled up while McNeill got the house in order. By the time normality was restored in March, Danny McGrain was ready to take his place again after an 18-month absence – and in the captain's role. He had returned to the side in a friendly match against Estoril in Portugal, on a valuable January excursion which helped keep the players match-fit.

During the early part of the League season, no club had broken clear of the pack so that Celtic were still in contention along with Dundee United and Rangers, when the League programme re-commenced. Brushing aside a Scottish Cup defeat by Aberdeen, they hit a good run of League results until meeting Rangers at Hampden early in May, of this extended season. Rangers won 1–0 to take a one point advantage with four games remaining. Celtic pressed on more in hope than expectation, and secured victories over Partick Thistle, St Mirren and Hearts before arriving at their last game of the season – against Rangers at Celtic Park on 21 May. The position was clear. Victory would give Celtic the title while anything less would leave Rangers, with two games still remaining, firmly in the driving seat.

It turned out to be one of the most memorable Celtic performances of recent times. Rangers led 1–0 at half-time and title hopes seemed to have evaporated when Doyle was sent off for retaliation shortly after the interval. Lennox came on as a substitute, and Celtic threw everything into attack. Midway through the half, Roy Aitken headed an equalizer and the Celtic Park roar of encouragement reached new heights. Sensationally, George McCluskey put Celtic 2–1 up after 75 minutes. Now they were 15 minutes away from the title. Joy was short-lived, for Rangers promptly equalized. Seven minutes remaining, and the Rangers defence got into a tangle over a cross from McCluskey. Jackson ended up sending the ball past his own keeper, McCloy. Seldom had the outcome of a League title hung so precariously. If Celtic, with ten men, lost a goal at this stage they were finished. If they could hold firm, the title was theirs. They held firm and, indeed, in the final minute Murdo MacLeod nearly took the roof off McCloy's net with a 20-yard drive which put the issue beyond doubt. It was a night of joy unconfined. Billy McNeill's first season as manager had been climaxed with a League title won in the most dramatic of circumstances. 'It was truly a magnificent affair,' the following week's board meeting agreed. 'Our supporters had been dancing on the terracing, reminiscent of the triumph of 1967.' The Celtic team was: Latchford, McGrain, Lynch, Aitken, McAdam, Edvaldsson, Provan, Conroy (Lennox), McCluskey, MacLeod and Doyle. Roy Aitken, hero of the day, describes it as 'far and away the best game I have played in'.

McNeill knew, however, that the whole Celtic Park set-up still needed strengthening. In his second season as manager there was a quarter-final exit from the League Cup, at the hands of ever-improving Aberdeen. But League progress was good and Celtic were clear leaders as 1980 dawned.

The return to the European Cup had been exciting, with the first expedition to Albania – a country about which little was known by the outside world, and which was not prepared to allow Scottish supporters or journalists in for the game. In spite of these much-publicized features of the trips, the Celtic directors noted that they were 'received with the utmost friendship and courtesy in Tirana' and the team returned home with an acceptable one-goal deficit. Confusion surrounded the Albanian journey to Glasgow for the return leg, as their visas lay unclaimed in Belgrade until they picked them up in the course of the journey to Glasgow. Then they arrived at Heathrow, without having made hotel arrangements but fortunately, director Chris White had travelled south in anticipation of such difficulties. This unusual build-up contributed to a 47,000 crowd assembling at Celtic Park, to give the unworldly Albanians a genuinely warm welcome, and to cheer a 4–1 victory for the home side. Celtic then qualified for the quarter-finals with an unexpectedly tight 3–2 aggregate win over Dundalk, the Irish champions. The prospect of a tie with Real Madrid in March whetted the winter appetite of team and supporters.

In time for the European Cup tie, McNeill plunged into the transfer market to spend £250,000 on bringing Frank McGarvey from Liverpool. It was a club, and indeed Scottish, record fee. All was still well on the home front, with Celtic eight points ahead in the League, when Real Madrid came to Glasgow on 5 March. In front of a 67,000 crowd, goals from McCluskey and Doyle gave Celtic a 2–0 lead. A fortnight later, however, in the frenzied atmosphere of a packed San Bernabeu stadium, Celtic lost an early goal and eventually went out 3–2 on aggregate, bitterly disappointed and aggrieved over weak refereeing. The exit from Europe was bad enough, but it also seemed to trigger a loss of form in the League. On 5 April, Celtic lost to Aberdeen in a game which ended defender Tom McAdam's career after he had suffered concussion. Then they went twice to Dundee, to lose 3–0 to United and 5–1 to the Dens Park club. From a seemingly impregnable position, Celtic were on their way to throwing away the Premier League title, which Aberdeen eventually snatched by a solitary point. On 10 May, however, some amends were made when George McCluskey scored in extra time to beat Rangers 1–0 in the Scottish Cup Final. The team at Hampden that day in front of a 70,303 crowd was: Latchford, Sneddon, McGrain, Aitken, Conroy, MacLeod, Provan, Doyle (Lennox), McCluskey, Burns and McGarvey.

The aftermath of the game provided one of the most disgraceful scenes in recent Scottish football memory, and brought a sentence of great injustice upon Celtic. The joyful Celtic players rushed towards their own supporters at the final whistle, to acknowledge their celebrations. Some Celtic supporters came onto the track, and the area behind the goal. From the other end, however, there came a malevolently-intended invasion. As the SFA's own report acknowledged: 'There was no question of celebration in the minds of the fans who invaded from the west end of the ground. They had violence in mind . . .' A pitched battle ensued, with mounted police charging around the centre of the pitch. The police, in Celtic's view, bore considerable responsibility for having only a few officers on duty at the Celtic end at the final whistle. A more realistic presence could have prevented the small and good-natured incursion. But the SFA made no differentiation between the clubs in the punishment handed out – fines of £20,000 each.

The 1980/1 season opened with a testimonial match against Manchester United for Danny McGrain, ten years after he had entered the Celtic first-team. He may well have ended up at Celtic Park only because a Rangers scout who watched him when he was making a youthful name with Queen's Park Victoria XI assumed (wrongly) that Daniel Fergus McGrain could not possibly be of Protestant stock! During the intervening period, he had come to epitomize the Celtic traditions of boundless energy, considerable skill, determination and loyalty, overcoming his diabetic condition and very serious injuries in the process. By common consent, McGrain was one of the world's best full-backs and he would end up as the most-capped player in Celtic's first century. He had been from the same vintage as Hay, Connelly, Dalglish and Macari but was now the only Celtic Park 'survivor' of that formidable group; proud of the fact that he never asked for a transfer throughout his long career at Celtic Park.

Celtic regained the Premier League title in season 1980/1 – the second such triumph under McNeill's management. But the season had started indifferently and relations between the manager and board, particularly chairman Desmond White, had begun to deteriorate. McNeill, as a player, had got on well with White. 'He was always very kind to me. Half an hour before a European Cup tie, I could ask for a couple of tickets for friends and he would always oblige. It was a good relationship, and I had a lot of respect for Desmond,' McNeill recalls. But McNeill as a manager was ambitious, sometimes impetuous, and sceptical about White's insistence that Celtic lived on a financial knife-edge. Though the supporters knew nothing about it, matters almost came to a head on 14 November 1980, when a pre-meeting between manager and directors took place, immediately before the shareholders' annual general meeting. The business was to 'discuss the gap that had developed between Mr McNeill and the chairman' and the manager was offered the opportunity to resign. He declined. Five days later, Celtic went out of the League Cup to Dundee United.

By January 1981, Desmond White was seeking economies in the running of the club on items such as 'youth trips, Seamill Hydro, scouting and managerial expenses to England, Ireland etc., and petrol consumption'. The club was now a £1 million per year business, and White feared that there could be a substantial loss on the season, partly because of an early and undistinguished exit from the European Cup-Winners Cup to Roumanian opponents. The directors agreed that 'these issues fell on relatively deaf management ears and in our opinion [there was] an unrealistic approach to the seriousness of the problem'. By May, Celtic had won the League title, by seven points from Aberdeen, but had gone out of both the Scottish Cup and League Cup at the semi-final stage to Dundee United. Success had become such a familiar trapping of Celtic Park that a season in which the League title was won was not necessarily regarded as a satisfactory one.

Desmond White complained bitterly at a board meeting that wages had doubled since McNeill's arrival, while gates were going down because of the economic recession in the country. The secretary of the Supporters' Association, George Delaney, was called in for a dressing down. He had written in the *Celtic View* that McNeill must have the directors' full support in buying players and had complained about a rise in the price of season tickets. 'Mr Delaney observed that the supporters thought that Celtic FC had lots of money. The chairman pointed out that possibly the supporters thought that, but that he, Mr Delaney, should know better, as he had information at times not available to the supporters.' In the event, the annual general meeting held in September 1981 heard that the club had broken even.

There was clearly a gulf between the McNeill approach, and the fiscal caution which Desmond White believed to be essential to the club's long-term well-being. McNeill tried to re-build a bridge when he told the annual meeting in September 1981 that he had been one of the Kelly Kids and he would like to see now a group of White Kids. The Celtic Boys' Club was playing an increasingly important part in that process, while John Kelman had taken charge of scouting the previous year. Season 1980/1 had seen the emergence of Charlie Nicholas as an enormous creative and goal-scoring talent – 'the most exciting player I have ever worked with,' says McNeill – while Pat Bonner, from Co. Donegal, had been confirmed as a first-class goalkeeper after Peter Latchford was injured, and Mark Reid emerged as a valuable home-reared defender. But by this time, the differences between manager and chairman had been exacerbated by matters unrelated to money. McNeill had run into a series of disciplinary problems, both for indiscreet comments about referees, and over a too-public altercation with a journalist for which the club fined him £500. Looking back on this period, McNeill admits that he was trying to be the club's greatest supporter as well as its manager. The austere Desmond White found such incidents unacceptable, and tensions mounted.

In spite of this background, season 1981/2 produced Celtic's 33rd League Championship success and the third in four campaigns under McNeill. They led from the start and ended up two points ahead of Aberdeen. Though both Frank McGarvey and Charlie Nicholas sustained leg-breaks in the course of this season, a relatively settled side had developed under McNeill, with Bonner, Reid and MacLeod ever-present throughout. McGrain, Aitken, McAdam, Sullivan, Burns and McCluskey were not far behind. It was a very good blend of youth and experience and a teenager with a famous Celtic surname attracted instant rave notices – Paul McStay made his first-team debut against Queen of the South in a Scottish Cup tie on 23 January 1982, and was soon playing with the midfield guile of a veteran. Once again, however, the cup competitions proved unrewarding. Celtic went out of the European Cup in the first round to Juventus, going down 2–0 in Italy after Murdo MacLeod had given them a slender first-leg lead. In the League Cup, they failed to qualify from their section for the quarter-finals and in the Scottish Cup, there was a fourth round defeat by Aberdeen.

The last day of the League season was reached with Celtic needing to avoid defeat by St Mirren in order to be sure of retaining the title. The situation was that, if Celtic lost 1–0, a five goal victory for Aberdeen over Rangers at Pittodrie would be enough to give them the title. By half-time, there were no goals at Celtic Park while Aberdeen were 4–0 up! It was not until the 63rd minute that George McCluskey scored the goal which relieved the tension, and Celtic finished as 3–0 winners. At the end of the game, the Celtic support tempered the joy of the occasion by chanting the name of Johnny Doyle, the popular winger who had been killed by an electrical accident in his home early in the season.

Having led Celtic to three Premier League titles and one Scottish Cup success during his four seasons as manager, Billy McNeill's tenure should have been extremely secure. In fact, however, relationships were still very difficult behind the Celtic Park façade. The following season opened with the directors taking umbrage over reported comments by the manager, in Holland for a warm-up tournament, about the need to buy two defenders and the board's alleged unwillingness to part with the necessary money. It was agreed to call McNeill before a board meeting in order that he might learn of the directors' displeasure. According to the minute of the meeting held on 26 August 1982, the directors told the manager that they did not want a repeat of such publicity. He responded that he was not responsible for the headlines that appeared. 'The directors unanimously interpreted such outpourings to the press as an obvious attempt to bring pressure on them to spend.'

In season 1982/3, Celtic raced to a League Cup triumph, goals from Nicholas and MacLeod helping them to a 2–1 victory over Rangers in the Hampden Final of 4 December. By then, however, they were again out of the European Cup in spite of having secured one of their best European results in years – a 4–3 aggregate victory over Ajax, Cruyff and all, in the first round after being held to a 2–2 draw at Celtic Park. George McCluskey scored the winning goal in Amsterdam – another reminder of just how significant a player he was during a period when he tended to be over-shadowed by other more publicized figures. Celtic then faced Real Sociedad of Spain with some confidence, but two late goals in the away leg left them with an uphill struggle at Celtic Park. Celtic's commitment to attack led to the loss of a goal midway through the first-half and, though they won the leg 2–1, they were out of Europe in anti-climactic circumstances.

The battle for the Premier League title was a particularly exciting one, with Dundee United, Aberdeen and Celtic racing neck and neck from start to finish. There was the first New Year's Day victory at Ibrox in 62 years to enthuse over – 2–1 with goals from McStay and Nicholas – but Celtic were dropping too many points against moderate opposition. Their hopes of a third title in a row were eventually destroyed inside three April days – a 3–2 home defeat from Dundee United and a Mark McGhee goal which beat them at Pittodrie took the initiative away from Celtic. On the last day of the season, they were dependent on United slipping up in a Dens Park derby. It did not happen and, although Celtic finished with a memorable 4–2 win over Rangers at Ibrox after being 2–0 down, United's 2–1 victory gave them their first ever title by a point.

In mid-April, Celtic had lost the Scottish Cup semi-final to Aberdeen by a single goal. Charlie Nicholas was missing from the side and this fuelled rumours that his days at Celtic Park were drawing rapidly to a close. Behind the scenes, Billy McNeill was involved in a vigorous rearguard action to keep him, and a remarkable package was put together. Nicholas was offered £400 per week; a £20,000 signing-on fee; a £20,000 interest-free loan and £10,000 to be paid into a pension fund, to yield him £170,000 at the age of 35. The lure of London was too strong, however, and Nicholas signed for Arsenal on 9 June 1983. For Billy McNeill, it was a bitter blow. 'I told Charlie as a manager and as a friend that it wasn't the right thing for him to do at that time,' he recalls.

The month of June 1983 really was an extraordinary one at Celtic Park. First, while McNeill was on holiday, a telephone call to Celtic Park informed the club that Sunderland were willing to sell striker Ally McCoist for £210,000. The significance of the call was not appreciated, and no action was taken. 'There appeared to be a lack of proper negotiations on our part,' the directors concluded. McCoist signed for Rangers instead, with devastating effect. When Nicholas finally opted for Highbury, Billy McNeill promptly signed Brian McClair from Motherwell for £70,000, and re-signed Murdo MacLeod and Mark Reid, both of whom had been looking for improved terms. A Rangers bid for MacLeod had been in the offing. Towards the end of the month, reports appeared about the fact that Manchester City had been showing an interest in obtaining McNeill's own services, at a salary of around £40,000. The *Sunday Mail* of 27 June carried a story which speculated about the manager's dissatisfaction over his level of remuneration, but which contained only one direct quote. 'I find it disappointing that I've never been offered a contract by my present employers,' McNeill was quoted as saying. The back-page story might have been a rather naïve attempt to force Celtic's hand, but it had quite the opposite effect. All the tensions which had developed between manager and chairman during the previous three years now exploded.

At 1 p.m. the following day, the Celtic directors – apart from Jack McGinn, who was on holiday – met in the Ambassador Restaurant to determine their response to the *Sunday Mail* interview. The meeting then moved to Desmond White's office in Bath Street and McNeill was summoned to be present. An uncompromising message was spelt out to him. No Celtic manager in the past had felt the need of a contract, and they were not prepared to negotiate one with McNeill. Neither were the directors prepared to discuss wages with him. McNeill recalls: 'That Monday, when I went up to meet the board of directors, I could not believe what was happening.' A public negotiating gambit had backfired. His position as Celtic manager was now impossible, and three days later he joined Manchester City. Desmond White's justification of the club's response was minuted thus: 'No man is greater than Celtic and had we acceded to Mr McNeill's demands there would have been, in our opinion, no living with the manager.' The affair gave rise to fierce debate in the press and wherever Celtic supporters met, with McNeill gaining general support in the court of public opinion.

In the long run, his departure may have been in the manager's own best interests. He would return to Celtic Park four years later, with a wider range of experience and a more relaxed temperamental approach. 'But at the time,' he recalls, 'I was very bitter. That bitterness lasted for about a year. I found it difficult to understand what had happened and I still think there were outside influences at work, driving the wedge between myself and the chairman.' He also recognizes, however, that the faults in letting relationships drift towards the final break-down were not all on one side. Public reaction to the affair dismayed Desmond White. He remained convinced that the club had treated McNeill fairly, and that the application of bargaining pressure through the media was something that could not be tolerated. For him, it was really as simple as that. In the present author's last conversation with him, White reflected on his many years of good relations with McNeill and puzzled over where it had all gone wrong. Two strong wills had met, and the outcome was to neither's satisfaction.

On 4 July 1983, David Hay was appointed as Celtic manager with Frank Connor – a former Celtic reserve goalkeeper, who had returned to the club as a reserve coach – as his assistant. John Clark, who had expected to be offered the managerial position on McNeill's departure, left with a golden handshake. Hay was well enough regarded by the Celtic support, but his managerial pedigree was modest. He had been with Motherwell for just one season and had led them to promotion, but had then decided to move to another job in the United States, before the Celtic offer came along. George McCluskey was the next admired face to leave Celtic Park; he was sold to Leeds for £140,000 in mid-July. In the early days of season 1983/4, Hay signed Jim Melrose – a former Partick Thistle favourite – from Coventry and full-back Brian Whittaker from Thistle. Jimmy Johnstone returned to Celtic Park as a part-time coach. In November, the very promising Stirling Albion forward, John Colquoun, moved to Celtic Park.

But the season turned out to be a disappointment, with Celtic finishing as runners-up in each of the three major domestic tournaments. Aberdeen had become the leading lights of Scottish football and won the League with seven points to spare. In the Scottish Cup Final, Alex Ferguson's formidable side completed the double by beating Celtic 2–1 in extra time, after Roy Aitken had been sent off early in the game. A remarkable League Cup Final had been lost 3–2 to Rangers in extra time. Celtic came back from 2–0 down to equalize with an 89th minute penalty, but McCoist completed his hat-trick during the additional period. In the UEFA Cup, Celtic beat Aarhus of Denmark and, more memorably, Sporting Lisbon thanks to a 5–0 second-leg win in Glasgow, before losing 2–1 at home to Brian Clough's Nottingham Forest after a goalless first leg. The fact that no honours were won in Hay's first season did nothing to remove the doubts of the supporters, though 31 goals from Brian McClair confirmed the wisdom of McNeill's last signing, and Paul McStay's consistent brilliance prompted reports that Inter Milan were prepared to pay £2 million for him.

At the end of the season, Whittaker was sold to Hearts and Hay signed a forward, Alan McInally, from Ayr United. Hay made approaches for David Narey of Dundee United, Neale Cooper of Aberdeen and even Joe Jordan of Verona, but none of these came to anything. The supporters were restive, particularly when Celtic went out of the League Cup at the hands of Dundee United, but there was general approval when Hay succeeded in signing Maurice Johnston, a lethal striker who had gone south from Partick Thistle to Watford little more than a year earlier. The fee of £400,000 was a Scottish record. Aberdeen were clearly the best side in Scotland at this time, and they again won the Premier League by seven clear points from Celtic. However, Hay's first success as Celtic manager came on 18 May 1985, when the team came from behind to win the 100th Scottish Cup Final in a breathtaking confrontation with Dundee United at Hampden Park. Most who were there still cannot fathom how Celtic managed to come back from the dead.

United were a goal ahead and suffering no threat when Davie Provan, just

14 minutes from the end, sent a perfect free-kick inside the left-hand post of goalkeeper Hamish McAlpine to equalize. Eight minutes later, Frank McGarvey simply bowed his head to connect with a cross from Roy Aitken and the ball flew home for the winner. Given Celtic's uncanny penchant for success on special occasions, victory was perhaps pre-ordained. Celtic supporters did not, however, interpret this isolated success as evidence of renaissance. Indeed, the season had been marked by an episode which was to blight Hay's brief career as Celtic manager and lead, effectively, to two seasons of unhappy failure in European competition – the yardstick by which the supporters measured the quality of each Celtic side, season by season.

As fiascos go, Celtic's Cup-winners Cup confrontations with Rapid Vienna in the winter of 1984 were collectors' items. Celtic had beaten Ghent in the first round, but then ran into a rough-house in Vienna. The Austrians won 3–1, but it was the manner of accomplishment which outraged the Celtic party. A savagely high tackle by Kienast, Rapid's resident delinquent, put Frank McGarvey out of the game. Yet only Alan McInally was sent off, for his first foul of the game. The Austrian team's behaviour was inflamed by the touchline promptings of their Yugoslav coach, Otto Baric, a man who had immersed himself in the waters of controversy at other times and in other places. Two weeks later in Glasgow, Celtic turned on an inspired performance and goals from McClair and MacLeod had equalized the tie on aggregate by half-time. Then Tommy Burns scored a third goal in the 68th minute, and all hell broke loose.

Burns had won the chase for a 50–50 ball with goalkeeper Ehn, prompting outrageous Austrian protests. Very soon afterwards, the brutal Kienast floored Burns with the referee unsighted, but was sent off on the testimony of a linesman. It seemed impossible that the referee could order him off without awarding a penalty, but he did. The referee's incredible tolerance of Rapid's protests undoubtedly helped to lead to serious trouble. With 14 minutes remaining. Celtic were awarded a penalty and the game was stopped for 10 minutes as players and officials argued and gesticulated near to the Jungle touchline. Eventually, missiles were thrown and Weinhofer, the Rapid substitute, collapsed holding his head. Television pictures seemed to confirm that he had not been struck, and an ambulance-man at the scene swore that there was no sign of injury. But the ruse was to succeed. Peter Grant missed the penalty, Celtic won on aggregate – and Weinhofer left the ground with his head swathed in bandages.

The news of a protest to UEFA by the Austrians surprised nobody, but confidence in Glasgow was high, and proved justified when the European authorities found in Celtic's favour on every count except one. The Scots were fined £4,000 and Rapid £5,000, while Kienast was suspended for four matches and manager Baric banned from the touchline for three European matches because of his behaviour. But, because the UEFA Committee vote had been split – information to which none of the parties should have been privy in any case – the Austrians were encouraged to appeal.

Nobody could believe it when the appeal – heard by only three members of a 21-strong committee with some claiming they knew nothing of the meeting – was upheld. Despite the fact that Rapid officials (including their doctor) changed their testimony three times, the match was ordered to be replayed at least 100 miles from Celtic Park and, to complete the perverse way in which the business was handled, the original fine imposed on Rapid was doubled.

The play-off took place at Old Trafford, home of Manchester United, in front of 51,500 and the football – with Celtic sadly out of form and Pacult scoring the only goal – was the least notable element of the match. For the first time in their distinguished European history, Celtic had officially lost both legs of a tie. More seriously, two spectators, in separate incidents, committed assaults on two Austrian players in circumstances which made the local police look shamefully neglectful.

The first man was allowed to climb a fence and run fifty yards before knocking goalkeeper Feurer to the ground in his own goal. The second was actually in custody – being held by the arms at the touchline near the players' tunnel – when he was allowed to swing his leg and kick goalscorer Pacult as he left the field at the end. That meant another worrying afternoon in Zurich, as UEFA deliberated this latest incident. But Celtic's and their fans' generally impressive record over the years prevented the dreaded ban. The club was fined £17,000 and ordered to play their next home European match behind closed doors. It was rather a malodorous sequence of events which left many Celtic men uneasy about the way the directors and management of the club had handled the entire affair, most notably their unseemly haste to agree to the play-off. Most of those who had been at Celtic Park for the second match had argued that the club should make a dignified withdrawal in protest, rather than effectively admit guilt to an offence which appeared not to have been committed.

The season ended on a high note with the Scottish Cup victory over Dundee United. But, as Hay searched for a title-winning side, he sold John Colquhoun to Hearts – a serious misjudgement as it transpired – Mark Reid to Charlton and Frank McGarvey to St Mirren. The UEFA injustice had its impact on the following season, also. Celtic were drawn in the Cup-Winners Cup against Atletico Madrid and a Mo Johnston goal secured a good 1–1 draw in Spain. The return leg on 2 October had to be played behind closed doors, as part of the Old Trafford punishment, and Celtic flopped in the unreal atmosphere of a virtually empty stadium. A first half goal put Atletico in a strong position and when Celtic went 3–1 down on aggregate after 71 minutes, the writing was on the wall. Roy Aitken pulled back one goal but there was no prospect of Celtic winning an aggregate lead. It was, without doubt, one of the most miserable afternoons spent at Celtic Park in many a long year, and the harshest retribution of all for the club's minimal responsibility for the Rapid Vienna mess. Celtic went out of the League Cup early, losing to Hibs in a penalty shoot-out in the quarter-final after a 4–4 draw. The Edinburgh club also triumphed in the Scottish Cup quarter-final tie, a last-minute goal giving them a 4–3 win over Celtic.

These undistinguished reverses heightened the sense of unease which had prevailed among the Celtic support since McNeill's sudden departure. A few good youngsters – notably defender Derek Whyte – were breaking through into the first team. But, in spite of the presence of high quality players like Burns, McClair, McStay and Johnston, the feeling persisted that Celtic were well short of having a top-class side. David Hay's laid-back approach sometimes appeared to be carried to excess, and he was left in sole command when he parted company with assistant manager Frank Connor in February 1986. Hay was a pleasant and thoughtful man, who preferred to treat players as adults and felt ill at ease with Connor's rough diamond approach. However, he did not always communicate effectively and his reliance on the players' own common sense was sometimes ill-rewarded. The impression developed of a club which lacked direction and discipline. Quite unexpectedly, however, Celtic won the Premier League title on the last day of season 1985/6 – as effective a way as any of heading off criticism in the short-term.

After a poor start to the season, Hearts hit a great streak of form and were on top by the turn of the year. Celtic took only 22 points from their first 18 games but the cut-throat nature of the competition meant that they were still well in touch. However, Hearts continued to go well until they started to drop nervous points in the last few games of the season, while Celtic put in a strong finish. The last day was reached on 3 May 1986, with Celtic needing to win handsomely against St Mirren at Love Street – and then depend on Hearts losing to Dundee at Dens Park. That was precisely what happened. Two goals from Brian McClair, two from Mo Johnston and one from Paul McStay put Celtic 5–0 up after 54 minutes. It was a performance with which no team in the country could have lived. With Celtic's part of the job done in style, attention on the Love Street terraces turned almost exclusively to the transistor radios. To the grief of the Hearts supporters, their team conceded two goals inside the final seven minutes. It was Celtic's title – and the terracing celebrations were of Lisbon vintage. Even in these extraordinary circumstances, David Hay found it difficult to be demonstrative.

# 20

# WHO OWNS CELTIC?
## *Shareholdings and Personalities*
## *through the Years*

NE of the myths about the story of Celtic is that some form of secrecy surrounds the question of who owns the club. Nothing could be further from the truth, since the entire picture of shareholding in Celtic is a matter of public record, freely available at Companies House in Edinburgh. Celtic were incorporated as a private limited company in 1897 with a nominal share capital of £5000, in 5000 shares of £1 each. There were, at that time, 201 members of the club and each was allocated a £1 share. In recognition of his outstanding services, John Glass was awarded an additional 100 fully paid-up shares, so that 301 were initially distributed. The remaining 4699 were sold to members for ten shillings each, according to ability to purchase. A further share issue of 5000 £1 shares was created in the following year, to raise capital for the club. Once again these were sold for ten shillings, so that there were then 301 fully-paid and 9699 half-paid shares in circulation.

Inevitably, the great majority of share-buyers were the businessmen of Glasgow's East End. The men who emerged from these early issues as the largest shareholders in Celtic were to be the initiators of lines of succession which have survived to the present day. This was true of James Grant, an Irish publican and engineer who had made his fortune mining diatomite in the Antrim hills and who had acquired 801 shares – almost one-twelfth of the total – by 1898. James Kelly, the player turned publican, held 450 shares by the same time. The Glass shares would soon act as a foundation for the

174

White interest in the club, while the Shaughnessy shares have served to retain the Celtic connection within the law firm which continues to carry that name. The full list of significant Celtic shareholders in 1897 and 1898, with addresses, occupations and shareholdings in each year is shown in the table below.

There were at that time many shareholders who held only one or two shares in the club. Many of these have also been retained within families, for sentimental reasons, down to the present day. Movement of these small shareholdings has not generally been a significant factor within the club's affairs, though there is evidence that Willie Maley – who had not been one of the original large shareholders – did build up a substantial holding by the

**Breakdown of Celtic shareholdings, 1897/8**

| Name | 1897 | 1898 | Occupation | Address |
| --- | --- | --- | --- | --- |
| John Allison | 100 | 200 | Masseur | 40 Hyde St, Manchester |
| James Cairns | – | 400 | – | 14 South Portland St |
| John Campbell | – | 100 | – | 379 Saracen St |
| John Colgan | 100 | 200 | Cattle dealer | 48 Whitehill St |
| Thomas Colgan | 150 | 300 | Publican | 16 Whitehill St |
| James Cronin | – | 100 | – | Bridge St, Alexandria |
| Bernard Crossan | 100 | 100 | Grocer | 12 Graeme St |
| Michael Docherty | 100 | 100 | Comm. agent | 161 Stockwell St |
| David Doyle | – | 100 | – | Bellshill |
| Michael Dunbar | 150 | 300 | Publican | 429 Gallowgate |
| Thomas Dunbar | 100 | 250 | Salesman | 429 Gallowgate |
| William Flynn | 200 | 400 | Comm. agent | 125 Hospital St |
| John Glass | 100 | 401 | Manager | 597 Gallowgate |
| Patrick Glass | 200 | 401 | Builder | Fairholm Villa, Shawlands |
| James Grant | 400 | 801 | Publican | 49 St Vincent St |
| James Kelly | 200 | 450 | Publican | Stonefield, Blantyre |
| Terence Lynch | 100 | 100 | Brewer | Crownpoint |
| Alex McCann | – | 100 | – | Bellshill |
| David McKillop | – | 100 | – | Kilmarnock |
| James McKillop | 100 | 200 | Egg merchant | 45 Apsley Pl |
| John McKillop | 200 | 400 | Publican | West Nile St |
| William McKillop | 200 | 400 | Restaurateur | West Nile St |
| John H. McLaughlin | 150 | 300 | Publican | Hamilton |
| David McLoskey | 200 | 400 | Traveller | Antrim Terr., Belfast |
| Thomas Moore | – | 100 | – | 97 Quarry St, Hamilton |
| Thomas Nelson | 100 | 200 | Cattle dealer | Bellgrove |
| John O'Hara | 100 | 300 | Publican | 351 Gallowgate |
| Peter Paterson | – | 100 | – | High St |
| John Rafferty | 100 | 201 | Fish salesman | Fish market |
| Joseph Shaughnessy | 300 | 651 | Lawyer | 83 Bath St |
| Peter Souness | – | 100 | – | Motherwell |
| John Warnock | 100 | 201 | Publican | 568 Springburn Rd |

1930s through small acquisitions, his position as club secretary putting him in a strong position to do this. In general, however, the pattern has been of the big shareholdings acting as magnets to further significant blocks of shares, reinforcing the pattern of control by a few families.

This process has been assisted at various points in the club's history by amendments to its constitution. Article 18 of the first Articles of Association in 1897 stated: 'The Executors or Administrators of the deceased shall be the only persons recognised by the Company as having any title to his share.' There was no control over whom the shareholding could subsequently be transferred to. But to this was added Article 18A by a special resolution at the annual general meeting of 1933. This decreed that the executor of a deceased shareholder's estate must notify the club within six months of whom the shares were to be transferred to. The nominated person would then 'require to be approved of by the directors, and failing a tender of such transfer within the said period, the directors shall have the right to purchase the holding of the deceased member either on their own behalf or on behalf of any other shareholder of the Company'. This tightened the directors' grip over whom shares could be transferred to, and effectively eliminated the prospect of any unwelcome 'outsider' acquiring a significant stake in Celtic. In 1947 the time limit for transfers was reduced to three months.

The list of directors with shareholdings in 1901 was as follows:

J. H. McLaughlin 300; John Glass 301; John O'Hara 390; John McKillop 460; James Grant 801; Michael Dunbar 372; James Kelly 560.

The O'Hara lineage was first to go when John O'Hara, the club's first secretary at its inception, died in 1904 and most of the family shareholding went to John Glass. His place on the board was taken by a Belfast man – Thomas Colgan, described as a publican but with varied business interests in Glasgow, who would soon marry into the Grant family. He and his brother John – a well-known cattle dealer in Belfast – had been shareholders from the outset.

John Glass died in 1906. By curious coincidence, Celtic's founding president passed away within a few days of the Irish hero of whom he had been a close associate and who had laid the centre turf at the new Celtic Park. The connection was recognized in the *Glasgow Star and Examiner*'s headline: 'The Deaths of Michael Davitt and John Glass'. Of Glass, the obituarist wrote that the Home Rule movement had lost 'one of its oldest, most loyal and generous members', while 'in sporting circles, he was a central and admired figure', never missing a Celtic meeting since the club's inception. John H. McLaughlin went further and described Glass as 'the founder and originator of the club'. It was at this point that Thomas White entered the scheme of things.

White was Glass's protégé, both in Irish political circles and in relation to

Celtic. The Home Government Branch of the Irish National League had taken over the *Glasgow Star and Examiner* in 1903, and White, who had briefly been chairman of the Branch, became a director – thus embarking on a publishing connection that was to be lifelong. Yet when he became a director of Celtic in 1906, after inheriting Glass's 401 shares, he was only twenty-two years of age, yet already a qualified lawyer. Of Irish origins, his family was already well established in Glasgow and his widowed mother owned a scrap-metal business in Dennistoun. The young Tom White would organize the affairs of the business each morning, before heading off to his law classes at Glasgow University and his wider public activities.

Another of the club's founders, Joseph Shaughnessy, also died in 1906. He had been a bailie in Rutherglen and legal adviser to Celtic from the start. He was also, the obituary noted, 'constantly consulted by the leaders of the trade unions in Scotland'. His son John subsequently succeeded him on the board.

In 1909, another strong link with the earliest days was broken through the death of John H. McLaughlin, only in his forties. For someone who apparently knew nothing of football in 1888, he had made a remarkable contribution not only to Celtic but to the development of football in Scotland, having championed the cause of open professionalism and the creation of a Scottish League. His shareholding was broken up, and no member of that family subsequently held office within Celtic – though an interest has survived to the present day.

The most active acquirer of shares in the pre-First World War period was James Kelly, who had become chairman in 1909. A man of extensive business interests – including the cinema in its pioneer days – he appears to have bought out William Flynn, a commission agent, who had been another of the early large shareholders. Tom White, who succeeded Kelly as chairman, was also building up his interest from several sources. The deaths of John McKillop and James Grant, both founding directors, in 1914 left only James Kelly and Michael Dunbar of the original board. An interesting name flits briefly across the scene in the same year, with Pat McGinn, an egg merchant of 22 Maitland Street, acquiring 370 shares from an Irish source – although the present-day chairman declines to claim this as proof of a long-standing family involvement!

In 1920 there was another issue of shares, raising the nominal share-capital value of the club from £10,000 to £25,000, although only 10,000 of the new £1 shares were taken up. All of these were fully paid, and distributed almost exclusively among existing shareholders on a pro rata basis.

The powerful McKillop shareholding was recognized in 1921 when John McKillop, an insurance agent, was elected to the board on the death of Michael Dunbar. Otherwise, the directorship remained unchanged during the 1920s and there were no major shifts in the balance of power. The death of James Kelly in 1931 led to his son Robert being made a director in his place, and to a division of the large Kelly shareholding among at least six members of the family. It seems very likely that the amendment to the constitution, to require directors' approval of share transfers, was prompted at this time by the steady rise in Willie Maley's share interest. By 1932 he owned 228 shares and acted as trustee for a further 212. Maley's position as secretary put him in the front line for information about potential share transfers – a situation of which he took advantage, and which contributed to a deteriorating relationship between himself and Tom White. The requirement to transfer shares within six months or else risk having them pass to directors or their nominees seems to have prompted James Grant's executor – Thomas Colgan, who had been sitting on the former director's shareholding for twenty years – to transfer a large part of it to Thomas Devlin, a trawler owner from Leith, in 1933.

The next significant development was the retirement of Tom Colgan to Toomebridge in 1940. (John McKillop retired from the board the following year but there was no replacement for either, the opportunity being taken to cut the number of directors to three – Tom White, Robert Kelly and John Shaughnessy.) The 'Toomebridge connection' is complex but important. Tom Colgan had married in 1906 a daughter of James Grant, whose family roots were in Toomebridge. However, Mrs Colgan died on the birth of their daughter Mary a short time later. From a young age, Mary lived at Toome House, Toomebridge, with her aunt and uncle – Neil and Felicia Grant, both of whom were unmarried. From the 1920s to the 1950s, Mary and her aunt Felicia would make occasional expeditions to Glasgow for major Celtic occasions although, according to surviving relatives, the ladies' interest in the sport was distinctly limited. Mary's cousin, Brian Grant, recalls joining in these expeditions, which took the Toomebridge party to the Bank Restaurant before and after the game, on to the team bus and even into the dressing rooms! When Tom Colgan retired both from business in Glasgow and as a Celtic director in 1940, he took up residence in Toome House with his daughter and the Grants. He died in 1946 and the Colgan shares were left to Mary who thus became – when the transfer was completed in 1949 – the holder of 1103 fully-paid and 1150 part-paid shares, making her the 'third force' in Celtic behind only the Kellys and Whites.

Tom White died in 1947 at the age of sixty-three, never having fully recovered from an attack of pneumonia which had been brought about by his bravely rescuing a bather from the sea. In later life he had concentrated upon his law practice and his Celtic interest, although his political and social interests had not entirely subsided. He had been a very close friend and associate of John Wheatley, the first Labour Minister of Health whose other crucial contribution to British politics had been to argue successfully for the compatibility of socialism with Catholicism at a time when the church hierarchy was resistant to that concept. Wheatley was a partner in the printing firm of Hoxon and Walsh, which was involved in the Labour movement and church work, as well as publishing the *Glasgow Eastern Standard*. Shortly after the First World War the firm found itself in difficulty and Wheatley sought Tom White's advice. The Celtic chairman joined the business and remained involved until the time of his death. A fluent and witty orator, he was very much in the tradition of the Celtic pioneers as a man with many dimensions to his character.

Desmond White became a director on the death of his father, while Tom Devlin Jnr also joined the board in 1949. After Col. Shaughnessy's death in 1953, after 41 years as a director, the Kelly–White–Devlin triumvirate sustained itself without additions until 1963. Meanwhile the Toomebridge connection had moved on a few stages – with the ultimate effect of concentrating a huge Celtic shareholding in the hands of one elderly Irishwoman. Sean Fallon recalls, from a team tour of Ireland during the early 1950s, being told by Robert Kelly that the two ladies, Felicia Grant and Mary Colgan, had expressed a desire to meet the 'three Irish boys' in the team – Peacock, Tully and Fallon. The chairman then took them to visit Toome House. A local hotel which the Grant family owned was also a regular stopping-place for Celtic parties over many years.

In 1956 Mary Colgan died, shortly after returning from a trip to the United States with Felicia. The Colgan shareholding was divided between her aunt and uncle. Then the substantial McCloskey shareholding in Belfast also passed to the Grants. As a result of all this, when Neil Grant died in the early 1960s his sister Felicia found herself the owner of 1705 fully-paid and 1752 half-paid Celtic shares – the biggest ownership block, accounting for more than one-sixth of the total shares issued. The fact that Robert Kelly, whose own family holding was of a similar size, maintained a very close personal relationship with the Toomebridge shareholders, and held their proxies, ensured that his power base within the club was unchallengeable throughout the period of his chairmanship. These are the facts behind the legend of the 'old lady in Ireland' who, according to the vague awareness of a generation of Celtic supporters, held the ultimate say in the club's fortunes.

The first 'new name' on the board for more than thirty years was added in 1964, when James Farrell – a partner in the Shaughnessy law firm – was invited to become a director, and was given clearance to acquire 534 former Shaughnessy shares which were at that time held in trust. He had just been instrumental in bringing to fruition the Celtic Development Fund, which would later attract large amounts of money into the club's coffers for the specific purpose of financing ground improvements. The board remained four-strong throughout the next memorable decade in the club's history.

Robert Kelly was knighted in 1969 in the wake of the European Cup triumph, and stepped down from the chairmanship a few months before his death in 1971 to make way for Desmond White. Sir Robert was the club's first president when he died. The Archbishop of Glasgow, the Most Reverend James Donald Scanlan, said at his funeral: 'His finest quality was his unshakeable determination, exemplified by his father before him, to maintain the highest standards in the face of adverse criticism and niggling opposition . . . He and his fellow directors had never forgotten that the Celtic Football Club was founded in the cause of charity.' This was indeed true, and it is perhaps an appropriate point at which to comment upon Celtic's respect for the charitable aspect of the club's tradition.

Over the years, Celtic have contributed very large amounts to charitable causes – both by playing games on behalf of specific funds and, more generally, by quietly giving donations in response to routine appeals and, occasionally, major disaster funds. Sean Fallon, who attended board meetings over many years, recalls that 'there was never a meeting which didn't end with agreement to give donations here and there'. It is a practice which is well maintained up to the present day and while nobody claims that Celtic's prime reason for existing is to raise money for charity – an unworldly expectation – there cannot be any football club in Britain or beyond which can claim anywhere near their record as givers to causes outside football.

In 1973 Felicia Grant died in St John's Nursing Home, Belfast – and so a substantial part of the Grant/Colgan shareholding returned to a member of the family in Scotland. She left half of her shareholding – 852 fully-paid and 877 part-paid shares – to her nephew James Grant, a seafarer with his home in Stepps, Lanarkshire. The son of her brother Tommy Joe, a colourful character who had departed for Canada many years previously, Mr Grant was the chief engineer on board a vessel berthed in Leningrad when news reached him that he had inherited a large Celtic shareholding – though it was far short of the 5000 shares reported at the time. The suggestion that he had overnight become the largest Celtic shareholder made good copy, but it was well wide of the mark. The less spectacular truth was that shares had been accruing steadily over the post-war years to the directors and their families, and by the mid 1970s the White, Kelly and Devlin shareholdings each substantially outweighed Mr Grant's remarkable inheritance. The remaining Grant shares were scattered amongst ten other relatives of Miss Felicia Grant, in County Antrim, Ontario and Michigan!

In 1982 two new directors were appointed – Desmond White's son Christopher and Jack McGinn, the club's commercial manager who had gone to the Celtic board in the early 1960s with the idea of creating a newspaper called the *Celtic View*. Having received official blessing for the then novel idea of a club newspaper, he edited it from 1965 to 1979 when he was appointed commercial manager. The integrity and competence of service which he provided to the club was recognized through an invitation to join the board. McGinn had held no shares in the club prior to becoming a director. This was a real break with the Celtic tradition of keeping directorships within a very close circle, based on the 'lines of inheritance'. Subsequently, Tom Grant – son of James Grant who had inherited the 'Irish' shares – was also co-opted. A young man with a lively interest in football, he renewed the Grant presence in the Celtic boardroom after a break of almost seventy years.

Desmond White died in 1985 after fourteen years as chairman. Again, he had lived a varied life, which allowed him to place football in a wider social context. As his *Celtic View* obituary observed:

In an age when too many mediocrities see football as a well-publicised avenue to self-aggrandisement, Desmond White was the absolute contrast – a well-rounded human being whose prime interest happened to lie in football. Where else would one find the chairman of a football club who read avidly of science and astronomy in his leisure time; who could speak of having found his deepest sense of contact with the infinite at the tops of mountains; who had the perspective on life and human behaviour which can only come from such diversity of interests?

White had exercised positive influence on a whole range of matters crucial to Scottish football, during a period when its future was by no means secure. He had a good claim to being regarded as the architect of the Premier League; he had put Celtic in the forefront of a campaign to save Hampden Park as Scotland's national stadium; he was an influential member of the MacElhone Committee which advanced the ideas for countering crowd trouble at Scottish football grounds that were subsequently embraced in the Criminal Justice (Scotland) Act. During the last years of his life he sustained a highly effective campaign for rating parity between Scottish properties and those in the rest of the UK. His prime concern was for football grounds, but the ramifications went far wider. The last game which he saw before his death, while on holiday in Greece, was the one in which Celtic won the 100th Scottish Cup Final.

On Desmond White's death in 1985, the mantle of chairman passed to Tom Devlin who had served quietly as a director for thirty-six years. It was an appointment which crowned his Celtic connection but proved to be regrettably brief, as he died just over a year later. At this point the directors turned to Jack McGinn – already a full-time worker for the club, who had succeeded Devlin as vice-chairman and whom they saw as the man best able to fulfil a modern chairman's role at Celtic Park. It was an appointment that McGinn had neither sought nor expected, and it was a remarkable tribute that the major shareholders on the board should have united in deciding to place their trust in him, rather than divide over the dynastic right to succeed.

Prior to the appointment of Tom Devlin, which was in recognition of extremely long service, two Kellys and two Whites had shared the chairmanship of Celtic from 1909 to 1985. Now Jack McGinn took over, after less than four years as a director and with no family pedigree in the Celtic hierarchy. It was an appointment indicative of a new era in football. He is under no illusions about the fickleness of public opinion and the near-inevitability of its being directed at some stage against the men who are believed to hold the purse-strings and the ultimate power in a football club.

I was there as a youngster when the supporters were shouting at Tom White, not long after the war. Then I heard Bob Kelly taking some terrible abuse in the early sixties from the crowd in front of the directors' box. Desmond White got it because, after all the great success, the club hit problems in the late seventies. Even Tom Devlin had to take some stick during his short time in office.

The early days of the Jack McGinn era at Celtic Park brought an unprecedented willingness to spend on a large scale in order to invest in success – while in no way departing from the perennial belief in the wisdom of relying mainly on home-grown talent. To some extent it has been a case of crossing a generation gap away from that rigid belief, and in other ways the commendable product of a more cautious financial era in which there can be no justification for the books not balancing in each and every season. Modern football conditions, it has been recognized, require a little more risk-taking than has generally been regarded as acceptable by Celtic.

The Celtic board has never divided, in modern times at least, along lines which demanded a count of share-based power. But the control of shares has, with very few exceptions, determined which individuals should have behind-the-scenes control over Celtic's fortunes. The twists and turns have led to a greater concentration of control, but the most striking factor is still the continuity of leading names, rather than the changes which have occurred.

*A full Celtic Park for a game against Hibs in 1961. Frank Haffey comes out to punch the ball, a goalkeeper who could inspire or infuriate*

*Skipper Billy McNeill is on top of the world after victory over Dunfermline in the 1965 Scottish Cup Final – the triumph that began Celtic's glory decade. Left to right J. Young, J. Hughes, J. Clark, W. McNeill, B. Auld, T. Gemmell, R. Lennox, C. Gallagher, J. Fallon*

*The Celts celebrate victory over Dundee United in the 100th Scottish Cup Final in 1985. The two goal scorers, Davie Provan (left) and Frank McGarvey take their lap of honour*

LEFT: *Sir Robert Kelly, known to many as 'Mr Celtic', was chairman of the club from 1947 to shortly before his death in 1971. An unashamed traditionalist, his was the ultimate authority at Parkhead, even on matters concerning team selection*
RIGHT: *The current chairman, Jack McGinn, who led Celtic into the great centenary season, pictured in front of the new-look Celtic Park frontage*

*A winning combination. Jock Stein, the great motivator, with one of his greatest triumphs, Jimmy Johnstone, a devastating winger from whom Stein managed to coax magnificent performances in vital matches*

*Billy McNeill and the Celtic family. Two of the 'elder statesmen' – Neil Mochan and Jimmy Steele – are in the foreground*

*What a team! Billy McNeill and his assistant, Tommy Craig, celebrate the winning of the League and Cup double in centenary year*

# 21

## THE RETURN OF CAESAR
### And the Centenary Celebrations

EASON 1986/7 had turned into a nightmare for Celtic. At the outset, they were faced with a very significant new challenge, when Rangers changed the whole tempo of Scottish football by recruiting Graeme Souness as manager and engaging in a policy of spending what they considered to be as much money as was required to guarantee success. In an entirely new development, big-name English players like Chris Woods, Terry Butcher and Graham Roberts found their way to Ibrox. Scottish football was plunged into a ferment of excitement by these developments, and much of the speculation inevitably concentrated on how Celtic would react to them. When the new-look Rangers promptly won the first available competition, the League Cup, the impression began to form that here indeed was an invincible force in Scottish football – with the power of money certain to sweep aside everything that stood in its way.

Certainly, it took some time for this pattern to assert itself in the race for the Premier League. Celtic went sixteen games without defeat to build up a clear lead by December. But then everything started to go wrong while, at the same time, Rangers hit an even longer run of consistency. The Celtic support watched with an increasing sense of foreboding as a ten-point lead was steadily whittled away. In the Scottish Cup, Celtic survived an epic three-game third round against Aberdeen, but then exited to Hearts. Just as worrying as the loss of form on the field was the steady build-up of problems off it. With the contracts of a number of key players due to expire at the end of the season, there was non-stop speculation about David Hay's ability to hang onto the players in question – particularly Mo Johnston, Murdo MacLeod and Brian McClair. As Johnston's form shaded off and disciplinary problems involving the player increased, it became increasingly apparent that McClair was the more important man to Celtic's long-term thinking, and that Hay's ability to persuade him that his future lay at Celtic Park would be a litmus test of his standing.

The inexorable progress towards the loss of the Premier League title came to a head in the second last game of the season, when Celtic lost at home to Falkirk, by 2–1, a result that summed up the unhappiness which had descended upon the club. The final League game of the season was at Tynecastle, and Celtic lost 1–0. It was Danny McGrain's final appearance as a Celtic player and Ian Paul of the *Glasgow Herald* summed up the great career thus:

The Celtic man really is quite remarkable when you consider the traumas he has overcome during a senior career that began as Celtic were winning the European Cup in 1967. As well as learning to live with, and indeed conquer, the drawbacks of diabetes, he came back from a horrible skull injury to become one of the finest full-backs this country has produced. Yet there he was on Saturday, still urging himself on, still trying always to use the ball sensibly.

Celtic's proneness to accident at this time was further exemplified when the intimation to McGrain that he was to be given a free transfer was made in an offhand sort of way, which the Celtic directors immediately recognized as a 'botch-up' which should be redeemed as quickly as possible. In the end, McGrain moved to Hamilton Academicals where his coaching experience proved of immediate value.

Two months before the end of the season, the Celtic directors were beginning to see the writing on the wall for David Hay as the prospects for a season without honours, on the eve of the club's centenary celebrations, grew all too real. The first inkling from the minutes of the board meetings came on 19 March 1987, when James Farrell 'reported that he had received information that Billy McNeill would be interested in leaving Aston Villa and returning to Celtic'. For some of Farrell's colleagues, the previous acrimonious parting with McNeill was of too recent memory and the matter was not pursued at this stage. But, by late April, with the League title all but gone, a consensus had developed that changes would have to be made. In addition to the players whose names were increasingly being linked with other clubs, the contracts of Bonner and McStay were about to expire. There was, at this point, little to suggest that any player of stature could be

THE RETURN OF CAESAR

persuaded to remain at Celtic Park. At the same time, David Hay's thoughts of buying players such as Johnny Sivebaek, Liam Brady and Aberdeen's Alex McLeish were coming to nothing.

On 8 May, events had been given impetus by the sacking of Billy McNeill as manager of Aston Villa, to whom he had moved ten months earlier from Manchester City. It was a moment of near-despair for McNeill. He was forty-six years of age and living in Cheshire and this was, he recalls, the low-point in his career. He contemplated the possibility of a move to the Middle East, and by 15 May he was engaged in discussions with Airdrie about the possibility of him taking over at Broomfield. Neither of these options greatly appealed to a man who had scaled the heights of professional football. Meanwhile, David Hay was going about his team-building plans and, on 20 May, he at last plunged into the transfer market to sign Mick McCarthy, the Irish international centre-half, from Manchester City for £450,000. But events were now moving quickly behind the scenes, though the Celtic board was still discussing whether their move for a successor to Hay should be directed at McNeill or at Lou Macari, by now manager of Swindon Town. By the time a special board meeting was held on 26 May, in the Bath Street office, it was unanimous that McNeill should be the target.

The following day, Jack McGinn and McNeill – who was in Glasgow for a Lisbon Lions reunion – met in the unsalubrious setting of a Clydebank car park. The terms on which the deal should be done were more or less sorted out. The scene then shifted that evening to the home of McNeill's old friend, Mike Jackson, where the full Celtic board was present to approve what had been agreed and to welcome back one of the most popular figures in the club's history. The following morning, Jack McGinn offered David Hay the opportunity to resign, which he turned down. So he was sacked. A press conference was convened for Celtic Park at 5 p.m. and, with true drama, Billy McNeill was announced as the new Celtic manager. Though the country was in the midst of a General Election campaign, politics were swept off the front pages by the sensational news. McNeill enthused:

To say I'm happy doesn't begin to describe how I feel. I'm as excited as I was thirty years ago when I first joined the club as a player. To me, they are the best. This is my club, and I can say that after being with two major English teams. Believe me, they do not compare with this club. I hope I have matured in the four years I have been away. I certainly believe that I have learned a lot as a manager. This is the third time I have joined Celtic and none of the magic has worn off.

The sense of excitement was shared by the Celtic support who could now see some prospect of a challenge to imperious Rangers developing in the season ahead. But nobody underestimated the scale of the problems which included the fact that a significant proportion of Celtic's most valuable players were still determined to look to pastures new. Murdo MacLeod, Mo Johnston and Brian McClair – who had scored 122 goals in his four seasons with Celtic – would all depart. During the summer, McNeill busied himself in the transfer market, bringing Andy Walker from Motherwell for £350,000, full-back Chris Morris from Sheffield Wednesday for £125,000, and – a particularly shrewd move – the vastly experienced Billy Stark from Aberdeen for a mere £75,000. As the players reassembled for training, McNeill made clear that a tighter disciplinary regime would operate at Celtic Park than in recent times, though it soon became apparent that this would be based on mutual respect between manager and players. Roy Aitken, whose own contract was quickly renewed by McNeill although it still had two years to run, says: 'Straight away, there was more of a settled atmosphere. Whereas through much of the previous season, there had been all this talk about transfers, now everyone knew that they were going to be at Celtic Park for the next few years.'

The team which McNeill built was in the real Celtic tradition, to which the manager was so much attached. 'Chris Morris, Anton Rogan and Derek Whyte are all natural forward-going players,' says Aitken, looking back on the season. 'We are the only team in Scotland that plays with three men up, to maintain the free-flowing style.' But before all the pieces fell into place, there were to be two more major excursions into the transfer market. Celtic did not make a great start to their centenary season. On 1 August, the new-look side lost 5–1 to Arsenal in a challenge match at Celtic Park. Then 42,000 turned out to witness a testimonial game for Tommy Burns, against Kenny Dalglish's Liverpool, which Celtic lost by a single goal. This event provided the opportunity for Danny McGrain and Davie Provan to salute the Celtic support. It was an important act of reconciliation with the veteran full-back, who had missed the chance to say a proper farewell at the end of the season because of the way in which his free transfer had been handled. No less warm was the reception for Provan, whose career had been cut short by the onset of a viral illness, which robbed him of energy and made it impossible for him to contemplate playing professional football again. He was to stay on the staff, to assist with the coaching of young players.

Celtic won the first League meeting of the season with Rangers 1–0, thanks to a Stark goal and this was psychologically important given the hype which continued to surround the Ibrox club. But during September there were serious set-backs which made it clear that there would be no instant miracle for McNeill. In the League Cup, Celtic went out in the quarter-final to Aberdeen and, even more disappointingly, the UEFA Cup campaign was extremely brief. Goals by Walker and Whyte helped Celtic to a 2–1 first-leg lead over Borussia Dortmund but, in West Germany, they could hold out for only 64 minutes against a side which included Murdo MacLeod – and ended up losing 2–0. This left them free, as the euphemism goes, to concentrate on the League, but it was apparent to McNeill that the attack needed strengthening – and he knew exactly the players whom he wanted to bring to Celtic Park. Big money was involved, but the Celtic board was now of a mind to spend. Indeed, the extraordinary thing was that they could almost balance the books in the season's transfer dealings because of the outflow of players which had occurred shortly after McNeill's arrival. This was in spite of the fact that the club felt 'robbed' by the tribunal finding that Manchester United should pay only £850,000 for McClair who, in this age of vast transfer fees, might reasonably have been regarded as being worth twice that amount.

In October, McNeill and Jack McGinn travelled south to tie up the transfer of Frank McAvennie from West Ham for £750,000. The player's form had declined slightly after an outstanding first season in London, following his transfer from St Mirren. McNeill had, however, a great respect for the player and believed that his sharpness as a striker could be restored. Meanwhile, McNeill was continuing to show interest in Joe Miller, the young Aberdeen winger, who was also attracting the attention of Liverpool and Manchester United. By November, Aberdeen – resigned to losing the player – decided to settle for a firm bid, rather than await a tribunal finding on what Miller was worth. This worked to McNeill's advantage, and he quickly secured McGinn's agreement for a £650,000 offer. Part of the attraction for the manager of both McAvennie and Miller was that they were both 'Celtic men' by instinct and upbringing. They were both fulfilling the ambitions of youth by signing for the club, and that was the kind of guaranteed commitment which McNeill knew could make the difference between success and failure of such big-money signings. His faith was justified and, as Roy Aitken says, 'the reason that things went so well for us was that all of the new signings fitted in straight away'.

By early October, Celtic had fallen into third place in the League table, behind Aberdeen and Hearts. But from that point onwards, success was to be virtually uninterrupted. The second meeting of the season with Rangers, at Ibrox, turned out to be an extraordinary affair which earned an unwelcome place in the annals of Scottish football because it led to four players ending up in the criminal courts. The game flared up when Rangers goalkeeper Woods and McAvennie clashed inside the penalty area. There was nothing very violent about the incident, but Butcher and Roberts both rushed into the fray. Woods, McAvennie and Butcher were all sent off while Roberts – who was extremely fortunate to escape the referee's attention – went into goal for Rangers. The rest of the game was played out in a tense atmosphere, and Rangers came from 2–0 down to force a draw. Astonishingly, the procurator fiscal's office in Glasgow initiated breach of the peace charges against the four players after the game had been shown on television. The affair dragged on throughout the season before McAvennie was eventually found not guilty; Woods and Butcher were fined; and the charge against Roberts was found 'not proven'. It was an incursion by the law into football which was welcomed by very few.

As 1987 drew to a close, Billy McNeill delighted the Celtic support by tying up long-term contracts with Aitken, Paul McStay and Peter Grant. By this time, the restlessness had disappeared from Celtic Park, to be replaced by a keen sense of purpose. The League points kept piling up while Celtic's rivals showed signs of uncertainty.

A 2–1 defeat by Dundee United on 24 October 1987 would be the last piece of bad news for Celtic supporters during the centenary season. By 28 November, when they beat Hibs 1–0 at Easter Road, Celtic were on top of the Premier League and that is where they stayed. A 42,000 crowd turned out at Celtic Park two days later to pay tribute to Davie Provan, who played for just eight minutes of his own testimonial match against Nottingham Forest. Celtic lost 3–1, but there was a nostalgic interlude when Kenny Dalglish – by now manager of Liverpool – came on as substitute for Paul McStay. On the Saturday, it was back to serious League business with Frank McAvennie, proving to be a golden buy, scoring all four goals against Morton at Cappielow. When Celtic won the 2 January fixture against Rangers, through two more McAvennie goals, the prospects for the League title began to look very good indeed. There was a series of close results and uncertain performances, but the important fact was that Celtic continued to accumulate the points while their rivals slipped up. The decisive game in the campaign, televised live on a Sunday afternoon, fell on 20 March against Rangers at Ibrox. Celtic rose magnificently to the occasion in an electric atmosphere. Paul McStay put them ahead with a memorable goal, which Bartram quickly equalized for Rangers. Instead of holding out for the draw which would have sufficed, Celtic kept going forward and a marvellous corner from Tommy Burns, headed on by Rogan, was chested home by Walker to put Celtic virtually beyond reach in the title race. Roy Aitken says: 'We went into that game with everyone assuming that we would play for a draw. But we knew that if we could come out of it with a win, we would open up a six-point lead at the top of the table. The tactics that day were outstanding and for us to come back and score again after losing the equalizer really said something about the character of the team.'

Celtic went thirty-one games without defeat before on 16 April, Hearts beat them 2–1 at Tynecastle to postpone the tying up of the League title. This had the beneficial effect, however, of allowing a capacity Celtic Park crowd to be present the following Saturday when a 3–0 victory over Dundee ensured that Celtic would be champions of the Scottish League in their centenary season – an achievement which had seemed improbable in the extreme, twelve months previously. There were great scenes of green and white celebration as the crowd sang 'Happy Birthday' to Celtic. For Billy McNeill – whose status as 'Caesar' was reinforced among the fans – it was a particularly poignant occasion. It was the 13th Scottish League title he had been involved in; nine as a player and four as a manager and, to lead Celtic to this achievement, he had emerged from the abyss of unemployment. There was special praise too for his assistant, Tommy Craig, who had arrived at Celtic Park a few months before McNeill's return. The two men had agreed to work together on an experimental basis, but Craig – a pleasant personality with a first-class football mind – had soon become the ideal partner in an irrepressible management team.

Meanwhile, the Scottish Cup campaign had been going smoothly following an uncomfortably close shave with lowly Stranraer back in January. Celtic won at home only by an early McAvennie goal and survived a missed penalty, to avoid the indignity of a replay. A Billy Stark goal then beat Hibs in a replay, after a goalless draw at Celtic Park. A capacity crowd at Firhill saw goals from Walker, Burns and Stark account for Partick Thistle. Thus Celtic qualified for the semi-finals and a Hampden meeting with Hearts, which produced one of the most remarkable finishes which the national stadium has witnessed. With just three minutes remaining, Celtic trailed by a single goal. The late assault which had been restored as one of the Celtic hallmarks was in full swing – and produced two goals, from Mark McGhee and Andy Walker, to carry the team into the Final. Billy McNeill attributed this stunning victory to 'appetite, dedication and pride – that's why we win games late'.

The scene was then set for the Final on Saturday 14 May. It was, in every sense, a glorious day. But Celtic's confidence about achieving the club's 11th League and Cup double in the centenary season was dented when Kevin Gallacher put Dundee United ahead early in the second half. For a time, Celtic seemed to be having difficulty in mounting the fight-back which everyone expected. With twenty minutes remaining, McGhee and Stark came on as substitutes and the flow of play was transformed – proof of a masterly tactical move by McNeill. With fifteen minutes remaining, Rogan made progress down the left and crossed for McAvennie to head past Thomson. The minutes ticked away and extra time seemed likely – in itself a welcome enough relief for the Celtic support. But there was now a built-in inevitability to the course of events. With almost the last attack of the game, McAvennie saw an opening in the Dundee United defence and shot through it into the Hampden net. The final whistle blew and a work of footballing fiction could not have produced a more astonishing climax to the game, the season and the century with honour.

# STATISTICAL APPENDIXES

**This section contains statistics up to the end of the 1987/8 season.**

## 1. CELTIC'S RECORD IN ALL COMPETITIONS

|  | Played | Won | Drew | Lost | For | Against |
|---|---|---|---|---|---|---|
| League | 2,995 | 1,832 | 586 | 577 | 6,726 | 3,231 |
| Scottish Cup | 432 | 301 | 72 | 59 | 1,111 | 415 |
| League Cup | 335 | 217 | 47 | 71 | 808 | 387 |
| European Competition | 123 | 65 | 23 | 35 | 228 | 118 |

*Record Victory*
  11–0 v. Dundee, 26 October 1895
*Record Defeat*
  0–8 v. Motherwell, 30 April 1937
*Highest Individual Goals' Aggregate in a Season*
  Jimmy McGrory, 50, 1935/6
*Highest Scorer in Total Aggregate*
  Jimmy McGrory, 397, 1922–38
*Most Goals in a League Match*
  Jimmy McGrory, 8 v. Dunfermline, 14 January 1928

*Record Scottish League Appearances*
  Alec McNair, 583, 1904/5–1924/5
*Record European Appearances*
  Billy McNeill, 69, 1962/3–1974/5
*Most Capped Player*
  Danny McGrain, 62
*Highest Home Attendance*
  92,000 v. Rangers, 1 January 1938
*Scottish League Record Attendance*
  Rangers v. Celtic, 118,567, 2 January 1939
*European Club Match Record Attendance*
  146,433 v. Aberdeen, Scottish Cup Final at Hampden Park, 24 April 1937
*European Cup Record Attendance*
  135,826 v. Leeds Utd, European Cup Semi-Final at Hampden Park, 15 April 1970

Celtic kept a clean sheet in 26 of their 38 League matches in season 1913/14.
  The record for the longest run without defeat in the Scottish League is held by Celtic who won 49 and drew 13 matches between 13 November 1915 when they lost 0–2 to Hearts at Tynecastle and 21 April 1917 when they lost 0–2 at home to Kilmarnock.

### League Champions *35 times*

1893, 1894, 1896, 1898, 1905, 1906, 1907, 1908, 1909, 1910, 1914, 1915, 1916, 1917, 1919, 1922, 1926, 1936, 1938, 1954, 1966, 1967, 1968, 1969, 1970, 1971, 1972, 1973, 1974, 1977, 1979, 1981, 1982, 1986, 1988.

### League, Runners-up *22 times*

1892, 1895, 1900, 1901, 1902, 1912, 1913, 1918, 1920, 1921, 1928, 1929, 1931, 1935, 1939, 1955, 1976, 1980, 1983, 1984, 1985, 1987.

### Scottish Cup Winners *28 times – a record*

1892, 1899, 1900, 1904, 1907, 1908, 1911, 1912, 1914, 1923, 1925, 1927, 1931, 1933, 1937, 1951, 1954, 1965, 1967, 1969, 1971, 1972, 1974, 1975, 1977, 1980, 1985, 1988.

### Scottish Cup, Runners-up *15 times*

1889, 1893, 1894, 1901, 1902, 1926, 1928, 1955, 1956, 1961, 1963, 1966, 1970, 1973, 1984.
*The Cup was withheld in 1909, after two drawn games with Rangers, owing to a riot.*

### Scottish League Cup Winners *9 times*

1956–57, 1957–58, 1965–66, 1966–67, 1967–68, 1968–69, 1969–70, 1974–75, 1982–83.

### Scottish League Cup, Runners-up *10 times*

1964–65, 1970–71, 1971–72, 1972–73, 1973–74, 1975–76, 1976–77, 1977–78, 1983–84, 1986–87.

**Trebles** *2*

1967, 1969.

**Doubles** *11*

1907, 1908, 1914, 1954, 1967, 1969, 1971, 1972, 1974, 1977, 1988.

**European Cup Winners**

1967.

**European Cup, Runners-up**

1970.

**Coronation Cup Winners**

1953.

**St Mungo's Cup Winners**

1951.

**Empire Exhibition Cup Winners**

1938.

**Glasgow Cup Winners** *29 times including once as joint winners*

## 2. LEAGUE RECORD YEAR BY YEAR

| Season | Played | Won | Drew | Lost | For | Against | Points | Pos. |
|--------|--------|-----|------|------|-----|---------|--------|------|
| 1890–1891 | 18 | 11 | 3 | 4 | 48 | 21 | 21* | 3rd |
| 1891–1892 | 22 | 16 | 3 | 3 | 62 | 21 | 35 | 2nd |
| 1892–1893 | 18 | 14 | 1 | 3 | 54 | 25 | 29 | 1st |
| 1893–1894 | 18 | 14 | 1 | 3 | 53 | 32 | 29 | 1st |
| 1894–1895 | 18 | 11 | 4 | 3 | 50 | 29 | 26 | 2nd |
| 1895–1896 | 18 | 15 | 0 | 3 | 64 | 25 | 30 | 1st |
| 1896–1897 | 18 | 10 | 4 | 4 | 42 | 18 | 24 | 4th |
| 1897–1898 | 18 | 15 | 3 | 0 | 56 | 13 | 33 | 1st |
| 1898–1899 | 18 | 11 | 2 | 5 | 51 | 33 | 24 | 3rd |
| 1899–1900 | 18 | 9 | 7 | 2 | 46 | 27 | 25 | 2nd |
| 1900–1901 | 20 | 13 | 3 | 4 | 49 | 28 | 29 | 2nd |
| 1901–1902 | 18 | 11 | 4 | 3 | 38 | 28 | 26 | 2nd |
| 1902–1903 | 22 | 8 | 10 | 4 | 36 | 30 | 26 | 5th |
| 1903–1904 | 26 | 18 | 2 | 6 | 69 | 28 | 38 | 3rd |
| 1904–1905 | 26 | 18 | 5 | 3 | 68 | 31 | 41 | 1st† |
| 1905–1906 | 30 | 24 | 1 | 5 | 76 | 19 | 49 | 1st |
| 1906–1907 | 34 | 23 | 9 | 2 | 80 | 30 | 55 | 1st |
| 1907–1908 | 34 | 24 | 7 | 3 | 86 | 27 | 55 | 1st |
| 1908–1909 | 34 | 23 | 5 | 6 | 71 | 24 | 51 | 1st |

\* *Had 4 points deducted for fielding an ineligible player*
† *Won Championship play-off against Rangers 2–1*

| Season | Played | Won | Drew | Lost | For | Against | Points | Pos. |
|---|---|---|---|---|---|---|---|---|
| 1909–1910 | 34 | 24 | 6 | 4 | 63 | 22 | 54 | 1st |
| 1910–1911 | 34 | 15 | 11 | 8 | 48 | 18 | 41 | 5th |
| 1911–1912 | 34 | 17 | 11 | 6 | 58 | 33 | 45 | 2nd |
| 1912–1913 | 34 | 22 | 5 | 7 | 53 | 28 | 49 | 2nd |
| 1913–1914 | 38 | 30 | 5 | 3 | 81 | 14 | 65 | 1st |
| 1914–1915 | 38 | 30 | 5 | 3 | 91 | 25 | 65 | 1st |
| 1915–1916 | 38 | 32 | 3 | 3 | 116 | 23 | 67 | 1st |
| 1916–1917 | 38 | 27 | 10 | 1 | 79 | 17 | 64 | 1st |
| 1917–1918 | 34 | 24 | 7 | 3 | 66 | 26 | 55 | 2nd |
| 1918–1919 | 34 | 26 | 6 | 2 | 71 | 22 | 58 | 1st |
| 1919–1920 | 42 | 29 | 10 | 3 | 89 | 31 | 68 | 2nd |
| 1920–1921 | 42 | 30 | 6 | 6 | 86 | 35 | 66 | 2nd |
| 1921–1922 | 42 | 27 | 13 | 2 | 83 | 20 | 67 | 1st |
| 1922–1923 | 38 | 19 | 8 | 11 | 52 | 39 | 46 | 3rd |
| 1923–1924 | 38 | 17 | 12 | 9 | 56 | 33 | 46 | 3rd |
| 1924–1925 | 38 | 18 | 8 | 12 | 77 | 44 | 44 | 4th |
| 1925–1926 | 38 | 25 | 8 | 5 | 97 | 40 | 58 | 1st |
| 1926–1927 | 38 | 21 | 7 | 10 | 101 | 55 | 49 | 3rd |
| 1927–1928 | 38 | 23 | 9 | 6 | 93 | 39 | 55 | 2nd |
| 1928–1929 | 38 | 22 | 7 | 9 | 67 | 44 | 51 | 2nd |
| 1929–1930 | 38 | 22 | 5 | 11 | 88 | 46 | 49 | 4th |
| 1930–1931 | 38 | 24 | 10 | 4 | 101 | 34 | 58 | 2nd |
| 1931–1932 | 38 | 20 | 8 | 10 | 94 | 50 | 48 | 3rd |
| 1932–1933 | 38 | 20 | 8 | 10 | 75 | 44 | 48 | 4th |
| 1933–1934 | 38 | 18 | 11 | 9 | 78 | 53 | 47 | 3rd |
| 1934–1935 | 38 | 24 | 4 | 10 | 92 | 45 | 52 | 2nd |
| 1935–1936 | 38 | 32 | 2 | 4 | 115 | 33 | 66 | 1st |
| 1936–1937 | 38 | 22 | 8 | 8 | 89 | 58 | 52 | 3rd |
| 1937–1938 | 38 | 27 | 7 | 4 | 114 | 42 | 61 | 1st |
| 1938–1939 | 38 | 20 | 8 | 10 | 99 | 53 | 48 | 2nd |
| 1939–1940‡ | 5 | 3 | 0 | 2 | 7 | 7 | 6 | 4th |
| 1946–1947 | 30 | 13 | 6 | 11 | 53 | 55 | 32 | 7th |
| 1947–1948 | 30 | 10 | 5 | 15 | 41 | 56 | 25 | 12th |
| 1948–1949 | 30 | 12 | 7 | 11 | 48 | 40 | 31 | 6th |
| 1949–1950 | 30 | 14 | 7 | 9 | 51 | 50 | 35 | 5th |
| 1950–1951 | 30 | 12 | 5 | 13 | 48 | 46 | 29 | 7th |
| 1951–1952 | 30 | 10 | 8 | 12 | 52 | 55 | 28 | 9th |
| 1952–1953 | 30 | 11 | 7 | 12 | 51 | 54 | 29 | 8th |
| 1953–1954 | 30 | 20 | 3 | 7 | 72 | 29 | 43 | 1st |
| 1954–1955 | 30 | 19 | 8 | 3 | 76 | 37 | 46 | 2nd |
| 1955–1956 | 34 | 16 | 9 | 9 | 55 | 39 | 41 | 5th |
| 1956–1957 | 34 | 15 | 8 | 11 | 58 | 43 | 38 | 5th |
| 1957–1958 | 34 | 19 | 8 | 7 | 84 | 47 | 46 | 3rd |
| 1958–1959 | 34 | 14 | 8 | 12 | 70 | 53 | 36 | 6th |
| 1959–1960 | 34 | 12 | 9 | 13 | 73 | 59 | 33 | 9th |
| 1960–1961 | 34 | 15 | 9 | 10 | 64 | 46 | 39 | 4th |
| 1961–1962 | 34 | 19 | 8 | 7 | 81 | 37 | 46 | 3rd |
| 1962–1963 | 34 | 19 | 6 | 9 | 76 | 44 | 44 | 4th |

‡ *Competition abandoned after outbreak of war*

| Season | Played | Won | Drew | Lost | For | Against | Points | Pos. |
|---|---|---|---|---|---|---|---|---|
| 1963–1964 | 34 | 19 | 9 | 6 | 89 | 34 | 47 | 3rd |
| 1964–1965 | 34 | 16 | 5 | 13 | 76 | 57 | 37 | 8th |
| 1965–1966 | 34 | 27 | 3 | 4 | 106 | 30 | 57 | 1st |
| 1966–1967 | 34 | 26 | 6 | 2 | 111 | 33 | 58 | 1st |
| 1967–1968 | 34 | 30 | 3 | 1 | 106 | 24 | 63 | 1st |
| 1968–1969 | 34 | 23 | 8 | 3 | 89 | 32 | 54 | 1st |
| 1969–1970 | 34 | 27 | 3 | 4 | 96 | 33 | 57 | 1st |
| 1970–1971 | 34 | 25 | 6 | 3 | 89 | 23 | 56 | 1st |
| 1971–1972 | 34 | 28 | 4 | 2 | 96 | 28 | 60 | 1st |
| 1972–1973 | 34 | 26 | 5 | 3 | 93 | 28 | 57 | 1st |
| 1973–1974 | 34 | 23 | 7 | 4 | 82 | 27 | 53 | 1st |
| 1974–1975 | 34 | 20 | 5 | 9 | 81 | 41 | 45 | 3rd |
| 1975–1976 | 36 | 21 | 6 | 9 | 71 | 42 | 48 | 2nd |
| 1976–1977 | 36 | 23 | 9 | 4 | 79 | 39 | 55 | 1st |
| 1977–1978 | 36 | 15 | 6 | 15 | 63 | 54 | 36 | 5th |
| 1978–1979 | 36 | 21 | 6 | 9 | 61 | 37 | 48 | 1st |
| 1979–1980 | 36 | 18 | 11 | 7 | 61 | 38 | 47 | 2nd |
| 1980–1981 | 36 | 26 | 4 | 6 | 84 | 37 | 56 | 1st |
| 1981–1982 | 36 | 24 | 7 | 5 | 79 | 33 | 55 | 1st |
| 1982–1983 | 36 | 25 | 5 | 6 | 90 | 36 | 55 | 2nd |
| 1983–1984 | 36 | 21 | 8 | 7 | 80 | 41 | 50 | 2nd |
| 1984–1985 | 36 | 22 | 8 | 6 | 77 | 30 | 52 | 2nd |
| 1985–1986 | 36 | 20 | 10 | 6 | 67 | 38 | 50 | 1st§ |
| 1986–1987 | 44 | 27 | 9 | 8 | 90 | 41 | 63 | 2nd |
| 1987–1988 | 44 | 31 | 10 | 3 | 79 | 23 | 72 | 1st |

§ *Won on Goal Difference*

# 3. SUMMARY OF SCOTTISH CUP FINALS

| | |
|---|---|
| 1888–1889 | lost to Third Lanark 1–2 |
| 1891–1892 | beat Queens Park 5–1 |
| 1892–1893 | lost to Queens Park 1–2 |
| 1893–1894 | lost to Rangers 1–3 |
| 1898–1899 | beat Rangers 2–0 |
| 1899–1900 | beat Queens Park 4–3 |
| 1900–1901 | lost to Hearts 3–4 |
| 1901–1902 | lost to Hibernian 0–1 |
| 1903–1904 | beat Rangers 3–2 |
| 1906–1907 | beat Hearts 3–0 |
| 1907–1908 | beat St Mirren 5–1 |
| 1908–1909 | Cup withheld after two drawn matches with Rangers 2–2, 1–1 |
| 1910–1911 | beat Hamilton 2–0 after 0–0 |
| 1911–1912 | beat Clyde 2–0 |
| 1913–1914 | beat Hibernian 4–1 after 0–0 |
| 1922–1923 | beat Hibernian 1–0 |

1924–1925   beat Dundee 2–1
1925–1926   lost to St Mirren 0–2
1926–1927   beat East Fife 3–1
1927–1928   lost to Rangers 0–4
1930–1931   beat Motherwell 4–2 after 2–2
1932–1933   beat Motherwell 1–0
1936–1937   beat Aberdeen 2–1
1950–1951   beat Motherwell 1–0
1953–1954   beat Aberdeen 2–1
1954–1955   lost to Clyde 0–1 after 1–1
1955–1956   lost to Hearts 1–3
1960–1961   lost to Dunfermline 0–2 after 0–0
1962–1963   lost to Rangers 0–3 after 1–1
1964–1965   beat Dunfermline 3–2
1965–1966   lost to Rangers 0–1 after 0–0
1966–1967   beat Aberdeen 2–0
1968–1969   beat Rangers 4–0
1969–1970   lost to Aberdeen 1–3
1970–1971   beat Rangers 2–1 after 1–1
1971–1972   beat Hibernian 6–1
1972–1973   lost to Rangers 2–3
1973–1974   beat Dundee United 3–0
1974–1975   beat Airdrie 3–1
1976–1977   beat Rangers 1–0
1979–1980   beat Rangers 1–0 (a.e.t.)
1983–1984   lost to Aberdeen 1–2 (a.e.t.)
1984–1985   beat Dundee United 2–1
1987–1988   beat Dundee United 2–1

# 4. SUMMARY OF
# SCOTTISH LEAGUE CUP FINALS

1956–1957   beat Partick Thistle 3–0 after 0–0
1957–1958   beat Rangers 7–1
1964–1965   lost to Rangers 1–2
1965–1966   beat Rangers 2–1
1966–1967   beat Rangers 1–0
1967–1968   beat Dundee 5–3
1968–1969   beat Hibernian 6–2
1969–1970   beat St Johnstone 1–0
1970–1971   lost to Rangers 0–1
1971–1972   lost to Partick Thistle 1–4
1972–1973   lost to Hibernian 1–2
1973–1974   lost to Dundee 0–1
1974–1975   beat Hibernian 6–3
1975–1976   lost to Rangers 0–1
1976–1977   lost to Aberdeen 1–2 (a.e.t.)
1977–1978   lost to Rangers 1–2 (a.e.t.)
1982–1983   beat Rangers 2–1

1983–1984   lost to Rangers 2–3 (a.e.t.)
1986–1987   lost to Rangers 1–2

# 5. SUMMARY OF EUROPEAN RESULTS

*1962–63 Fairs Cup*
   Valencia (2–4, 2–2)
*1963–64 European Cup-Winners' Cup*
   Basle (5–1, 5–0), Dinamo Zagreb (3–0, 1–2), Slovan Bratislava (1–0, 1–0),
   M.T.K. Budapest (3–0, 0–4)
*1964–65 Fairs Cup*
   Leixoes (1–1, 3–0), Barcelona (1–3, 0–0)
*1965–66 European Cup-Winners' Cup*
   Go Ahead Deventer (6–0, 1–0), A.G.F. Aahrus (1–0, 2–0), Dynamo Kiev
   (3–0, 1–1), Liverpool (1–0, 0–2)
*1966–67 European Cup*
   Zurich (2–0, 3–0), Nantes (3–1, 3–1), Vojvodina (0–1, 2–0), Dukla Prague
   (3–1, 0–0), Internazionale Milan (2–1)
*1967–68 European Cup*
   Dynamo Kiev (1–2, 1–1)
*1968–69 European Cup*
   St Etienne (0–2, 4–0), Red Star Belgrade (5–1, 1–1), A.C. Milan (0–0, 0–1)
*1969–70 European Cup*
   Basle (0–0, 2–0), Benfica (3–0, 0–3*), Fiorentina (3–0, 0–1), Leeds United
   (1–0, 2–1), Feyenoord (1–2)
*1970–71 European Cup*
   Kokkola (9–0, 5–0), Waterford (7–0, 3–2), Ajax (0–3, 1–0)
*1971–72 European Cup*
   Boldklub 1903 (1–2, 3–0), Sliema Wanderers (5–0, 2–1), Uijpest Dosza
   (2–1, 1–1), Internazionale Milan (0–0, 0–0†)
*1972–73 European Cup*
   Rosenberg Trondheim (2–1, 3–1), Uijpest Dosza (2–1, 0–3)
*1973–74 European Cup*
   T.P.S. Turku (6–1, 3–0), Vejle B.K. (0–0, 1–0), Basle (2–3, 4–2), Atletico
   Madrid (0–0, 0–2)
*1974–75 European Cup*
   Olympiakos (1–1, 0–2)
*1975–76 European Cup-Winners' Cup*
   Valur (2–0, 7–0), Boavista (0–0, 3–1), Sachsenring Zwickau (1–1, 0–1)
*1976–77 UEFA Cup*
   Wisla Krakow (2–2, 0–2)
*1977–78 European Cup*
   Jeunesse d'Esch (5–0, 6–1), S.W.W. Innsbruck (2–1, 0–3)
*1978–79 Failed to Qualify for European Competition*
*1979–80 European Cup*
   Partizan Tirana (0–1, 4–1), Dundalk (3–2, 0–0), Real Madrid (2–0, 0–3)
*1980–81 European Cup-Winners' Cup*
   Diosgyeori Miskolc (6–0, 1–2), Politechnica Timisoara (2–1, 0–1‡)

★  *Won on toss of coin*          †  *Lost on penalties*          ‡  *Lost on Away Goals Rule*

*1981–82 European Cup*
  Juventus (1–0, 0–2)
*1982–83 European Cup*
  Ajax (2–2, 2–1), Real Sociedad (0–2, 2–1)
*1983–84 UEFA Cup*
  A.G.F. Aahrus (1–0, 4–1), Sporting Lisbon (0–2, 5–0), Nottingham Forest
  (0–0, 1–2)
*1984–85 European Cup-Winners' Cup*
  K.A.A. Ghent (0–1, 3–0), Rapid Vienna (1–3, 3–0§, 0–1)
*1985–86 European Cup-Winners' Cup*
  Atletico Madrid (1–1, 1–2)
*1986–87 European Cup*
  Shamrock Rovers (1–0, 2–0), Dynamo Kiev (1–1, 1–3)
*1987–88 UEFA Cup*
  Borussia Dortmund (2–1, 0–2)

Celtic have played against teams from 26 European countries since season
1962–63

| Country | Played | Won | Drew | Lost | For | Against |
|---|---|---|---|---|---|---|
| Albania | 2 | 1 | 0 | 1 | 4 | 2 |
| Austria | 5 | 2 | 0 | 3 | 6 | 8 |
| Belgium | 2 | 1 | 0 | 1 | 3 | 1 |
| Czechoslovakia | 4 | 3 | 1 | 0 | 5 | 1 |
| Denmark | 8 | 6 | 1 | 1 | 13 | 3 |
| East Germany | 2 | 0 | 1 | 1 | 1 | 2 |
| England | 6 | 3 | 1 | 2 | 5 | 5 |
| Finland | 4 | 4 | 0 | 0 | 23 | 1 |
| France | 4 | 3 | 0 | 1 | 10 | 4 |
| Greece | 2 | 0 | 1 | 1 | 1 | 3 |
| Holland | 7 | 4 | 1 | 2 | 13 | 8 |
| Hungary | 8 | 4 | 1 | 3 | 15 | 12 |
| Iceland | 2 | 2 | 0 | 0 | 9 | 0 |
| Italy | 9 | 3 | 3 | 3 | 6 | 5 |
| Luxembourg | 2 | 2 | 0 | 0 | 11 | 1 |
| Malta | 2 | 2 | 0 | 0 | 7 | 1 |
| Norway | 2 | 2 | 0 | 0 | 5 | 2 |
| Poland | 2 | 0 | 1 | 1 | 2 | 4 |
| Portugal | 8 | 4 | 2 | 2 | 15 | 7 |
| Republic of Ireland | 6 | 5 | 1 | 0 | 16 | 4 |
| Romania | 2 | 1 | 0 | 1 | 2 | 2 |
| Spain | 12 | 2 | 4 | 6 | 11 | 20 |
| Switzerland | 8 | 6 | 1 | 1 | 23 | 6 |
| U.S.S.R. | 6 | 1 | 3 | 2 | 8 | 8 |
| West Germany | 2 | 1 | 0 | 1 | 2 | 3 |
| Yugoslavia | 6 | 3 | 1 | 2 | 12 | 5 |
| | 123 | 65 | 23 | 35 | 228 | 118 |

§ *UEFA ordered match to be replayed*

# 6. SCOTTISH CUP WINNING TEAMS

*1892 (beat Queens Park 5–1)*
Cullen; Reynolds, Doyle; Maley, Kelly, Gallacher; McCallum, Brady,
Dowds, McMahon, Campbell

*1899 (beat Rangers 2–0)*
McArthur; Welford, Storrier; Battles, Marshall, King; Hodge, Campbell,
Divers, McMahon, Bell

*1900 (beat Queens Park 4–3)*
McArthur; Storrier, Battles; Russell, Marshall, Orr; Hodge, Campbell,
Divers, McMahon, Bell

*1904 (beat Rangers 3–2)*
Adams; McLeod, Orr; Young, Loney, Hay; Muir, McMenemy, Quinn,
Somers, Hamilton

*1907 (beat Hearts 3–0)*
Adams; McLeod, Orr; Young, McNair, Hay; Bennett, McMenemy, Quinn,
Somers, Templeton

*1908 (beat St Mirren 5–1)*
Adams; McNair, Weir; Young, Loney, Hay; Bennett, McMenemy, Quinn,
Somers, Hamilton

*1911 (beat Hamilton 2–0 in replay)*
Adams; McNair, Hay; Young, McAteer, Dodds; McAtee, McMenemy,
Quinn, Kivlichan, Hamilton

*1912 (beat Clyde 2–0)*
Mulrooney; McNair, Dodds; Young, Loney, Johnstone; McAtee, Gallacher,
Quinn, McMenemy, Brown

*1914 (beat Hibernian 4–1 in replay)*
Shaw; McNair, Dodds; Young, Johnstone, McMaster; McAtee, Gallacher,
McColl, McMenemy, Browning

*1923 (beat Hibernian 1–0)*
Shaw; McNair, W. McStay; J. McStay, Cringan, McFarlane; McAtee,
Gallacher, Cassidy, McLean, Connolly

*1925 (beat Dundee 2–1)*
Shevlin; W. McStay, Hilley; Wilson, J. McStay, McFarlane; Connolly,
Gallacher, McGrory, A. Thomson, McLean

*1927 (beat East Fife 3–1)*
J. Thomson; W. McStay, Hilley; Wilson, J. McStay, McFarlane; Connolly,
A. Thomson, McInally, McMenemy, McLean

*1931 (beat Motherwell 4–2 in replay)*
J. Thomson; Cook, McGonagle; Wilson, McStay, Geatons; R. Thomson,
A. Thomson, McGrory, Scarff, Napier

*1933 (beat Motherwell 1–0)*
Kennaway; Hogg, McGonagle; Wilson, McStay, Geatons; R. Thomson,
A. Thomson, McGrory, Napier, H. O'Donnell

*1937 (beat Aberdeen 2–1)*
Kennaway; Hogg, Morrison; Geatons, Lyon, Paterson; Delaney, Buchan,
McGrory, Crum, Murphy

*1951 (beat Motherwell 1–0)*
Hunter; Fallon, Rollo; Evans, Boden, Baillie; Weir, Collins, J. McPhail,
Peacock, Tully

*1954 (beat Aberdeen 2–1)*
Bonnar; Haughney, Meechan; Evans, Stein, Peacock; Higgins, Fernie,
Fallon, Tully, Mochan
*1965 (beat Dunfermline 3–2)*
Fallon; Young, Gemmell; Murdoch, McNeill, Clark; Chalmers, Gallagher,
Hughes, Lennox, Auld
*1967 (beat Aberdeen 2–0)*
Simpson; Craig, Gemmell; Murdoch, McNeill, Clark; Johnstone, Wallace,
Chalmers, Auld, Lennox
*1969 (beat Rangers 4–0)*
Fallon; Craig, Gemmell; Murdoch, McNeill, Brogan (Clark); Connelly,
Chalmers, Wallace, Lennox, Auld
*1971 (beat Rangers 2–1 in replay)*
Williams; Craig, Brogan; Connelly, McNeill, Hay; Johnstone, Macari, Hood
(Wallace), Callaghan, Lennox
*1972 (beat Hibernian 6–1)*
Williams; Craig, Brogan; Murdoch, McNeill, Connelly; Johnstone, Deans,
Macari, Dalglish, Callaghan. Substitute: Lennox (not used)
*1974 (beat Dundee United 3–0)*
Connaghan; McGrain (Callaghan), Brogan; Murray, McNeill, P. McCluskey;
Johnstone, Hood, Deans, Hay, Dalglish. Other substitute: Lennox
*1975 (beat Airdrie 3–1)*
Latchford; McGrain, Lynch; Murray, McNeill, P. McCluskey; Hood,
Glavin, Dalglish, Lennox, Wilson. Substitutes: Callaghan and MacDonald
(not used)
*1977 (beat Rangers 1–0)*
Latchford; McGrain, Lynch; Stanton, MacDonald, Aitken; Dalglish,
Edvaldsson, Craig, Conn, Wilson. Substitutes: Burns and Doyle (not used)
*1980 (beat Rangers 1–0)*
Latchford; Sneddon, McGrain; Aitken, Conroy, MacLeod; Provan, Doyle
(Lennox), G. McCluskey, Burns, McGarvey. Other substitute: Davidson
*1985 (beat Dundee United 2–1)*
Bonner; W. McStay, McGrain; Aitken, McAdam, MacLeod; Provan,
P. McStay (O'Leary), Johnston, Burns (McClair), McGarvey
*1988 (beat Dundee United 2–1)*
McKnight; Morris, Rogan; Aitken, McCarthy, Whyte (Stark); Miller,
McStay, McAvennie, Walker (McGhee), Burns

# 7. SCOTTISH LEAGUE CUP WINNING TEAMS

*1956–57 (beat Partick Thistle 3–0 in replay)*
Beattie; Haughney, Fallon; Evans, Jack, Peacock; Tully, Collins,
W. McPhail, Fernie, Mochan
*1957–58 (beat Rangers 7–1)*
Beattie; Donnelly, Fallon; Fernie, Evans, Peacock; Tully, Collins,
W. McPhail, Wilson, Mochan
*1965–66 (beat Rangers 2–1)*
Simpson; Young, Gemmell; Murdoch, McNeill, Clark; Johnstone, Gallagher,
McBride, Lennox, Hughes

*1966–67 (beat Rangers 1–0)*
Simpson; Gemmell, O'Neill; Murdoch, McNeill, Clark; Johnstone, Lennox, McBride, Auld, Hughes (Chalmers)

*1967–68 (beat Dundee 5–3)*
Simpson; Craig, Gemmell; Murdoch, McNeill, Clark; Chalmers, Lennox, Wallace, Auld (O'Neill), Hughes

*1968–69 (beat Hibernian 6–2)*
Fallon; Craig, Gemmell (Clark); Murdoch, McNeill, Brogan; Johnstone, Wallace, Chalmers, Auld, Lennox

*1969–70 (beat St Johnstone 1–0)*
Fallon; Craig, Hay; Murdoch, McNeill, Brogan; Callaghan, Hood, Hughes, Chalmers (Johnstone), Auld

*1974–75 (beat Hibernian 6–3)*
Hunter; McGrain, Brogan; Murray, McNeill, P. McCluskey; Johnstone, Dalglish, Deans, Hood, Wilson. Substitutes: Lennox and MacDonald (not used)

*1982–83 (beat Rangers 2–1)*
Bonner; McGrain, Sinclair; Aitken, McAdam, MacLeod; Provan, P. McStay (Reid), McGarvey, Burns, Nicholas. Other substitute: G. McCluskey

# 8. OTHER MAJOR CUP WINNING TEAMS

## Empire Exhibition Cup 1938
*First Round* beat Sunderland 3–1 after 0–0 (a.e.t.)
*Semi-Final* beat Hearts 1–0
*Final at Ibrox*
Celtic 1 Everton 0 a.e.t.   Attendance: 82,000
Scorer Crum (97)
*Celtic* Kennaway; Hogg, Morrison; Geatons, Lyon, Paterson; Delaney, MacDonald, Crum, Divers, Murphy
*Everton* Sagar; Cook, Greenhalgh; Mercer, Jones, Thomson; Geldard, Cunliffe, Lawton, Stevenson, Boyes

## Coronation Cup 1953
*First Round* beat Arsenal 1–0
*Semi-Final* beat Manchester United 2–1
*Final at Hampden*
Celtic 2 Hibernian 0   Attendance: 117,060
Scorers Mochan (28), Walsh (87)
*Celtic* Bonnar; Haughney, Rollo; Evans, Stein, McPhail; Collins, Walsh, Mochan, Peacock, Fernie
*Hibernian* Younger; Govan, Paterson; Buchanan, Howie, Combe; Smith, Johnstone, Reilly, Turnbull, Ormond

## European Cup 1967
*First Round* beat F.C. Zurich (2–0, 3–0)
*Second Round* beat Nantes (3–1, 3–1)
*Quarter-Final* beat Vojvodina (0–1, 2–0)
*Semi-Final* beat Dukla Prague (3–1, 0–0)

*Final at Estadio Nacional, Lisbon*
Celtic 2 Internazionale Milan 1    Attendance: 55,000
Scorers Gemmell (63), Chalmers (85)
        Mazzola pen. (7)
*Celtic* Simpson; Craig, Gemmell; Murdoch, McNeill, Clark; Johnstone,
Wallace, Chalmers, Auld, Lennox
*Internazionale* Sarti; Burgnich, Facchetti; Bedin, Guarneri, Picchi; Bicicli,
Mazzola, Cappellini, Corso, Domenghini

# 9. SCOTTISH INTERNATIONAL APPEARANCES
## up to v. England, May 1988

| | |
|---|---|
| Aitken, R.   39 | Groves, W.   2(3) |
| Auld, R.   3 | Haffey, F.   2 |
| Battles, B.   3 | Haughney, M.   1 |
| Bell, J.   5(10) | Hay, D.   27 |
| Bennett, A.   3(11) | Hay, J.   7(11) |
| Blessington, J.   4 | Hogg, R.   1 |
| Brogan, J.   4 | Hughes, J.   8 |
| Browning, J.   1 | Hunter, A.   2(4) |
| Burns, T.   8 | Johnston, M.   10(19) |
| Campbell, J.   12 | Johnstone, J.   23 |
| Cassidy, J.   4 | Kelly, J.   7(8) |
| Chalmers, S.   5 | Kennaway, J.   2 |
| Clark, J.   4 | Kennedy, J.   6 |
| Collins, R.   22(31) | King, A.   4(6) |
| Connelly, G.   2 | Lennox, R.   10 |
| Craig, Jim   1 | Loney, W.   2 |
| Craig, Joe   1 | McArthur, D.   3 |
| Crerand, P.   11(16) | McAtee, A.   1 |
| Cringan, W.   5 | McAvennie, F.   1(5) |
| Crum, J.   2 | McBride, J.   2 |
| Dalglish, K.   47(102) | McClair, B.   4(5) |
| Deans, J.   2 | McGarvey, F.   5(7) |
| Delaney, J.   9(13) | McGonagle, W. P.   6 |
| Divers, J.   1 | McGrain, D.   62 |
| Divers, J.   1 | McGrory, J.   7 |
| Dodds, J.   3 | McInally, T.   2 |
| Dowds, P.   1 | McKay, D.   14 |
| Doyle, D.   8 | McKeown, M.   2 |
| Evans, R.   45(48) | McLaren, J.   2(3) |
| Fernie, W.   12 | McLean, A.   4 |
| Gemmell, T.   18 | McLeod, D.   4 |
| Gilchrist, J.   1 | MacLeod, M.   5(7) |
| Glavin, R.   1 | McMahon, A.   6 |

*Totals in brackets indicate total caps won.*
*Players such as Pat Stanton, who did not win any caps as a Celtic player, have not been
included in the above list.*

McMenemy, J. 12
McNair, A. 15
McNeill, W. 29
McPhail, J. 5
McStay, P. 29
McStay, W. 13
Macari, L. 6(24)
Madden, J. 2
Maley, W. 2
Marshall, H. 2
Meechan, P. 1
Miller, W. 6
Mochan, N. 3
Murdoch, R. 12
Murphy, F. 1
Napier, C. 3(5)
Nicholas, C. 6(19)
Orr, W. 3

Paterson, G. 1
Provan, D. 10
Quinn, J. 11
Russell, D. 4(6)
Scarff, P. 1
Simpson, R. 5
Smith, E. 2
Somers, P. 4
Storrier, D. 3
Thomson, A. 3
Thomson, J. 4
Thomson, R. 1
Walker, A. 1
Wallace, W. 4(7)
Whyte, D. 2
Wilson, Peter 4
Wilson, Paul 1
Young, J. 1

*Derek Whyte became the 100th Celtic player to represent Scotland when he made an appearance v. Belgium (14.10.87).*

*Ireland Internationalists*
P. Bonner, S. Fallon, J. Foley, C. Gallagher, J. Haverty, P. Kavanagh, M. McCarthy, C. Morris, P. Turner
*Northern Ireland Internationalists*
F. Collins, W. Cook, P. Gallacher, P. Kavanagh, A. McKnight, S. Mulholland, R. Peacock, A. Rogan, C. Tully
*Icelandic Internationalist*
J. Edvaldsson
*United States Internationalist*
J. Kennaway
*Canadian Internationalist*
J. Kennaway

## 10. SCOTTISH LEAGUE INTERNATIONALISTS

R. Auld

J. Baillie, B. Battles, R. Beattie, A. Bennett, J. Blessington, T. Bogan, J. Brogan, J. Brown, J. Browning, W. Buchan

T. Callaghan, J. Campbell, J. Cassidy, S. Chalmers, J. Clark, R. Collins, G. Connelly, P. Connolly, P. Crerand, W. Cringan

J. Delaney, J. Divers, J. Dodds, T. Dunbar

R. Evans

W. Ferguson, W. Fernie

P. Gallacher, C. Geatons, T. Gemmell, J. Gilchrist, J. Gilhooly

D. Hamilton, M. Haughney, D. Hay, J. Hay, J. Higgins, H. Hilley, J. Hodge, R. Hogg, H. Hood, J. Hughes, T. Hynds

J. Johnstone, P. Johnstone

J. Kelly, J. Kennaway, J. Kennedy, A. King, T. Kiernan, W. Kivlichan

R. Lennox, W. Loney, W. Lyon

A. McAtee, D. McArthur, P. McAuley, J. McBride, J. McFarlane,
W. McGonagle, D. McGrain, J. McGrory, A. McLean, D. McLeod,
A. McMahon, J. McMenemy, A. McNair, W. McNeill, J. McPhail, J. McStay,
W. McStay, J. Madden, W. Maley, J. Mallan, A. Martin, P. Meechan,
W. Miller, R. Murdoch, F. Murphy

C. Napier, W. O'Neill

G. Paterson

J. Quinn

A. Rollo, D. Russell

C. Shaw, R. Simpson. P. Somers, J. Stein, D. Storrier

A. Thomson, J. Thomson, R. Thomson

W. Wallace, P. Wilson

J. Young

## 11. SIX-FIGURE TRANSFER DEALS

| Date | Player | From | To | Fee £ |
| --- | --- | --- | --- | --- |
| Jan 1973 | Lou Macari | Celtic | Manchester Utd | 200,000 |
| Jul 1974 | David Hay | Celtic | Chelsea | 250,000 |
| Aug 1977 | Kenny Dalglish | Celtic | Liverpool | 400,000 |
| Sep 1978 | Davie Provan | Kilmarnock | Celtic | 120,000 |
| Nov 1978 | Murdo MacLeod | Dumbarton | Celtic | 100,000 |
| Mar 1980 | Frank McGarvey | Liverpool | Celtic | 250,000 |
| Jun 1983 | Charlie Nicholas | Celtic | Arsenal | 750,000 |
| Jul 1983 | George McCluskey | Celtic | Leeds Utd | 140,000 |
| Aug 1983 | Jim Melrose | Coventry | Celtic | 100,000 |
| Oct 1984 | Maurice Johnston | Watford | Celtic | 400,000 |
| Nov 1985 | Mark McGhee | S.V. Hamburg | Celtic | 150,000 |
| May 1987 | Mick McCarthy | Manchester City | Celtic | 450,000 |
| Jun 1987 | Maurice Johnston | Celtic | Nantes | 373,600 |
| Jun 1987 | Murdo MacLeod | Celtic | Borussia Dortmund | 220,000 |
| Jun 1987 | Brian McClair | Celtic | Manchester Utd | 850,000 |
| Jul 1987 | Andy Walker | Motherwell | Celtic | 350,000 |
| Jul 1987 | Alan McInally | Celtic | Aston Villa | 250,000 |
| Jul 1987 | Chris Morris | Sheffield Wed | Celtic | 125,000 |
| Oct 1987 | Frank McAvennie | West Ham | Celtic | 750,000 |
| Nov 1987 | Joe Miller | Aberdeen | Celtic | 650,000 |

## 12. MANAGERS LEAGUE RECORD (1897–1988)

| Name | Played | Won | Drew | Lost | Champion-ships won |
|---|---|---|---|---|---|
| Willie Maley 1897–1940 | 1431 | 907 | 286 | 238 | 16 |
| Jimmy McStay 1940–45 | | | | | |
| *No official League games were played during this period* | | | | | |
| Jimmy McGrory 1945–65 | 601 | 282 | 134 | 185 | 1 |
| Jock Stein 1965–75 1976–78 | 421 | 296 | 66 | 59 | 10 |
| Sean Fallon 1975–76 | 36 | 21 | 6 | 9 | – |
| *He was in charge for one season while Jock Stein recovered from injuries sustained in a car crash* | | | | | |
| Billy McNeill 1978–83 first spell | 180 | 114 | 33 | 33 | 3 |
| David Hay 1983–87 | 152 | 90 | 35 | 27 | 1 |
| Billy McNeill 1987– second spell | 44 | 31 | 10 | 3 | 1 |

## 13. CHAIRMEN OF THE CLUB

| | |
|---|---|
| Dr J. Conway | 1888–1890 |
| John Glass | 1890–1897 |
| J. H. McLaughlin | 1897–1909 |
| James Kelly | 1909–1914 |
| Thomas White | 1914–1947 |
| Robert Kelly | 1947–1971 |
| Desmond White | 1971–1985 |
| Tom Devlin | 1985–1986 |
| Jack McGinn | 1986– |

## 14. SCOTTISH FOOTBALL WRITERS PLAYER OF THE YEAR

| | | | |
|---|---|---|---|
| 1965 | Billy McNeill | 1967 | Ronnie Simpson |
| 1969 | Bobby Murdoch | 1973 | George Connelly |
| 1977 | Danny McGrain | 1983 | Charlie Nicholas |
| 1987 | Brian McClair | 1988 | Paul McStay |

## 15. SCOTTISH P.F.A. PLAYER OF THE YEAR

| | | | |
|---|---|---|---|
| 1980 | Davie Provan | 1983 | Charlie Nicholas |
| 1987 | Brian McClair | 1988 | Paul McStay |

## 16. SCOTTISH P.F.A. YOUNG PLAYER OF THE YEAR

1983    Charlie Nicholas

## 17. SCORING MILESTONES

| | | |
|---|---|---|
| 2,000th League goal | – | Adam McLean |
| 3,000th    ,, | – | Jimmy McGrory |
| 4,000th    ,, | – | Jimmy Delaney |
| 5,000th    ,, | – | Frank Brogan |
| 6,000th    ,, | – | Bobby Murdoch |
| 7,000th    ,, | – | Brian McClair |

*Calculations include unofficial results from games played during the Second World War*

# INDEX